Liberia, South Carolina

Liberia, South Carolina

An African American Appalachian Community

· ·

JOHN M. COGGESHALL

The University of North Carolina Press Chapel Hill

This book was published with the assistance of the H. Eugene and Lillian Youngs Lehman Fund of the University of North Carolina Press. A complete list of books published in the Lehman Series appears at the end of the book.

© 2018 The University of North Carolina Press
All rights reserved
Set in Charis and Lato by Westchester Publishing Services
Manufactured in the United States of America

The University of North Carolina Press has been a member of the Green Press Initiative since 2003.

Library of Congress Cataloging-in-Publication Data
Names: Coggeshall, John M., author.
Title: Liberia, South Carolina : an African American Appalachian community / John M. Coggeshall.
Description: Chapel Hill : University of North Carolina Press, [2018] | Includes bibliographical references and index.
Identifiers: LCCN 2017044368 | ISBN 9781469640846 (cloth : alk. paper) | ISBN 9781469640853 (pbk : alk. paper) | ISBN 9781469640860 (ebook)
Subjects: LCSH: African Americans—South Carolina—Liberia—History. | Appalachians (People)—South Carolina—Liberia. | Appalachian Region, Southern—Race relations. | Clarke, Mable Owens. | Liberia (S.C.)—History. | Owens family.
Classification: LCC E185.912 .C64 2018 | DDC 305.896/073075723—dc23
LC record available at https://lccn.loc.gov/2017044368

Cover illustration: Emerson "Empse" Kemp at his home in Liberia (photo courtesy of Joseph Reece).

This book is dedicated to the memory of Katie Owens and her friends, her neighbors, and her descendants, past and present—especially to her great-granddaughter, Mable Owens Clarke.

Contents

A gallery of illustrations and maps follows p. 120.

Preface

Just after reaching the crest of the hill, with a small country church and prominent greenish-gray boulders to the right, I stopped my car by the side of the road one afternoon and let the view envelop me—there, about four miles ahead, stretched the thousand-foot-high wall of the Blue Ridge Mountains, framed by the massive rocky dome of Table Rock to the left and the sharp cliff of Caesar's Head to the right. Before me lay a beautiful little valley, threaded by a small stream. As I stopped to take in the pastoral scene, a white car came down the driveway of a brick bungalow to the left, and a middle-aged African American woman leaned her head out of the car's window and asked, "May I help you?" I told her I was a researcher from Clemson University, and that I was looking for the community called "Liberia," in northern Pickens County, South Carolina. "This is it," she replied. "My name is Mable Owens Clarke, and my family has been here for five generations."

From that moment on, Mable Clarke and I became partners in this project (with her permission, and reflective of our partnership, I often refer to her by her first name in this story). I had seen the name "Liberia Road" on a Pickens County map, and had thought that place name seemed unusually out of place in an Appalachian borderland region traditionally priding itself on a Scots-Irish and German settlement history. So, that May afternoon, I set out to discover the locality for myself, and by coincidence I met the descendant of one of the oldest black families in the area—in fact, the last remaining black extended family in Liberia. Mable Owens Clarke is the youngest daughter of Christopher Owens, who was the oldest son of William Owens, who was the youngest son of Katie Owens, a woman born into slavery sometime around 1840. The story of Katie Owens, her descendants, and her neighbors and friends in Liberia and the surrounding area is the subject of this book. This small African American community, tied to other African American and Euro-American communities in Pickens and Greenville Counties (see map 2), also reflects the larger story of African Americans in the South in general and helps confirm the presence of otherwise "invisible" blacks in southern Appalachian regions.

This book reflects an interdisciplinary approach to the community's history and to its place in the history of South Carolina and in the nation generally. As an anthropologist, I rely heavily on the cultural information of contemporary residents and their immediate memories. At the same time, historians contextualize the story throughout varied time periods, and sociology and black feminist theory add important perspectives. Political science and philosophy offer critiques of general conceptions of power and resistance that manifest directly in the Liberia story. I hope the story of Liberia, rather than being an impersonal history or an ahistorical ethnography, is an "ethnography through time," an oral history occupying a niche between both disciplines, connecting multidisciplinary theoretical ideas to local people and events and creating a story that is accessible to both academics and a general audience.

Through the story of Liberia, the reader will discover a group of people with the strength of character and the will to persist that reflect, in an even larger frame, the indomitability of the human spirit. I think it is a story worth telling.

A Note on the Text

Rather than correcting the grammar of recorded speech, the book uses verbatim quotes. It is recognized that grammatical errors may occur in actual human speech, and these errors are not corrected in the text, to avoid distractions and to preserve authenticity. For unusual constructions in recorded speech, however, [sic] is used. Since many descriptions, stories, and commentaries are based on direct interviews with area residents, quotes may be attributed directly to informants (see appendix 3) or, for more controversial material, to a more general speaker (see note 76, chapter 1). Otherwise "unattributed" quotes are from direct interviews with area residents conducted by the author.

Acknowledgments

In many ways, this book has reminded me of what I love most about being an anthropologist—the opportunity to help give voice to those whose voices may have been ignored or overlooked, and to restore dignity and respect to those lives.

From the moment in May 2007 when I first met Mable Owens Clarke, I have been privileged to be able to help her tell the story of the Liberia community. I could not have written this book without her help, and I am forever grateful for her patience, encouragement, and commitment. After Mable and I had negotiated terms for this research project, she introduced me to numerous informants, accompanied me on virtually every interview trip, and continued to offer her thoughts and criticism as I wrote drafts of this manuscript. While I have done my best to reconcile alternate perspectives on "truth," it is possible that some facts or events in this story may remain uncertain. This is to be expected in oral history. At the same time, I take full responsibility for the statements in this book.

In addition to Mable Clarke, I want to thank other members of the Liberia community, including Mable's late brothers A. C. and Grover Owens (who died during the research process), the entire Owens family, and the Reverend Chester Trower and his congregation at Soapstone Baptist Church. I would also like to thank those other residents of Greenville, Pickens, and Oconee Counties, black and white, who volunteered their time and memories for the interviews that have enhanced significantly the story of Liberia. I want to remember especially the late Edgar Smith, one of those white neighbors.

The Harry Hampton Memorial Wildlife Fund, partnered with the South Carolina Department of Natural Resources, provided $9,500 and the Clemson University Research Investment Fund Program added another $6,000 to support the more general "Jocassee Gorges Cultural History Project," under which I interviewed Liberia's residents. Almost all of this money paid the Clemson University undergraduate students who transcribed the interview tapes, and I am grateful to the professionalism and patience shown by Whitney Anderson, Maggie Dunn, Katie Herring, Megan Kindy,

Sarah Moore, Amanda Moser, John Powell, Kristin Richardson, Jessica Shomper, Paige Wartko, Nathan Weaver, Ashley White, and Eric Willis. Sarah Moore also edited and perfected the maps and kinship chart for this volume.

My original intention was to present the story of Liberia as a privately printed booklet, but as I discussed the project with my then-department chair, Ellen Granberg, she encouraged me to see the story within a broader historical, social, and theoretical context. I am indebted to Ellen for challenging me to "think bigger." A written agreement between Mable Clarke and myself guarantees that all royalties from the sale of this book will be returned to the Liberia community to help in historical preservation, restoration, and interpretation.

Friends and colleagues have read various drafts of chapters and/or the entire manuscript, and I am grateful for the thoughtful and helpful suggestions from Roosevelt Aiken, Dilshan Fernando, Charlotte Frisbie, Lucy Jackson Bayles, Meredith McCarroll, Janet Robertson McIlvaine, Cathy Robison, Cindy Roper, and the Rev. Chester Trower. I would also like to thank Annette Calzone and her colleagues at Westchester Publishing Services for their technical editing, and Clemson undergraduates Shannon Dunn, Brittany George, Katrina Moore, Christina Morrison, and Nahla Muldrow for helping me proofread the final copy. Thanks, too, to Mike Taber, who constructed the index. I also appreciate the comments from four anonymous reviewers from various university presses, who helped me extend the theoretical direction of the manuscript and rethink some details. I want to thank especially historian Bruce Baker, who reviewed the manuscript thoroughly, expanded my research and writing greatly, and helped me to improve the manuscript significantly. Bruce also identified the long-forgotten date of the Soapstone Church burning, and for that discovery I am forever grateful.

Finally, I want to thank all of the historical residents of Liberia, especially Katie Owens, Joseph McJunkin, Emerson Kemp, and Chris and Lula McJunkin Owens, for having the courage, fortitude, and vision to establish, sustain, and defend the Liberia community for over a century and a half. Readers of this book will come to learn what this community represents today because of the sacrifices of these and other individuals in the past. To all those who struggle for justice and dignity, I hope this story adds to that legacy.

Liberia, South Carolina

1 Shifting Paradigms

Understanding the Liberia Community

· ·

Prologue

"Your church is on fire!" the woman shouted, as she pounded furiously on the door of the rural house one peaceful Saturday evening in April 1967. Alarmed, the African American residents raced out the door and stood, horrified and helpless, at the sight—on top of the hill, the small wooden Soapstone Baptist Church blazed uncontrollably. Someone called the only available help—a volunteer fire brigade from a small crossroads hamlet. Everyone rushed up the hill to help. Suddenly—"Boom!" and a nearby black-owned vacant house also exploded in flames. "Look," someone somberly announced. There, scratched into the dirt of the church parking lot, were the chilling words: "The KKK has paid you a visit."

Rebuilt with widespread community help, Soapstone Baptist Church continues to meet, supported in part by monthly fish fries hosted by Mable Owens Clarke (great-granddaughter of the freed slaves who founded Liberia). During a recent fish fry, Mable hosted a tour of the older slave Soapstone Cemetery for a white male local historian (not all graves are those of slaves; see appendix 1). Traditional, white-dominated histories have maintained (incorrectly) that Appalachian antebellum whites (including those in South Carolina's Upstate) held few or no slaves, and this local historian operated on that same assumption. As Mable shared her family's oral history about how freed slaves had settled in the surrounding area, the white man abruptly asked, "Where did the slaves come from?" knowing (correctly) that massive numbers of freed slaves were not transported from other regions to the Upstate after 1865. Frustrated and embarrassed by his challenging tone, and unaware of his unstated assumptions, Mable could only reply, "Originally Africa, I guess." Assuming Mable's own family story was incorrect, the local historian then dismissively scoffed, "You'd better learn your history!"

Within the old cemetery lies a hand carved soapstone tombstone, with the inscription "Chanie Kimp [sic] / Died / Aug. 6, 1884 / Age 60 ye." According to a private family document, the enslaved black woman named Chaney was bequeathed to James Hester by his father in 1844, along with her son, Emerson. Emerson grew up to become Hester's "boss slave" and later lived in the Liberia community with his mother, Chaney. Emerson Kemp as an older man is shown in the photo on the cover of this book (and see figure 8), standing in front of his Liberia home. While he certainly looks distinguished and dapper, the most appealing aspect of the photo is his body posture, standing almost jauntily for the photographer, exemplifying what historian W. J. Megginson described as "persistence and perseverance," characteristic of blacks in Upstate South Carolina.[1]

All three stories together illustrate the two principal themes traced through this book. The first theme uncovers the "hidden transcripts," or the social and cultural strategies of black persistence and resistance, creating a "countermemory" parallel to white-constructed local historical "truth." Local whites argue (as Mable's cemetery visitor did) that antebellum white landowners in South Carolina's mountains owned few or no slaves, that postbellum black settlement in the mountains was sparse or nonexistent, and that local whites and blacks have interacted peacefully throughout the centuries. On the other hand, Mable's oral history challenges all of those assumptions, as represented by the stalwart stance and visible presence of former slave Emerson Kemp. The second theme, one more generally shared with Appalachian whites as well, examines the powerful tie that pulled Mable, Emerson, and many of their relatives back to their ancestral lands. These themes will be presented largely from the perspectives of the black descendants of the freed local slaves who founded Liberia, offering a countermemory to explain the emotional tie to ancestral land these Upstate South Carolinians have felt, and continue to feel, centuries later.

Physical Setting

The Liberia "community," like a lot of rural communities, is less a legally delimited entity and more a culturally defined area of recognized neighborly ties.[2] The center of Liberia would be Soapstone Baptist Church (see map 3; figure 1), adjacent to several enormous slabs of greenish-gray soapstone rock. Standing atop the slabs, one has a stunning view—a yard-wide stream meanders through an open field in a bowl-shaped valley. To the left, the blacktop Liberia Road descends along a hillside. Above the valley, just slightly left, looms a gigantic flat-topped mountain, about four miles away, approximately 2,000 feet higher than the base, with a massive, curving exposed cliff sloping from the top to about halfway down, then disappearing in a blanket of green. This is Table Rock (see map 2; figure 1). From beyond Table Rock to the left and extending to the horizon on the right stretches the thousand-foot-high escarpment of the very edge of the Blue Ridge Mountains. Just to the right of a deep-cleft valley is another exposed cliff, Caesar's Head (see map 2). Invisible under vegetation near the base of Caesar's Head lies Bald Rock (see map 2), acres of exposed, curving, channeled granite, bare of trees and vegetation. The Blue Ridge wall then continues on to the right, farther into Greenville County. From a vantage point atop Soapstone Rock, in the shadow of the remains of ancient island arcs, volcanic cores, subterranean magma pools, and titanic continental collisions hundreds of millions of years ago, lies the bucolic Soapstone Baptist Church, the heart of Liberia.[3]

Theoretical Background

The story of the Liberia community is in some ways unique and thus is worthwhile presenting for that reason alone. But the story also illustrates two major theoretical streams in anthropology in particular and in the social sciences in general, and thus the story also contributes to the scholarly literature in two significant and interrelated ways.

First, while white local history preserved a version of Liberia's story, an alternative version always has existed simultaneously, often hidden from public perception and challenge and thus protected from erasure. What are the functions of such alternate histories, and how and why do they persist? What might these alternate histories reveal about black persistence in the area and for other communities in general? Liberia's blacks would appear to have had little power to resist or to manipulate their dominating white neighbors, especially given the political and economic reality of the nineteenth and (most of) the twentieth centuries. Yet, as those narrating Liberia's alternate story demonstrate, African Americans resisted this domination in every period of their apparent powerlessness. What forms did such resistance take, and what might scholars learn about the nature of power and the relations between dominated and dominating groups from this particular story? Might the alternative history of Liberia in fact serve as one of the ways by which the apparently less powerful regain some control of their lives? A second theme is also offered in this story. What explains the tremendous desire by many of Liberia's residents to hold lands their ancestors struggled so valiantly to obtain and retain? Might this desire also offer insights into the symbolic meaning of land for Appalachian groups in general?

The history of Liberia will explore these two general themes within the framework of theoretical trends in the social sciences.

At the core of the Liberia story lies an intriguing and often maligned period in American history: Reconstruction (approximately 1863–77). During this time, millions of formerly subjugated human beings entered the paid labor force; sought land and the means of production; and (males) voted, ran for, and held local, state, and national offices for the first time. In response to this newly gained freedom by blacks came multiple waves of crippling psychological, economic, political, and social backlash by most southern whites, supplemented by indifference and inaction by most northern whites. After barely a decade of implementation, Reconstruction rather abruptly ended, whites regained almost complete political and economic control, and civil rights for blacks plunged into almost a century of denial and delay. Given this retaliation and refutation of black rights by whites, why is this period so critically important?

Challenging earlier historical work that viewed Reconstruction as a failure, historian Eric Foner more recently has interpreted Reconstruction as fundamentally a contestation over black labor.[4] Immediately after the Civil War, Foner argued, freed slaves demanded complete economic and political freedom, terrifying southern whites.[5] Under "Presidential" Reconstruction, Foner continued, southern whites soon regained control over black labor. Angered by the potential restoration of southern white domination, Congress then initiated "Radical" Reconstruction, whereby blacks gained much greater political and economic freedom under direct federal protection. A stream of international and national economic, political, and cultural forces continually undermined Reconstruction, and southern whites demanded a return to white rule to "save" the South. After one of the most contentious presidential elections in U.S. history, Foner concluded, by 1877 southern whites had regained political and economic control of black labor—a control that persisted for several more generations.

Since Reconstruction had failed to integrate blacks into American political and economic equality or had been mired in political corruption and "misrule" (an older southern interpretation), earlier historians dismissed the period for a variety of reasons. However, perceiving the period through "the centrality of the black experience," Foner argued that black "demands for civil and political rights and their efforts to create schools, churches, and other institutions of freedom proved crucial for establishing the social and political agenda of Reconstruction."[6] Furthermore, Foner continued, Reconstruction opened doors for blacks that never completely closed again: a more tolerant (and industrializing) North became an economic refuge from hopeless poverty; Radical Constitutional amendments buttressed civil rights legislation and provided federal protection to enforce those rights generations later; black families preserved memories of "better days" of political equality; and all these forces combined to offer blacks an idealistic dream for an optimistic future.[7] Foner concluded that "in the family traditions and collective folk memories of the black community," an alternate history of Reconstruction survived.[8]

Historian Bruce Baker elaborated on Foner's idea of these contrastive white and black memories of Reconstruction. Baker described the hegemonic "memory" that most white southerners had of Reconstruction: a narrative about average whites pushed to extremes by black "radicals," and who then had no recourse but to overthrow that "tyranny" and restore "legitimate" control after 1876. Simultaneously, Baker continued, "well out of sight of the general public," in segregated spaces protected from white erasure, existed the "countermemory" of blacks. This alternate story consisted of several related threads: the relative success of black politicians under Reconstruction; the acquisition of land and freedom by blacks after the Civil War; and the violence perpetrated against blacks by the dominating white culture. The stories persisted in these hidden spaces as currents beneath the surface of public narratives, and provided support and justification for the resurgence of black pride and political strength that helped empower their New Deal economic recovery and fuel the civil rights movement.[9] "African-Americans . . . could look to their own family histories to see a shadow" of a world of racial equality, Baker explained, and thus stories of places like Liberia, as well as the actual lived experiences of people in that place, provided a critical comparison to the inequalities of contemporary life and a beacon of hope for the future.[10]

Baker's analysis borrowed from historian Fritz Ringer's elaboration of Pierre Bourdieu's concept of an "intellectual field." Ringer defined an intellectual field as a set of agents competing with each other "for the right to define, or to co-define what shall count as intellectually established and culturally legitimate."[11] While "memory" preserves the "truth" of the dominant group, "countermemory challenges this [elitist] hegemony by offering a divergent commemorative narrative representing the views of marginalized individuals or groups within the society": the conflict between the two strands of "truth" creates a "contested territory," Zerubavel added.[12] Specifically in the Liberia story, the "intellectual field" is the continual struggle between white and black tradition bearers for the right to define and to present the "truth" of the past. As will be shown, the dominant, public white memory of the region has been one of peaceful coexistence and minuscule black numbers, but the countermemory of local black residents has preserved a story of inequality and resistance for a much larger historical community.

The contestation between the discourses of memory and countermemory described by these historians reflects the larger contestation between cultural accounts of reality as exemplified by the work of postmodern anthropologists. For postmodern theorists, all descriptions of cultural reality (not just historical accounts) become relative. The concept of culture, James Clifford argued, is "composed of seriously contested codes and representations" that undermine "overly transparent modes of authority." Thus, cultural "truth" no longer is perceived as homogeneous but instead becomes contested between groups or "partial," depending on alternate points of view. Furthermore, Clifford continued, the delimitation of that contested cultural truth, in written form, also needs to be considered: "who speaks? who writes? when and where? with or to whom? under what institutional and historical constraints?"[13] Such nuanced descriptions of alternating realities influence the "epistemological groundings" of all ethnographic accounts, George Marcus and Michael Fischer concluded.[14] Statements of cultural reality, both present and past, thus depend on the perspectives of those describing that reality in oral and written form; different groups have slightly different perspectives. Feminist author bell hooks critiqued Marcus and Fischer's conclusions by noting that as white males, subconsciously they had offered a limited version of reality; hooks wanted to replace their authoritative white male voices with "the polyphonic nature of critical discourse" to include the voices of others, especially those with less power.[15] Examining these "subaltern viewpoints" enriches and complicates anthropological analysis, Ira Harrison and Faye Harrison added.[16] As Stephen Tyler acknowledged, underlying the entire postmodernist critique of objective description is "an ideology of power."[17] Those in power control the writing of history and the determination of "truth."

Beneath the contestation over alternate perspectives on truth (both present reality and past history) and the political power to establish and proclaim truth lie the deeper social consequences of that cultural inequality. As sociologist Patricia Hill Collins explained, "dominant groups aim to replace subjugated knowledge with their own specialized thought because they realize that gaining control over this dimension of subordinate groups' lives simplifies control."[18] In other words, the ability to control people politically and economically gives those in power the added ability to control history and culture, and the control of history and culture allows more powerful groups to justify and explain their position of political and economic domination. For example, white versions of the "failures" of black governance during Reconstruction justified to whites the overthrow of that governance and the introduction of even more restrictions on black freedom. After the restoration of white political and economic domination in South Carolina, whites also controlled the educational system and thus the writing of textbooks (and the documentation of cultural "truth"), compelling generations of black pupils to read of their ancestors' "ineffectiveness" at governing caused by the dominant white view of black cultural, social, and even biological inferiority. But, as will be seen, an alternative version of that white "truth" persisted as a countermemory in black communities, including in Liberia. This pernicious white control of the African American story is why journalist Ta-Nehisi Coates advocated for "a new story, a new history told through the lens of our struggle."[19]

Theoretical examinations of power and domination, however, demonstrate that power is quite frequently contested between groups, both ideologically (memory and countermemory, alternative cultural realities) and socially (political and economic). Here the thoughts of Michel Foucault and his critics may be enlightening. In many of his works, Foucault directly connected power with resistance: "There are no relations of power without resistances; the latter are all the more real and effective because they are formed right at the point where relations of power are exercised; resistance to power . . . exists all the more by being in the same place as power; hence, like power, resistance is multiple."[20]

Power may be both general and public and (simultaneously) visceral and personal, Foucault observed: "But in thinking of the mechanisms of power, I am thinking rather of its capillary form of existence, the point where power reaches into the very grain of individuals, touches their bodies and inserts itself into their actions and attitudes, their discourses, learning processes and everyday lives."[21] Outward from these capillary forms of personalized power, Richard Lynch explained, power coalesces into the forms of greater hegemonic control more easily recognized by social scientists (that is, political and economic power). In fact, Lynch suggested that Foucault recommended examining power "in its local and peripheral effects."[22] In subsequent chapters, readers will discover personal and local examples of black resistance to white domination.

Foucault described other forms of power that also may enlighten an understanding of the Liberia story. As Marcelo Hoffman explained, Foucault also wrote about "disciplinary power" in his depictions of prisons and asylums. In institutions like the "panopticon," Hoffman continued, hegemonic power manifests in part through continual surveillance and the judgment of those making observations, creating a "normalizing gaze" by which individuals are evaluated and assessed.[23] Moreover, even those being observed by the elites also observe each other, in effect reinforcing the surveillance even further. In this way, racial inequality during various historical periods became a norm for evaluating all black behavior, and every action by every black person was constantly monitored and evaluated by more-powerful whites and by black peers. On the other hand, one may also see why secretive enclaves, free from the prying eyes of hegemonic power, become critically important for subordinated groups.

Hegemonic power creates a body of general knowledge about that power, and both come to be embedded in individuals, Ellen Feder wrote.[24] Feder argued that Foucault described power relations as "'a dense web that passes through apparatuses and institutions, without being localized in them.'" Because of this enveloping sense of power relationships, Feder continued, just one term or event (Foucault's "capillary form" of power's existence) automatically fires into action the entire institutionalized "dense web" of inequality, because all the dominated and dominating individuals know and have embodied the knowledge of power and inequality so well. Thus, Feder concluded, the system reinforces the "truth" of the inequality as common knowledge. In other words, one white utterance of a derogatory racial term to one black woman in one southern commercial establishment in 1950, said at just the right time and with just the right tone of voice, instantly reminds her of every whispered story, every suffered indignity, every witnessed injustice, and the bitterness of that gendered political and economic inequality in every aspect of her daily life and in the lives of her family and friends.[25]

While it might appear that this black victim may have been powerless in this situation, she was not—at least not entirely. As Foucault noted, economic, political, and ideological inequalities generate resistance to those forms of inequality. Building on that idea has been political scientist James Scott, whose work also has informed historian Bruce Baker and sociologist Wilma Dunaway. Scott elucidated the mechanisms by which those ostensibly without power manage, disguise, manipulate, and transform their powerlessness into various forms of resistance. As Scott explained, although those without power face tremendous cruelty, arbitrary punishment, and very real inequalities, subordinates simultaneously create an alternate social world and accompanying critical narrative of the elites outside the purview of the elites themselves.[26] Scott described these places and narratives as "hidden transcripts," physical places and cultural creations that explicate the relationship between dominant and subordinate groups, allowing subordinates to retain their dignity and directly challenge the inequalities in (mostly) surreptitious ways. While elites have their own hidden transcripts, more difficult to access are the hidden transcripts of subordinates, for by definition they must publicly accept their inequality but simultaneously hide their insubordinate thoughts and acts of reprisal and retaliation. Scott sought to discover the "infrapolitics of the powerless," or all collective forms of resistance. Scott suggested that hidden transcripts also help to illuminate "those rare moments of political electricity" when formerly hidden transcripts burst into the public view in the form of rebellions.

In a more recent book, Scott applied his description of the strategies of subordinate groups to the hill tribes of Southeast Asia, who successfully have avoided complete incorporation by surrounding state-level societies for centuries.[27] While state-level societies may view these peoples as "archaic remnants" or "contemporary ancestors," the various hill tribes deliberately have utilized a variety of materialistic and ideological strategies to control their own access to their more powerful lowland neighbors. In addition to making their homes in "remote, marginal areas that are difficult of access," hill peoples adopt highly mobile subsistence strategies, avoid labor-intensive modes of production, maintain flexible social structures, and support value systems of egalitarianism that contradict those of totalitarian states.[28] These tribes even manipulate their oral traditions, oscillating between remembering and forgetting historical "truth" in attempts at self-preservation when faced with a "capricious and menacing political environment" exemplified by state social control.[29]

African Americans in the mountains of the rural South thus provide a way to test these "broad patterns" of resistance to hegemonic control. Moreover, the "remote" location of the Liberia community, in the hills beyond the hegemonic surveillance of white society, fits Scott's description of Southeast Asian hill tribes. Scott's detailed analysis of the forms and functions of the hidden transcripts of various subordinated groups has been extremely helpful in illuminating the challenges African Americans faced under white hegemonic control in the South during various historical periods, and the alternate forms of personal and group resistance blacks adopted.[30] On the other hand, Liberia's residents have not always avoided incorporation into general American society like Southeast Asian hill tribes have avoided state-level domination. Through various times in their history, rather,

Liberia's residents sometimes have sought such inclusion but often have been denied full acceptance. Combining both of Scott's works together, however, provides evidence for an image of Liberia's residents as sometimes seeking and sometimes avoiding contact with white society and sometimes being accepted into, and sometimes being denied acceptance into, that same overarching society. Scott recognized that "the ultimate value of the broad patterns" he outlined "could be established only by embedding them firmly in settings that are historically grounded and culturally specific."[31] The story of the Liberia community as a vehicle for black freedom offers precisely such an example.

"Southern historians have ignored freedmen's settlements" such as Liberia, historians Thad Sitton and James Conrad generalized, and their study of "freedom colonies" in Texas provides valuable parallels to a fuller understanding of Liberia's historical context.[32] Freedom colonies throughout the nation (primarily the South) formed after the Civil War as blacks deliberately sought enclaves away from white domination. Historian Loren Schweninger listed ten examples of these communities, excluding Texas but including South Carolina's "Promised Land" (see following discussion); most of these communities lasted only a generation or two, he noted.[33] In contrast, the Texas freedom colonies studied by Sitton and Conrad "long remained especially remote, informal, and unofficial—defensive black communities that went almost as unnoticed by white contemporaries . . . as by latter-day historians." Typically containing a church (or churches) and a school, these "unofficial places" "at the end of remote roads" were rarely visited by the federal census taker, county sheriff, or tax assessor; in fact, a "casual traveler might pass through one of these rural communities without even noticing that a community was there."[34] Likewise, folklorist Lynwood Montell characterized the isolated freed black community of Coe Ridge, Kentucky, as "almost inaccessible" and thus largely unknown to those beyond the immediate area.[35] "Freedmen's settlements were black enclaves that kept to themselves," Sitton and Conrad concluded, "and until the end of Jim Crow few whites wished—or dared—to live there."[36]

Instead of examining these remote, unnoticed black enclaves, most studies of African Americans in the rural South have focused on tenants and sharecroppers, primarily in the Piedmont Cotton Belt (although see Schweninger for both rural and urban property owners).[37] Sociologist Stewart Tolnay, for example, analyzed the lives of black farm families throughout the South during the twentieth century, while historian Gilbert Fite traced the progression of agricultural practices in the South after the Civil

War.[38] The "Behind the Veil" oral history project documented the "rich, complicated, heroic, and ultimately ambiguous texture of African American lives during the era of segregation." Unfortunately, "little has been written about the actual experience of black Americans during the age of segregation," the editors concluded.[39]

More specific studies of the region include that of historian Sharon Holt, who examined the strategies used by freedpeople in a North Carolina Piedmont county to establish independent households and communities.[40] Historian Mark Schultz described the nuances of Jim Crow racism in a lower Piedmont Georgia county, wondering why historians have insufficiently documented the lives of rural African Americans "who achieved more than marginal economic or personal independence," as well as situations where "African Americans were able to assert their dignity in the face of white oppression in the rural South."[41] Historian Debra Reid recognized the traditional scholarly focus on the Piedmont, Delta, and Pinelands, and urged that "more micro-level studies of individual and family experiences in and outside of heavily black-populated cotton-producing counties must be undertaken in order to understand fully the breadth of black landowning farm family experiences." Reid also recommended that historians adopt the methodology of oral interviewing, a "traditional anthropological approach," in order to allow historians "to deepen their understanding of black farm owners and their communities."[42]

Specifically for South Carolina, few historical ethnographic studies have been conducted. Historians Reid and Schweninger specifically cited the community of "Promised Land," in the lower Piedmont of South Carolina (just across the southeastern Abbeville County line, see map 1), documented by historian Elizabeth Bethel and described by novelist John Edgar Wideman. Another South Carolina Piedmont community study was conducted by sociologist Hylan Lewis on the "blackways" of the town of York (York County, see map 1), just southwest of Charlotte, North Carolina. Carol Stack, a cultural anthropologist, examined rural black communities in the Low Country of the Carolinas to understand the pull of recent return migration from the North. Sociologist William Falk described the contemporary pull of land ties in a pseudonymous African American community in South Carolina's Low Country, while rural sociologists Janice Dyer and Conner Bailey analyzed the critical importance of heirs' property to help rural African Americans, especially along the Carolina-Georgia coast, retain both their land and their cultural identity.[43]

Regardless of specific location, both white and black southern rural communities faced common problems during various historical periods of the past several centuries: the boll weevil, fluctuating farm prices, and soil exhaustion (to name a few). But unlike their white neighbors, blacks as a social group faced random and often horrific violence at the hands of whites as an attempt to maintain hegemonic control (blacks retaliated in myriad ways). In fact, journalist Ta-Nehisi Coates characterized white attempts to destroy black bodies as part of America's heritage.[44] Justifying this violence from a white perspective was the deeply rooted fear by southern whites of black violence directed against them. These white fears arose from stories about actual slave revolts (such as the one in Haiti) and from the "black male rapist" myth (rendered more terrifying because the act violated the formal cultural boundaries of rigid racial barriers).[45] However, as sociologists Stewart Tolnay and E. M. Beck found, white organized violence against blacks, especially between 1882 and 1930, significantly exceeded black assaults on whites; this "state-sanctioned terrorism" contributed structurally and symbolically to white domination over every black community, especially but not exclusively in the South.[46] The national disgrace of this racialized violence even entered popular culture. In 1939, Billie Holiday contrasted images of the magnolia-scented South with bulging-eyed lynching victims in her mournful ballad, "Strange Fruit": "Black bodies swinging in the southern breeze / Strange fruit hanging from the poplar trees."[47]

The murder of blacks by white mob violence appalled contemporary sociologist W. E. B. DuBois. Writing in the more progressive period after World War I, DuBois tried to explain the persistent nature of this horrific, racialized violence. In a series of articles in *The Crisis* (the journal of the NAACP [National Association for the Advancement of Colored People]), DuBois argued that southern lynchings were "a species of public amusement to which certain black districts and city slums are regularly treated." Whenever a black person committed a "serious" crime (as defined at that particular time by whites), whites often took the law into their own hands. Black resistance to this white vigilantism was met with even more white violence in retaliation, and reinforced the "black criminal" stereotype in white minds. DuBois equated this pattern of black resistance and white overwhelming and terrifyingly violent retaliation to the process of white colonization of native peoples in general. Whenever whites subdue native inhabitants anywhere in the world, DuBois noted, the natives are often redefined as the aggressors in a complete reversal of roles.[48]

Anthropologist Michael Taussig offered a case study and an explanation for the role reversal anticipated by DuBois.[49] In a study of European rubber exploiters in the upper Amazon rain forest, Taussig argued that the Europeans hired *muchachos* (native overseers) to work the plantations, expand territory, and exterminate the native population. In order to accomplish those tasks, the *muchachos* initiated stories of cannibalism about the natives, creating a "culture of terror" which then justified the overseers' enacting horrific tortures on the natives. Besides eliciting needed information, the purpose of torture "is the need to control massive populations through the cultural elaboration of fear." Torture also prevents retaliation by establishing an ideology "that sustained the precarious solidarity" of those in power by "beating out through the body of the tortured" some "truths" about "reality." Taussig described the curious "mimesis" of the "colonial mirror" that reflected the savagery attributed by the colonists to the Indians with that violence actually perpetrated by the colonists *on* the Indians. Torture, or "the space of death," becomes the "mediator *par excellence* of colonial hegemony."

Liberia's capacity as a test case to discover and explore hidden transcripts of resistance to hegemonic racism and the consequent "culture of terror" created by that racism lies in its location—the southern Appalachian foothills. In fact, some researchers have described blacks in Appalachia as "invisible."[50] In general, scholar Leon Williams believed that Appalachia "has been painted with the broad stroke of a white brush which has obliterated and distorted the contributions of its second largest population group." Historian Linda Culpepper argued that this whitewashing has occurred because mountain blacks did not fit the "academic paradigm or accepted image of southern mountaineers." In fact, the "whiteness" of Appalachia, sociologist Barbara Smith explained, has been created not by historical settlement patterns but instead by "active practices" designed to drive resident blacks from the region. Indeed, historian Steven Nash argued, northern travelers after the Civil War observed numerous blacks in the mountains, but these Appalachian residents disappeared from discourse (but often not from actual residency) by the late nineteenth century. Archaeologist Jodi Barnes, for example, documented a community of freed blacks in western Virginia that "became invisible" because of the twentieth century's focus on poverty-stricken mountain whites as Appalachia's typical residents. "The result," concluded scholar Wilburn Hayden, "is an unconsciously diminished depiction of the other groups' place or contributions to the region." Sociologist William Turner urged "intensified study" for communities and for cultures (such as blacks) that at that time had "never been studied."[51]

Fortunately, the scholarly picture focused on blacks in Appalachia has become somewhat more extensive during the past several decades, historian

John Inscoe observed. One of the areas of research Inscoe reviewed is that of community studies, and he specifically mentioned the work on Beech Creek, in Clay County, Kentucky. In Inscoe's volume, Jennifer Lund Smith documented the struggles of a North Georgia community during Reconstruction. From the mountains of western North Carolina come three stories: that of the Salem School in Elk Park (a Christian mission near the Tennessee border serving a small nineteenth-century black community), the Allen School in Asheville (a high school for the region's African Americans, functioning into the 1970s), and the black Junaluska community in Boone, virtually invisible due to "accommodation, caution, and isolation." Farther south, Linda Culpepper described a community of blacks living in Flat Rock, North Carolina (about twenty miles north of Marietta; see map 2), freed by their white Charlestonian owners who had traditionally vacationed in the mountains for generations. On their way to Flat Rock, Culpepper added, blacks could have stayed in the "Kingdom of Happy Land" just across the border in South Carolina, another isolated freedom colony, whose residents moved to Flat Rock as the Kingdom folded in the early twentieth century. The Maxwell community in northern Oconee County (see map 1) persisted into the late nineteenth century, and Liberia, in adjacent Pickens County, continues to this day.[52]

As anthropologist Antoinette Jackson argued, since these isolated black communities traced their founding to freed slaves, these enslaved lives must be acknowledged in community histories, especially when working with descendants.[53] The story of Liberia, then, begins before 1865, when the future residents were undocumented property. While reconstructing the lives of "people without history" is difficult, it may still be done. Historian W. J. Megginson and sociologist Wilma Dunaway systematically have reconstructed Appalachian slave life (including that in Pickens and Greenville Counties in South Carolina) by utilizing their discipline-specific research methodologies.[54] These general contributions enrich the beginnings of the Liberia story, enhanced by family stories from descendants.

"White sources do not document the pain, sufferings, deprivations, resentment, and anger felt by slaves," historian W. J. Megginson acknowledged, but the oral traditions of black Upstate families document such sufferings.[55] Preserved through generations, these stories of enslaved lives of individuals matter for several critical reasons. First, virtually all of Liberia's original inhabitants began their lives as slaves, including Emerson Kemp (described in the Preface) and at least two of Mable's great-grandparents on her mother's and father's sides. It is critical to respect, contextualize, and present these personal histories. Second, many local whites (such as the historian described in the Preface) deny or discredit the presence of significant numbers of blacks in northern Pickens County both before and after the Civil War; thus, any evidence of such presence should be documented. Third, the description of life under slavery for Liberia's founders forms a critical contrast to the twenty-first-century ideals of equality for Liberia's descendants, and this contrast makes the poignancy of Liberia's persistence even more dramatic. Fourth, the "Behind the Veil" researchers argued that the story of black resistance during the civil rights movement must begin in the segregated South; thus, the resistance of Liberia's residents to white oppression should begin with enslaved resistances by these same people before freedom. Finally, as anthropologist Antoinette Jackson recommended, "descendant knowledge within specific families and communities should be . . . longitudinal in scope. In so doing, memories of descendants of the enslaved, constructed in the contemporary present, constitute additional sources of knowledge that can contribute to rethinking" the traditional views of enslaved peoples. "There is much value in taking seriously the evidence we have of slavery at the most intimate and personal of levels," historian John Inscoe added, especially "the stories of individuals, of families, of communities, from whatever sources and perspectives they come to us."[56]

Inscoe has critiqued the social scientific literature describing blacks in Appalachia, with no mention of studies in South Carolina's mountains. Inscoe's overview also noted the relative lack of the discussion of "African-American agency": he encouraged future studies where "Appalachian blacks take center stage" and tell their stories in their own voices. The lives of "women, individually or collectively, black or white," also need to be documented with much greater detail, Inscoe suggested. Finally, Inscoe singled out two particular studies because they provided a "detailed reconstruction of the very lives of obscure individual blacks" (although not from South Carolina). He especially appreciated the "challenging detective work it took to piece together those stories" because they clarified "the region's black populace as fully engaged individuals who managed to better their lives and their families' lives." "As vast as the range of issues and experiences chronicled here" in his *Appalachians and Race* volume, Inscoe admitted, "the field of Appalachian race relations remains wide open."[57]

Given that much of the Liberia story centers on the lives of black women and often is presented in their own words, it is imperative to examine black feminist literature for additional insights. Several decades ago, bell hooks advocated for a "liberatory voice" for black women, a way of speaking that "demands that paradigms shift." Black women, hooks insisted, should be at the center of feminist discourse, so that black voices may enhance the discussion about "resistance, an affirmation of struggle."[58] In fact, sociologist Patricia Hill Collins criticized some of James Scott's earlier work on domination and resistance because he had overlooked black women's voices. Without these voices, Collins argued, it appears black women "willingly collaborate in their own victimization," and they most assuredly do not. By highlighting black women's responses to various types of domination in U.S. history, Collins concluded, "Black feminist thought helps reconceptualize social relations of domination and resistance."[59]

Patricia Hill Collins elaborated on bell hooks's earlier work, deliberately "shifting the center" of feminist theory from prevailing discussions of male patriarchy to the underdocumented but interrelated effects of race, class, and gender on female empowerment. Considering the relationships of these variables to each other, or their "intersectionality," makes these variables even more powerful. By "shifting the center" of the discussion, Collins continued, researchers better understand the critically important "motherwork" of black females, work that "recognizes that individual survival, empowerment, and identity require group survival, empowerment, and identity."[60]

According to Collins, "motherwork" for black females involves issues that typically do not affect white or middle-class females nearly as often.[61] For example, black females must expend significant time and energy to protect their children (and by extension those in the community) from physical harm, and have done so for centuries. Black females also have fought for centuries to control sexual access to their own bodies (especially during periods of hegemonic racial and gender inequality), and have had to raise a significant number of biracial children, often without the financial or social help of white fathers. Black mothers also have struggled to retain physical and emotional contact with their children, potentially lost to them because of slavery sales, out-migration for better employment, or incarceration under an unequal criminal justice system. Black mothers also have had to contest the cultural content of their children's minds, by resisting attempts by whites to impose alternate dialects, cultural values, and "truths" of historical events or racial inequalities. To survive and resist, black mothers become "othermothers," raising their own children alongside those in the community, instilling positive self-esteem, strategies of resistance, and lessons for community development in all of their charges. Thus, Collins concluded, seeing the world through the eyes of black women can "enrich our understanding of how subordinate groups create knowledge that fosters both their empowerment and social justice."[62]

Sources and Methods

The postmodern view of anthropology and oral history directly affects the analysis of the sources used for this story. As this theoretical perspective suggests, histories may be viewed as creations, in the sense that they consist of some (but not all) historical documents and some (but not all) eyewitness recollections. Even these documents and recollections are filtered through lenses—of age, race, gender, economic status, and social/historical context, for example (the "alternate truths," "contested history," or "countermemories" discussed earlier). Thus, the history of the Liberia community blends together a range of documents and memories from as wide a variety of sources as possible, both contemporary and past, to present as accurately (but imperfectly) as possible a critical story of this community.

One source, the U.S. Census, might appear to be an impeccable measure of population statistics, including the racial makeup of a region. But, considering the contemporary difficulties of defining "race" and the challenge of documenting the homeless and the extreme poor, problems of a century ago seem even more daunting. Viewed on websites like Ancestry.com (utilized for this book), the original census forms from the nineteenth century are interesting reflections of contemporary concerns.[63]

One standard variable was race, although the definition of "race," the number of possible categories, and even the designator (self or census taker) all varied with each census. The challenge to the recorder was differentiating between "black" and "mulatto," or "mulatto" and "white": where was the dividing line?[64] Even more crucially, of course, these designations were not neutral; in the highly segregated legal system of South Carolina in the late nineteenth and early twentieth centuries, individuals labeled "white" could eat, worship, court, marry, learn, work, sit, ride public transportation, and even urinate in places completely different from those labeled as "others" (for example, mulatto, black, or colored). And since a census form represented an official government document, a designation as one race immediately and permanently classified one and one's kin into a social and economic caste system. Occasionally, if one looks closely at the actual hand-recorded census forms, one can see a *W* with an *M* overwritten in darker color, or an *M* overwritten by a *W*. While these could be relatively innocuous clerical corrections, they also might reveal the chillingly critical social value embedded in a mere letter of the alphabet.

In the story of Liberia, many terms could be used to describe the residents who trace at least part of their ancestry back to Africa. Mable Owens Clarke explained the historical variety and emotional impact of these alternating labels during her own lifetime: "You know, we've had so many names, sometimes I try to figure out what name we are. . . . I don't know any other race that went through so many names as us. I mean truthfully, I started out in school as a little girl as being called a Negro. . . . Then it went from Negro to colored, and from colored to I guess we [are]—black. . . . I mean sometime you look in the mirror and you say, 'Now which one of these—what am I?' . . . With the whites—you've been white all of your life. . . . And it's just so confusing. . . . You have to wonder what [are] all these labels? Why is there change? . . . They haven't figured out yet . . . what race I am or where I am on this planet?"

Acknowledging the existence of the diversity of terms used to describe Mable's group (terms that vary by decade, by custom, by ethnicity, and by individual), this book uses "African American" and "black" interchangeably, recognizing the social construction of race well established by social scientists. For all such designations, the wishes of the story's principal consultant, Mable Owens Clarke, have defined the appropriate identifying labels for this group. Historical sources or personal recollections using other terms remain unchanged. It is acknowledged that the nineteenth-century term "mulatto" may convey negative connotations to some readers today, but the term was a formal census category for decades and appears in this story in appropriate historical contexts. Even more pejorative terms are used only sparingly, in the context of actual conversations, and with the approval of the African American readers. Likewise, "Euro-American" or "white" will be used to designate individuals of mainly European ancestry, again recognizing the probable intermixture of genes from varied groups.

The term "Indian" in local discussions of ethnic identity may not reflect what it might seem to indicate to general readers. While intermarriages and other types of sexual relationships along the Native American–British border in the Southeast certainly occurred, compounded by freed blacks and slaves held by both groups (see chapter 2), individuals described by informants as having "Indian blood" were more likely mixed race between whites and blacks. In order to avoid the embarrassment or shame of such illegal or negatively sanctioned parentage, both whites and blacks glossed over the awkwardness of explaining red-haired or light-skinned blacks as instead having "Indian" ancestry. While of course this was certainly possible, the designation of "Indian" more frequently provided a culturally acceptable label for problematic offspring. This nuanced reading of the "Indian" ethnic term provides an alternate "truth" for the Sam "Goob" Keith story presented in chapters 2, 3, and 4.

Local and regional newspapers might seem to be factual documentations of area events, but these sources, too, reflect the social inequalities of their times and the subjective enumeration of events considered by contemporary editors to be newsworthy. In Jennifer Smith's study of a post-Reconstruction black community in northern Georgia, for example, Smith discovered that the local paper "printed stories that either ridiculed the efforts of local African Americans or displayed a paternalistic attitude toward those it referred to as 'our colored people.' Some African Americans were singled out for their 'industry' and 'honesty.'" Historian Mark Schultz observed that white newspapers generally ignored blacks in the early twentieth century. If blacks were mentioned at all, W. J. Megginson noted for Upstate South Carolina, they frequently were linked with crimes or accidents.[65]

For decades, local papers like the *Pickens Sentinel* typically reported only the obituaries of "good" blacks. These obituaries frequently contained hints of the contemporary condescending attitude of many whites toward their black neighbors, as researchers had documented for other areas. For example, in the obituary for Lewis (Luke) Terrell, published in the *Sentinel* March 23, 1923 (p. 4), he was remembered as "a good old time darkey." The writer then offered an editorial comparison: "We sometimes think how much the old time colored people of latter days out strips [*sic*] the colored people of today in many ways." Of course, those "latter days" meant either the time of enslavement or the period of horrific racism during the late nineteenth century (see chapter 3).

These obituaries also glossed over "late unpleasantries" like slavery. In the obituary of Katie Owens (see figure 2), the February 23, 1928, issue of the *Pickens Sentinel* (p. 8) mentioned that "she made her home with some of the best families before the 60's." The wording of the story implied that Katie Owens made her home with the best families of her own free will. Left unstated, but known to every reader at the time, of course, was the fact that these "best families" *owned* Katie Owens. She "made her home" with them because she had no choice; she was their property. In this way, the brutality of slavery and the ownership of fellow human beings by even the "best families" disappeared from the printed record—but remained in the countermemory of Katie Owens and the other descendants of those slaves.

Local histories may be very good sources of information, both for what they include and for what they overlook. There are two histories of the Pumpkintown area, both written by whites descended from prominent local families. While both included some copies of documents and photographs, both also relied heavily on oral traditions passed through generations of family members and thus subject to the typical biases and misrepresentations of oral tradition explained in this chapter. For example, Bert Hendricks Reece, in her *History of Pumpkintown-Oolenoy*, mentioned in her foreword that the booklet is based on "written notes" that she took from "authentic information" told to her by her parents. Alma Lynch and Elizabeth Ellison, in *Echoes: Oolenoy-Pumpkintown*, recognized that "there is a lot of confusion about this early history, because there is not much proof other than information handed down from generation to generation. We try to present accurate facts," they assured readers. Bert Reece's son Josef, who had spent his childhood in the Oolenoy Valley, added interesting details from his boyhood recollections in his autobiography.[66]

Other families have lacked the resources, time, or professional training to collect, write, or publish their family histories. Even into the late nineteenth century, many African Americans in the area were still undereducated, with poor home storage facilities and no extra income for photography, and thus were unable to save extensive family correspondence or critical family documents. On the other hand, as the historians of the "Behind the Veil" project argued, "family and community efforts to preserve and pass down oral traditions were crucial to the survival of African American identity and heritage."[67] Fortunately, some black Upstate family histories have been collected on videotape or tape recorders at family reunions, but the tapes have never been condensed, organized, and published in a formal manner. For example, in 1983 James Monroe McJunkin taped his recollections of the stories told by his enslaved grandfather, Joseph.[68] James's daughter Angela McJunkin Young narrated these same stories. "Now I'm telling you the things that my Dad has passed on to all of us," she noted; "when we would have the McJunkin family reunion, when Daddy got—he would talk *so long* until they learned how to let Daddy give the history and eat at the same time!"

Logically, families wish to portray their ancestors as kind, heroic, insightful, generous, prosperous, and sober; thus any behaviors indicating brutality, cowardice, ignorance, selfishness, poverty, or intemperance would disappear in oral history and thus never be recorded. Family quarrels, criminal behavior, religious disputes, and financial difficulties fade with selected memory, and thus local histories typically distill the vagaries of normal human lives into paeans of one's own ancestors. Regional historian Frederick Holder acknowledged that these local histories reflected "the way the writers wished things to be . . . not the way things actually were." "Despite my best efforts and most earnest pleas for people to document the material they print," Holder lamented, "an amazing amount of material without substance continues to be published on/or about Pickens County."[69]

Compounding the challenges of finding the "truth" in local histories are the thick veils of race, class, and gender, contextualized by alternating historical periods. Local histories described prominent people, typically males, and rarely mentioned those of lower status. This included African Americans, both former slaves and freed residents. The two Pumpkintown local histories mentioned Liberia, but they drew almost exclusively on the memories of the Owens family (the family featured here as well). Little mention was made of other black communities in the area, nor was there any description of the complicated series of social interrelationships blacks faced as they negotiated the legal and social segregation that existed through much of this documented history. Of course, no mention is made in these local histories of any difficulties blacks faced or crimes committed against them. As with local newspapers, the portrait painted of racial lines by these local histories is one of complacency, cooperation, and harmony.[70] Thus, even though they are written, local histories are as influenced by selective memory as are oral histories. Given the ambiguity of "truth" in printed sources, how, then, should one "learn your history"?

Without documents such as courthouse land and tax records, historians have faced significant challenges of documentation, oral historians Thad Sitton and James Conrad commented, for "no documents meant no history. . . . Only in the living memories of elderly community residents did the vein of information run deep." Thus, they continued, "oral traditional history (accounts passed down from others) reach back before the documents and fill gaps in the records."[71] Oral history, however, may be modified by all of the factors described earlier in this chapter: the problems in local, county, state, and federal records; the influences of age, gender, race, and class on the perceptions of "truth" as individuals within those groups perceive it; and the varied ways these imperfect documents and imperfect people become woven into imperfect narratives with the editorial addition of fond memories and the deletion of negative events. Thus, oral historians struggle with the same postmodern issues as do anthropologists.[72] Nevertheless, as folklorist Lynwood Montell argued, "the story of any local group, as viewed by its people, is worthy of being recorded, for it can serve as a historical record in those areas where written accounts have not been preserved."[73] When used in this particular story, the documentation of historical incidents by means of oral sources must be weighed with the same care and caution as readers would weigh all other sources.

To supplement and enhance oral history, to provide "the sort of deep familiarity with a place and a way of life" requested by historian Bruce Baker, anthropologists document culture through ethnographic fieldwork.[74] Culture can be understood to be the ideas people have about their world, and the behaviors stemming from those ideas. Since culture is shared by a group, members share these ideas and behaviors, with allowance for individual variation and slight alternatives due to gender, class, race, and age, for example. In interviews, people can describe their culture in the past and the present, and these descriptions, with some variation, denote ways of life that were, and continue to be, typical of what most people believe and do. Cultural descriptions develop their validity and reliability precisely because they are shared by members of a society—what most people typically do (or did) most of the time. Unlike the necessity of oral history to describe a specific sequence of dates and events, cultural traditions are less susceptible to faulty memories but equally susceptible to the variances created by gender, class, race, and age. Such variation may be mitigated by collecting cultural traditions from a wider variety of people.

In fact, "leaving the archives to spend time in communities and with people directly impacted by the stories we tell is an essential part of anthropological research," Antoinette Jackson declared. Jackson recommended blending both oral history and ethnography, especially when documenting former enslaved communities. Adopting Jackson's methodology, the story of Liberia presented here utilizes "the archives" and the "memories of descendants of the enslaved, constructed in the contemporary present."[75] But the story of Liberia also relies on cultural traditions collected from whites as well as blacks, describing varied time periods, and representing both genders and a wide variety of ages (providing "multiple truths" and "polyphonic voices").[76]

A word of caution about "authenticity of voice" is in order. Given the critique of cultural description by the postmodernist anthropologists and oral historians, and the equally valid critique of the dominance of male voices by black feminists, who then has the authoritative position to speak for Liberia's residents? As Patricia Hill Collins argued, descriptions of the lives of black women should not come from the dominant discourse. Instead, she continued, researchers should rely on "personalized narratives, autobiographical statements, . . . and other personalized statements [in order to obtain] . . . the authentic standpoint of subordinated groups."[77] Black women today, Collins concluded, "insist on our right to define our own reality, establish our own identities, and name our history." However, blacks may not always be able to present their own "sense of the world."[78] Whites (and white males) can never fully comprehend the black (female) experience, but whites may describe that experience, as long as the latter recognize that they are not the exclusive authorities on that experience, hooks admonished.[79] In the Liberia story outlined in the following chapters, blacks offer their own story in their own words; at the same time, that story is presented alongside alternate voices, critiqued by outsider academics, and framed within a historical context, for a broader and more nuanced understanding of historical "truth."

Conclusion

The story of Liberia transcends Pickens County and even South Carolina, becoming not only a case study of an Appalachian African American community but also an opportunity to apply an array of theoretical perspectives to that case study. In order to tell the Liberia story, the chapters are organized chronologically and divided by significant local events. Following this introductory chapter, chapter 2 describes life in the Oolenoy Valley before 1865, documenting the lives of several enslaved individuals (for example, Katie Owens and Emerson Kemp) and several black family traditions depicting life under slavery. Chapter 3 covers the late nineteenth century to 1900, just after the birth of Katie Owens's grandson Christopher Owens, another main character in the story. Chapter 4 follows Chris Owens's life until 1940 and just before the birth of his youngest daughter, Mable, a third major character of the Liberia story. Chapter 5 describes Mable's childhood in Liberia until her departure for the North in the early 1960s. Chapter 6 focuses on the Soapstone Baptist Church fire in 1967 and its aftermath, and Chapter 7 portrays the Liberia community in recent decades. Chapter 8 offers a theoretical discussion of the centripetal force pulling Liberia's residents (and many Appalachian residents in general) back to their ancestral homes, as well as an epilogue. By following the history of the Liberia community from its origins in antebellum South Carolina into the twenty-first century, the book links two themes: the "hidden transcripts" of the countermemory of an overlooked minority group, and a possible explanation for the powerful tie to place the descendants of these people feel.

More specifically, the story of Liberia answers the requests of numerous oral historians to examine black family histories in order to discover examples of black activism, presenting the alternate truths of opposing versions of history. Moving beyond the hidden transcripts of life under slavery, Liberia's story expands the application of Foucault's concepts of power and resistance to examine personal stories of the hidden transcripts in African American life under Reconstruction, Jim Crow laws, and the dawning civil rights movement. In fact, Liberia becomes a hidden transcript itself, a protected enclave beyond white surveillance, much like Scott's Southeastern Asian hill tribes. Conceiving of Liberia as a hidden transcript also explains why some whites have tried so hard to destroy it over the decades, and why blacks have struggled so hard to prevent that from happening.

Under the generalized observation by dominant groups over subordinate ones during these two centuries, it also becomes possible to sense the racist culture of terror imposed by the dominant group for control, or to hear and feel what Foucault termed the capillary forms of inequality. On the other hand, in each chapter African Americans reveal details of the infrapolitics of the powerless, as they resist white domination in myriad ways in a setting that is historically grounded and culturally specific. Finally, Liberia's story helps to materialize a typically invisible Appalachian group in an overlooked geographical area and presents anthropological evidence for what numerous scholars claimed to be missing from earlier studies: black agency in managing their own lives, black voices (especially those of women) telling their own stories, and general black history (including life under slavery) coalescing from the stories of descendants of the enslaved. In the following chapters, readers will hear the voices of strong black othermothers who struggled generation after generation to improve their children's lives, and whose children (frequently daughters) in turn took up the next generation's struggle. In doing so, these black mothers improved their community and (ultimately in small part) their state and nation. As with the "Behind the Veil" project, Liberia's story demonstrates "how one generation makes possible the hopes of the next generation."[80] With this volume, the field of Appalachian race relations no longer remains as wide open as Inscoe once feared. The story of Liberia is an anthropologically grounded means by which another "people without history" (borrowing Eric Wolf's phrase) may enter the historical record and thus gain dignity and honor to their lives.

2 You Zip Your Lips

Life in Slavery

· ·

The human story of the settlement of the area that would be named the Oolenoy Valley began with the arrival of the first Native Americans, but this arrival and the subsequent cultural periods of Native occupation of the area remain a separate story, beyond the reach of Liberia's immediate history. It is important to note, however, that a Native American presence can still be detected in several ways, such as in the artifacts exposed during plowing, the partially shaped bowls and preforms on some soapstone boulders, and a few of the place names on the landscape (such as Oolenoy). Acknowledging that Native Americans were the area's original settlers, the time frame of this particular story opens with the arrival of the first Euro-Americans.

Before the "French and Indian War" of 1756, the western frontier of the American British colonies varied from north to south; in South Carolina relatively few white settlements extended into the upper Piedmont (see the shaded area on map 1). At this time, historian Rachel Klein made no mention of any settlements in Cherokee territory (what later became Pendleton District, including today's Pickens County). Sociologist Wilma Dunaway characterized this backcountry frontier as still lying at the periphery of European nations, with the Native Americans increasingly drawn into the world system through contact with present-day Charleston. Historian Theda Perdue documented significant ethnic intermarriage and cultural blending along this frontier, specifically between the Cherokee and British and American traders. Using material culture, archaeologist Mark Groover documented the interethnic cultural exchanges between Native Americans, Euro-Americans, and African Americans along the frontier at a site near modern-day Columbia, suggesting that the persistence of African American traditions may have been due to resistance and negotiation.[1]

By the end of the "French and Indian War" in 1763, historian Walter Edgar noted that the Cherokee had been pushed to the very edge of the colony but were still east of the Blue Ridge Mountains. During the summer of 1776, Edgar continued, Col. Andrew Williamson "led backcountry militia units against the Indians, [and] destroyed most of their towns east of the mountains. . . . In a short time the Cherokee were routed and sued for peace."[2] With the peace treaty of DeWitt's Corner in 1777, the Cherokee ceded upper South Carolina, including all of present-day Greenville County and most of Pickens and Oconee Counties.[3]

After the Revolutionary War, local historian Margaret Mills Seaborn wrote, the former Cherokee land in South Carolina was put up for sale or given as compensation for military service.[4] For his military service in the Revolutionary War, Gen. Andrew Pickens received a large tract of land that he named Hopewell, situated on the Seneca River several miles south of what later would become John C. Calhoun's plantation. In 1785, General Pickens cosigned the Treaty of Hopewell, which defined the South Carolina Cherokee boundary as a sliver of land delimited by a line from the "'top of the Oconee mountain till it shall strike Tugaloo river,'" the state boundary with Georgia.[5] Remaining Cherokee territory in South Carolina thus excluded the Oolenoy Valley, which had been opened for legal white settlement only after the end of the Revolutionary War in 1783. During the decade of the 1780s, central authority was weak, and whites regularly signed fraudulent treaties, trespassed on Indian lands, and murdered headmen and villagers.[6] The symbolic closing of the frontier in South Carolina came about twenty years later, when Oconee Station, the last frontier outpost (now in Oconee County), closed and the remaining Cherokee land was sold.[7]

While scholars have discussed the significant social presence and cultural (and racial) impact of the Cherokee on Appalachian race relations to the north and west of the Upstate (in North Carolina, Tennessee, and Georgia) throughout the late eighteenth and early nineteenth centuries, the Cherokee as a political entity disappear from South Carolina's local histories after the end of the Revolutionary War.[8] However, individual Native peoples do not. Many Upstate families today claim an "Indian" ancestor, but sometimes that ethnic label may disguise a more complicated genealogical past—for example, the curious case of Sam "Goob" Keith, described in this and in chapters 3 and 4.

By the late eighteenth century, small Euro-American settlements appeared in the Upstate, as scattered mountain farms and floodplain plantations. The invention of Eli Whitney's cotton gin in 1793 made possible the transformation of much of the interior of the state for cotton production, and South Carolina's economy increasingly became linked to the global market.[9] One of the most prominent Upstate planters, John C. Calhoun, emerged onto the national stage by the 1820s and became a vehement defender of states' rights and slavery.[10] As Calhoun and his northern coun-

terpart Daniel Webster sparred over these issues, Calhoun's fellow south-
erner Andrew Jackson forcibly removed from northern Georgia most of the
Cherokee (and many other southeastern indigenous peoples) during the
nation's "manifest destiny" of the 1830s. War on the southwestern border
over Texas, the discovery of gold in California, and the question of slavery's
expansion into the new U.S. territories on the eastern Great Plains swept
the national conscience. Compromises in the 1850s between North and
South only delayed the coming storm, historian Louis Wright observed. And
yet, on the eve of the Civil War, historian Walter Edgar acknowledged,
South Carolina "continued the economic pattern established more than
150 years earlier: an agricultural economy based upon staple crops produced for world markets by enslaved black labor."[11]

Settlement of the Oolenoy Valley

According to local tradition, one of the first Euro-American settlers to the
Oolenoy Valley was Cornelius Keith, a Scots immigrant to the United States.
Most likely, the pioneer was Keith's son, also named Cornelius. As some settlers before and many after them, the Keith party followed the Great Wagon
Road from Virginia down the front range of the Blue Ridge, through North
Carolina, and eventually to the Oolenoy Valley in South Carolina sometime after the Cherokee removal from most of South Carolina (1777) and
after the end of the Revolutionary War (1783).[12] Specifically, John M. Keith
(a direct descendant), documented in his family history that "on April 25,
1795, Cornelius Junior [son of the Keith immigrant] purchased 100 acres of
land from Colin Campbell in Pendleton District, South Carolina, on both
sides of the Oolinoy [sic] Creek." Any date earlier than that is "utterly beyond reason," John Keith asserted, because as scholars had noted, before
1777 the land had belonged to the Cherokee. Legend has it that Cornelius
Keith bought his land from a Cherokee leader ("Chief Woolenoy") for a pony,
but regional historian Fred Holder dismissed that story as showing "at best a
complete ignorance of history."[13] Validating John Keith's version of his own
family history, sociologist Wilma Dunaway found that at this time most of
the land in upper South Carolina was held by land speculators (such as Colin
Campbell) from whom actual settlers purchased their land titles.[14] Keith
eventually chose a hill on the north side of the Oolenoy River upon which to
build his permanent residence, while (apparently) his tract included land on
both banks of the river. Ambrose Reid, whose ancestors hailed from In-
verness, Scotland, also had built a home in the valley by 1812.[15]

The establishment of clusters of homes in the district that eventually became the upper part of Pickens County evolved into Pumpkintown, a small crossroads community named for the abundant squash an early traveler observed growing in the fertile floodplains of the Oolenoy River, "land so rich and fertile that one had to raise one's eyes to the blue sky to see how tall the corn grew." A later local historian, on the other hand, credited an inebriated Scots-Irish local resident (unnamed) who, growing tired of a debate for the community's name, waved his arm toward the "great fields of corn and immense pumpkins," swore and exclaimed, " 'Jest call 'er Punkin Town!' "[16]

At least two antebellum descriptions of the community exist, both from travelers visiting nearby Table Rock Mountain and Hotel (see map 2). On August 6, 1840, Mary Moragne and her group arrived at the crossroads and noted "to the left was a fertile valley of waving corn watered by a pretty little stream." About two years later, T. Addison Richards's party reached "the heart of the metropolis [Pumpkintown], and instead of a cozy little village, found only one old shed, save kitchen, barn, and a 'smithy.' "[17]

"This settlement was all Scotch, the families including many of noble name," according to Flora Keith Overman, a descendant of these same families. Although wealth accumulation and economic inequality locally were relative (especially in comparison to the plantation wealth of South Carolina's Low Country), scholars such as John Inscoe and Wilma Dunaway noted that prominent white families typically "dominated highland society" by means of their wealth, family connections, business interests, and governmental power.[18] In fact, Inscoe added, "there was a strong correlation between when [that is, how early] a family settled . . . and its eventual status within mountain society." Dunaway argued that such status inequality eventually created a "polarized Appalachian society in which the wealthy gentry amassed a majority of the acreage while more than half the settler households remained landless." Moreover, mountain plantation owners "possessed a higher comparative percentage of their region's total wealth compared to their [Low Country] plantation counterparts." Exemplifying this trend, Flora Keith Overman proclaimed that her ancestors, the Keith brothers, "grew and prospered and ruled and ran that section of South Carolina."[19]

In the neighboring (present-day) county of Greenville, Daniel McJunkin (a family also originally from Scotland) moved after the Revolutionary War to the Middle Saluda River in the upper Blue Ridge coves, according to (white) McJunkin family history. A local historian provided his middle school interviewers with an unnamed document that claimed that James McJunkin, also a Scots immigrant, had "traded the Indians a pony and some chickens for a section of this county," an area at the base of the Blue Ridge and along the South Saluda River. According to the same document, in 1791 Jeremiah Cleveland then bought a large part of this tract; a small community still bears his name. Two years earlier, farther upstream in the South Saluda River valley just north of Table Rock, another settler, Joshua Burgess, "traded a horse to a Cherokee Indian for 900 acres."[20]

Readers may have noticed that for the Keith, McJunkin, and Burgess legendary land purchases, the price to the Native Americans was one pony (and some chickens as change) for enormous tracts of land. In addition to the criticisms (mentioned earlier) about the land being unavailable for Euro-American purchase until after 1785 or so, all three stories portrayed Native Americans as ignorant of the value of their groups' geographical areas and oblivious to the implication of permitting white settlement; simultaneously, the legends also portrayed the Euro-American immigrants as extremely clever. Since ethnohistorians agree that by this time Native Americans in the Southeast, including the Cherokee, already had acquired horses, such single equine trades for large land tracts seem highly doubtful.[21] Space does not permit a more detailed critical examination of these settler and Native American tales, but it is highly likely that such legends collapsed or ignored decades of Native American treaty negotiations and removal prior to the appearance of the first permanent Euro-American settlements in the Oolenoy Valley.

To work these Upstate farms and plantations, many of the prominent white landowners who "ruled and ran" this section of upper Pickens County bought and sold slaves and profited from their labor and the products of their labor. Slavery as an institution in the mountain counties of the Appalachians has been well documented by scholars such as John Inscoe, Steven Nash, Wilma Dunaway, and W. J. Megginson, with most of the research being done in western North Carolina and Virginia but including present-day Pickens and Greenville Counties in South Carolina (see, for example, Dunaway's map and Megginson's book).[22] While Inscoe acknowledged a "quiltlike character" of varied degrees of acceptance in the area, southerners in general (and Appalachian whites more specifically) supported slavery, including white residents in Upstate South Carolina. After all, as Inscoe observed, western North Carolina and northeastern Georgia were closer to Pickens County than were Charleston and Savannah, and the Upcountry descendants of the Scots-Irish avoided the British-descended Low Country planters as much as possible.[23] Thus, descriptions of slavery in the Upstate much more closely resembled the institution in the Appalachian regions just to the north and west rather than descriptions of slavery on South Carolina's Low Country rice and cotton plantations.

Logically, Dunaway observed, Appalachian slaveholders "were the wealthiest, most powerful elites in the region," because "slaveholders monopolized land and held the dominant economic and sociopolitical positions in the region's local economies, and the wealthiest planter-merchant elites stood at the pinnacle of local status." Dunaway added that local slaveholders also "championed proslavery agendas rather than the social and economic interests of the nonslaveholders in their own communities." Ultimately, Dunaway concluded that even if most Appalachian whites did not participate directly in slave ownership, "local merchants and nonslaveholding farms benefited from the economic spin-offs from that trade."[24] Despite a "quiltlike" degree of varied acceptance for the institution of slavery, the antebellum Upstate economy, including individual landowners and all their white trading partners, benefited directly or indirectly from the labor and products of enslaved blacks.

According to the U.S. Slave Census, there were approximately 4,166 slaves in Pickens District (present-day Oconee and Pickens Counties) in 1860; at least "10–20 percent of the [overall] population," according to historian Scott Poole.[25] While the Pickens District numbers stretched over two present-day counties and included the large Seneca River floodplain plantations of national politicians like John C. Calhoun as well as the relatively smaller holdings of farmers like the Keiths in the Oolenoy Valley, contemporary scholars and the nineteenth-century census takers agreed that there were significant numbers of enslaved blacks living in the Upstate in general, and in upper Pickens County in particular, by the time the Civil War erupted in 1861.

According to Dunaway, approximately one-third of the families in the South Carolina mountain areas owned slaves, and that was generally true in the Oolenoy Valley area as well.[26] "I was told that there were only about 10 or 12 slaves or slave families held by other farmers in the [Pumpkintown] community," local historian Josef Reece recollected from his childhood stories; he could be reflecting his mother's memories as well. Family names of slave owners in the valley included descendants of the original families, who had become some of the region's larger landholders by the mid-nineteenth century: Sutherlands, Hesters, Burgesses, and Keiths (among others); Josef Reece added the Gowens and Owens families to his mother's list.[27]

According to the 1860 U.S. Slave Census for Pickens District (and in keeping with historians' generalizations), the actual numbers of slaves owned per person were relatively small: for example, James Sutherland owned seventeen slaves; John Sutherland, ten; Abraham Hester, eleven; Sarah Burgess, five; James Keith, thirteen; and Ambrose Reid, five. In a newspaper article from 1930, Flora Keith Overman (born in 1849) reflected on her Pickens District childhood: "Our family [the Keiths] lived on a large and well-equipped plantation of 1,300 acres. There were from 50 to 100 slaves who worked this farm, and for years made good crops and fed the family—black and white. We wanted for nothing; everything was plentiful. . . . Not anything ever disturbed us; the sun rose and set in peace and quietness every day for four sad, long years [the Civil War], for we were in the care of our faithful slaves. I say all honor to them!" Local historian Bert Hendricks Reece added a few more details: "The fair treatment of slaves seemed to have been the rule with all the Keiths. . . . Their rule was to give each member of the family a Negro girl, valued at $1,000 for a wedding gift."[28]

Flora Keith Overman recalled that her grandfather, William LaFoon Keith, "left his plantation at Table Rock in the valley of the Oolenoy for his slaves to run. His own slave was his overseer; never was there a hired white man over his plantation."[29] Dunaway noted that this practice occurred in about 10 percent of the mountain plantations: "In these cases, the slave foreman assumed the duties of an overseer to control the other laborers. Elderly [or inexperienced] owners often relied upon trusted slaves to direct and monitor outdoor work." For example, according to Sutherland family local history, James B. Hester (married in 1859) "owned a farm of fine bottom land" on the Oolenoy River, and during the Civil War, "his wife ran the farm." Undoubtedly, the young bride had a great deal of help. The story of Hester's "boss slave" Emerson (or "Empse"), described later in this chapter and in subsequent chapters, enlightens this statement.[30]

William Keith eventually moved to Old Pickens, the former county seat (now flooded by Lake Keowee), and his granddaughter Flora described the life of enslaved blacks from the perspective of their white owners: "Grandma had her colored housekeeper, Aunty Lucy and her mother, Aunt Jinny, was the cook. The yard was full of little negroes ready to run errands or do service all day long. . . . Our household slaves told me fairy tales, stories of boars in the winds, and many an old negro legend. My nurse was given to my mother when she married by her Grandfather, John Thompson. Her name was Caroline. . . . My mother was good to her slaves and always helped take care of the little negro babies born in the home quarters and in the plantation houses."[31] Local historian Bert Reece added: "These slaves remained devoted mostly to their 'white folks.' . . . The colored mammies seemed to love the white children as their own and gave them such devoted care." As early as 1836, local historians Alma Lynch and Elizabeth Ellison discovered, enslaved African Americans even attended Oolenoy Baptist Church, and according to the church minutes, eighteen blacks were members in June 1845.[32]

Terms for African Americans probably reflected what sociologist Bertram Doyle described as a restricted but still heartfelt level of affection by some whites for these enslaved individuals. "Certain of the old slaves, especially on the plantation, were addressed as 'Uncle,' usually with the Christian name. Next to 'mammy,' this title, perhaps, represented the highest respect paid to slaves by white persons." In the mountain counties more than the lower South, historian John Inscoe concluded, "genuine affection and intimacy often existed between individual blacks and their owners."[33] Such feelings may have occurred because mountain slaves had a wider variety of tasks and formed a smaller minority (and were thus viewed as less of a threat for rebellion); in addition, slaveholders themselves formed a minority of whites, and so came under greater scrutiny by their nonslaveholding neighbors.[34]

No known records exist specifically from the Oolenoy Valley detailing life in the slave quarters of the small plantations of the landed local gentry. However, general life of Upstate blacks under slavery has been well documented by historians and sociologists.[35] For most multi-slave Upstate plantations and farms, historian W. J. Megginson observed, "cabins may have been grouped together—probably not in a neat row, like many in the lowcountry, because of land contours. Cabins would likely have been erected on poor land," such as outside the main Oolenoy Valley. At this time, most slaves lived in small cabins with plank or dirt floors, with chimneys of sticks or mud. Sanitation problems (especially access to good drinking water) were magnified because slaves lived in crowded conditions.[36] Households grew some vegetable crops. Historian Walter Edgar noted that food consisted of "corn (cornbread, ash cake, mush, hominy, or grits), molasses, and whatever vegetables and meat they were able to provide for themselves." "In the best of times," Dunaway discovered, "most Appalachian slaves were underfed and malnourished, and their diets lacked many of the nutrients essential to good health."[37] Greenville County resident James Monroe McJunkin corroborated this information, for he had heard from his enslaved grandfather that slaves ate whatever they could get from their masters. "If the master asked them to eat beans, they got beans. They got whatever the master wanted them to eat."[38]

Despite their poor nutrition and health, slaves labored extensively. "Whatever he [the master] wanted done, they did it," James McJunkin continued. Based on her review of ex-slave narratives and slavers' journals, sociologist Dunaway provided additional details that supported McJunkin's recollections. For example, Dunaway cited the journal of a slaveholder just across the North Carolina line who described the typical activities of slaves. Enslaved women would "cut briars, plant pumpkin seed, pull flax, gather clover seed, dig sweet potatoes, sprout new ground, and hoe corn. Women harvested corn and fodder and stacked it at the ends of the rows, while males hauled it from the fields. Later women shucked and shelled the corn and packed the fodder into the barn. Men cut firewood and timber, while women carried it to the road and stacked it."[39] Dunaway found that "slave women worked alongside men at most productive economic tasks, including field work, meat production, tobacco manufacturing, milling, cotton ginning, and leather tanning." Women also "did most of the tasks necessary to manage a household, including meal preparation, cabin cleaning, food preservation, and caregiving to the young, the sick, the pregnant, and the dying." Historian John Blassingame supported Dunaway's findings, and anthropologist Mary Anglin added cloth making and clothing manufacture to the preceding list.[40]

As Oolenoy Valley resident Bert Reece suggested earlier, Dunaway found that "black midwives and experienced 'grannies' provided prenatal advice and tended postpartum mothers. . . . On many mountain plantations, 'old negro mammies' used their accumulated medical wisdom to treat everyone in the quarters, and sometimes on adjacent farms. The most expert slave healers were *conjurors* who were able to diagnose and treat complex conditions with herbal concoctions, charms, diets, and physical regimens. Combining African and Native American knowledge about indigenous plants, these healers used a variety of teas, poultices, and ointments derived from plants gathered from the woods or cultivated in garden parcels" (emphasis in original).[41]

Dunaway's analysis of ex-slave narratives and owner journals demonstrated that slaves created their own social and cultural worlds (borrowing James Scott's hidden transcripts concept) in order to reassert their own humanity, to keep African and generational traditions alive, and to defend themselves physically and emotionally. "Illiterate and denied any written history of their group's past," Dunaway noted, "they [mountain slaves] rooted themselves politically in an oral memory pool that refuted slave-holder myths that justified the oppressive system."[42] Sociologist Jillian Jimenez argued that grandmothers especially offered a "counternarrative to their grandchildren, one in which the owners had less power."[43] In Dunaway's analysis, households became *sustenance pooling structures* through which slaves organized self-provisioning, confronted external threats, and ensured the short-term survival and intergenerational reproduction of laborers." In addition, "cultural specialists . . . kept alive mountain slave traditions," and "weddings, funerals, weekend and holiday gatherings, work parties, and religious meetings" created social outlets and opportunities for slaves to rehumanize themselves and reassert their independent cultural identity.[44]

Undermining slave attempts at preserving their humanity was the fact that, like livestock, slaves could be sold regardless of marital or kin relations. While historians Edgar and Blassingame argued that masters encouraged their slaves to create families in order to provide stability, to prevent runaways, and to reproduce property, sociologist Dunaway had a differing perspective after reviewing the ex-slave narratives and slavers' journals. "Very few Appalachian slave marriages were publicly acknowledged," Dunaway discovered, "and the only record of parentage was maintained as part of masters' written inventories or mental notes."[45] All sources agreed with historian Walter Edgar that slavery as an institution eroded the strength of male slaves to be true heads of their families: "Shelter, clothing, food, and working conditions were all dictated by the owner. A man could not protect his wife or daughters from unwanted advances by overseers or owners. Every member of the family was subject to being disciplined, and children saw their parents whipped and vice versa."[46]

Following most slave sales, historian W. J. Megginson noted, Upstate slaves "found themselves living not much farther away," with families remaining in contact and thus "less permanently disrupted." However, individual family stories varied from this trend. Jane Hunter, an African American woman born in the Upstate in the late nineteenth century, remembered stories from her grandmother (enslaved in what is today Anderson County), who witnessed "the separation of families by chattel sale [and] . . . the tearing apart of her own soul when her mother was sold down the river to a new and unknown master."[47] The McGowens family's oral tradition from the Liberia area included a story about three full brothers who acquired three different last names because they had been owned by three different families (Lewis, Sutherland, and Burgess); through time, this common ancestry probably would have been forgotten. Angela McJunkin Young did not know the name of her great-grandfather's first wife or their children's names, because all "were sold as slaves" and thus lost to family history. As Dunaway had noted, the "emotional needs or kinship ties of slaves were not even recognized as anything like those experienced by their white oppressors." Ironically, Dunaway added, while Appalachian whites lauded the virtues of their own kinship networks and family history, "Appalachian masters destroyed black families in great numbers."[48]

It is difficult to trace the kinship ties and familial relationships of these enslaved Americans because before the Civil War, slaves had no last names except (occasionally) for the very old. James Monroe McJunkin reminded his young interviewers what that dehumanization felt like and meant to his own enslaved grandfather, Joseph: "Before that time we didn't have a name. I tell some people it was like that mule out there. I call him Tob. That's all he has is Tob. All he had then was Joseph. When freedom came he had to have a last name, so he chose McJunkin." McJunkin had been a kind master, so Joseph kept that name. However, because of the continual dissolution and breakup of families, Dunaway concluded that "very few Appalachian ex-slaves were able to maintain permanent surnames that reflected the identities of their biological fathers."[49]

The historical and sociological analyses of enslaved African Americans discussed earlier provide a general picture of life under slavery in the Upstate of South Carolina. But what can be learned of the personal histories of the actual human beings who lived in the Oolenoy Valley during this period but outside the boundaries of documented history? Fortunately, white-authored local histories occasionally acknowledged by name the presence of the human beings whose labor made possible a comfortable standard of living for many whites; occasionally, white-controlled news stories mentioned these people as well. Black oral tradition preserves some stories, too. These anecdotes and sketches offer the only documentary evidence for the otherwise rich lives of these human beings; moreover, this information had remained scattered in a variety of disparate sources. In this chapter, the stories are gathered together and placed into a historical and ethnographic context. The preserved tales provide brief, tantalizing glimpses into the lives of specific enslaved African Americans in the Oolenoy Valley, and illustrate and support some of the more general analytical points raised by scholars.

A few individuals were named and discussed. For example, Luke Terrell is mentioned as belonging to the Sutherland family in Bert Reece's local history (and eulogized in the *Pickens Sentinel* of March 23, 1923, p. 4). Another *Pickens Sentinel* obituary (February 23, 1928, p. 8) described a woman named "Aunt Katie" who "made her home with some of the best families [including the Sutherlands] before the [18]60's. These people were always 'my folks' to her. Her loyalty grew stronger as the years went by" (see also figure 2). In a will dated September 4, 1844, Alfred Hester bequeathed to his son James Hester a "Negro woman" named Chaney (valued at $500) and her son, Emerson. As a young adult, Emerson (or "Empse") became James Hester's "boss slave" (see also the prologue, figure 8, and cover photo); he "was considered a valuable person" according to his obituary in the *Pickens Sentinel* on December 29, 1927. As Dunaway noted about such important slaves, Emerson most likely was Hester's plantation manager, entrusted with a great deal of responsibility by Hester's young wife, and undoubtedly the reason why Hester "found plenty of corn in his crib and bacon in the smokehouse" when he returned from the Civil War. Megginson found that such black overseers typically belonged to "widows and [absent] professional men" and noted that "overseers are a virtually invisible component of the area's history."[50]

One of the more complex stories of enslaved African Americans appeared in Reece's local history of the Oolenoy Valley. "In the days of slavery," she wrote, the Keith family had been known to be kind to their slaves. She continued: "At one of these sales, a small negro boy named Goob was to be sold. He tugged at Mark [Marse/Master?] Keith's trousers and begged, 'You buy me, . . . You buy me.' Keith bought him and he afterwards was known as Goob Keith. He lived a long useful life." Local historians Alma Lynch and Elizabeth Ellison repeated the story, adding that "a man" offered fifty dollars more than the asking price, and successfully "carried Goob home with him."[51] In a local news story from the *Easley Progress* over a century later (August 30, 1967), about a visit by some locals reminiscing over "Goob" Keith's grave, a few more details of his life from this prewar time are revealed. The visitors remembered that Keith "told of being sold to one of the [white] Keith brothers of Pumpkintown for $1,000 when he was a lad of 13 years. He told of prospective buyers examining his muscles and making bids on him during the auction sale. This man took the name of Keith since all slaves had the last name the same as their owners. He was called Sam Keith, but later he was called 'Goob' as a nickname. How he came about being called this is a puzzle." The nickname may have been short for "goober," an African American word of African origin for "peanut."

Identifying these specific individuals in the slave records of the 1860 Census is virtually impossible, for no names were recorded for "property," only approximate dates of birth, because actual birth records were rarely kept for property, either. "Boss slave" Emerson, for example, could have been the eighteen-year-old male slave enumerated for James Hester, "Goob" might have been the seven-year-old boy owned by James Keith, and Aunt Katie might have been the eighteen-year-old female owned by Sarah Sutherland, another by James K. Sutherland, or the twenty-year-old female owned by "[Cor]Nelius" Keith.[52]

To the east of Table Rock and Caesar's Head, in present-day Greenville County, was another group of slaveholding families, including the Blythes and the McJunkins. In the 1860 U.S. Slave Census, Daniel Blythe owned thirty-five slaves, Absalom Blythe owned twenty-six, Sarah McJunkin owned three (including a forty-two-year-old man), and Daniel McJunkin owned one, a thirty-five-year-old man. According to the oral tradition of the (black) McJunkin family as narrated by a great-granddaughter, their family's patriarch was a man named Joseph, sold as a slave down in Georgia in 1820 (see appendix 2). Joseph had always told his descendants that he was from Liberia, in Africa. Since the colony (later country) of Liberia was founded by freed slaves returned to Africa right around that date, it is possible that Joseph came from that already-established colony, or a region nearby. It is also possible that he could have come from the region in Africa (on or before 1820) that later became known as the nation of Liberia. Dunaway observed that such "intergenerational transmission of stories about the African diaspora" reflected the strength of slave families through time.[53]

According to (black) McJunkin family tradition, Joseph eventually was bought by Absalom Blythe, who was said to be cruel to his slaves. The Blythes owned far more slaves per capita than the McJunkins (as mentioned earlier), and historian John Inscoe argued that the owners who had fewer slaves tended to be more lenient overall. Absalom Blythe took Joseph to River Falls, a plantation deep into a Blue Ridge valley, on the Middle Saluda River (see map 2) where a small cluster of homes still carries that name today. Joseph labored as a slave there for over forty years. Escape was impossible, since "paddy rollers" (patrollers) caught and punished runaway slaves. "So you just had to stay and suffer the consequences," grandson James Monroe McJunkin explained. James McJunkin's daughter added that one time Blythe told Joseph to catch another slave, but he refused to do it, sparking (she continued) "almost a war between the master and the master's companion. . . . [In fact], it was this firm stand that ended whipping [as punishment] on Absalom Blythe's plantation." Fortunately, sometime before the Civil War, Joseph and his half brother John were sold to the McJunkin family, and because these new owners treated the brothers better, eventually they took that last name as their own, a great-granddaughter explained.[54] These two men, Joseph and John, are most likely the two black males listed as owned by Sarah and Daniel McJunkin in the 1860 Slave Census.

Eventually, James Monroe McJunkin's tale continued, John was sold for $1,500 and worried that he would be taken farther south into Alabama. The (white) McJunkins begged the new owner not to take John farther south; "Oh, no; I would never do that," the new owner replied innocently. "They took the boat and traveled by river" down the Tennessee and then on to the Ohio, at which time John realized he had been tricked. He jumped overboard. "The owner and his dogs jumped in after him and [John] drowned them and escaped into Ohio, into free land." In a contemporary retelling of the story, Angela Young (James McJunkin's daughter) somberly concluded her history with "John was never heard of again." Meanwhile, Joseph stayed with his new owner, Young continued, but to safeguard other possible runaways, "Joseph remarked to the other slaves on the plantation, 'Now if one should decide to run away then the next one we aren't to report or tell on that one. In other words, you zip your lips!'"[55]

This family narrative, preserved for over a century and a half, illustrates several broader historical and theoretical issues. In her review of ex-slave narratives, Dunaway concluded that "impending sales or distant hires of family members triggered more than two-fifths of the successful escapes of Appalachian slaves to the North." Moreover, in order to prevent runaways, Dunaway found that Appalachian masters typically disguised their impending plans for sales of human beings. Joseph's admonition to his enslaved peers also suggests the immensity of Foucault's generalized surveillance, in which the slaves so embodied the dominant power inequality that they watched each other in order to maintain compliance. But upon closer inspection, the family story exemplifies Scott's public and hidden transcripts: for the former, one of the "rare moments of political electricity" where the oppressed overthrows the oppressor and gains freedom, and how the resistance by a slave to a master's command triggered "almost a war" but this "firm stand" successfully ended whipping on the plantation; and the hidden transcript where the inevitability of escape was acknowledged by the slaves, but their public response to that fact to the faces of their white masters was manifest silence and professed ignorance.[56]

"When the Civil War broke out," Angela Young continued, Joseph "predicted that the North was going to beat the South," and that angered some whites in the area so much that they plotted to kill him. One day Joseph's owner (who must have been Sarah McJunkin) sent him to Greenville on "Maude," the mule, to pay the taxes, and she cautioned him to be careful, for she feared for his life. On the return trip Joseph rode down a long hill on the road from Greenville (now U.S. Highway 276), and at the bottom of that hill, near the junction of present-day Long Shoals Road (north of the Gold Mine, see map 2), the mob lay in wait for him. Mrs. Young's voice quieted as she continued: "So when he came along and he saw the mob he said, . . . 'Whoa, Maude!' And then he said to the gentlemen, 'How are you gentlemen?' and tipped his hat. And my Dad said, 'And that's when the Lord paralyzed their hands' and they didn't kill him. And then he said, 'Get up, Maude,' and he went on back to the old home place."[57]

These family stories of the lives of slaves illustrate several critical cultural themes involving life in the days before emancipation, and thus support the theoretical concepts discussed in chapter 1. First, narratives told and preserved (orally or in writing) by whites exemplify the public memory or public transcript, painting African Americans as contented with their lives and their enslaved condition, especially as being contented with the white families who preserved the stories about them. As political scientist James Scott noted, the public transcript of domination becomes a "kind of self-hypnosis within ruling groups to buck up their courage, improve their cohesion, display their power, and convince themselves anew of their high moral purpose."[58] At the same time, without the benefit of hidden transcripts, it is impossible to know for certain whether the black "mammies" truly loved their white charges or they recognized that if they did not display the appropriate amount of affection, they might be sold "down in Alabama" and perpetually separated from their own children and spouses. Patricia Hill Collins has suggested that the "mammy" figure "symbolizes the dominant group's perceptions of the ideal Black female relationship to elite White male power." In such situations of unequal power, Scott added, "subordinates offer a performance of deference and consent while attempting to discern, to read, the real intentions and mood of the potentially threatening powerholder."[59]

Second, readers also get a glimpse of the complicated performance of social interaction played by blacks and whites under slavery. Historian W. J. Megginson described antebellum Upstate plantation life as "richly textured as well as multicolored"; blacks and whites played together as children and interacted together as adults, Megginson explained. Sociologist Bertram Doyle described this social interaction as "a well-recognized code of observances . . . between white persons and slaves."[60] Black nannies cared for their young white charges and entertained them with folk tales, nursed them with traditional cures, and fed them from cherished recipes. Especially on the small plantations, white farmers utilized slave labor while working side by side with them, splitting rails or shucking corn. Black and white adults both knew their respective places, but simultaneously freely interacted on a daily basis as they barbecued pigs over an open charcoal fire, swapped stories on a cool autumn night, or sipped moonshine on a shady front porch. Many oral traditions and social behaviors freely passed between castes of people who themselves were constrained by legal and social barriers.

As one could imagine, close interaction between males and females separated by a legal and social chasm that permitted the complete domination of one category over the other inevitably led to sexual encounters across the racial boundary. Lost to the hushed whispers of memory were the emotional, psychological, and social conditions of these encounters—were they consensual or coerced? And from whose perspective is this assessed, the master's or the slave's? As social historian George Tindall observed, "under the system of slavery there had sometimes been a degree of intimacy between the plantation owner, his sons, and the overseers and the female slaves." Sociologist Patricia Hill Collins has argued that "any sexual encounters between two parties where one has so much control over the other could never be fully consensual, even if the slave appeared to agree. Structural power differences of this magnitude limit the subordinate's power to give free consent or refusal." Collins added that this sexual degradation of female slaves allowed white women to uphold the "purity" of womanhood while adding to the general system of oppression and subordination within slavery. On the other hand, Collins observed, "to characterize interracial sex purely in terms of the victimization of Black women would be a distortion, because such depictions strip Black women of agency. Many Black women successfully resisted sexual assault while others cut bargains with their masters." Through all of these kinds of relationships, Tindall noted, "the greatest portion of the mulatto population came into existence."[61]

Given the general inequality between males and females in Victorian-era America, coupled with the enormous inequality between master and slave (as Collins noted earlier), one might expect these encounters never to have been recorded in white family histories.[62] No white informant ever has mentioned such forced relationships, and none appear in any printed local history. Yet, Dunaway found that "about 5 percent of all the slave narratives in the WPA [Works Progress Administration] collection include reports that the slave's father was white. . . . Moreover, one in ten Appalachian slave families was headed by a woman whose children were the outcome of her sexual exploitation by white males."[63] Preserved in the oral traditions of African American families, the stories persist.

For example, the family history of the Talleys documented a poignant story about their ancestor Rosa Talley: "Afraid of physical abuse if she resisted his advances, she complied to the will of a white man on the Reuben Talley Plantation in Travelers Rest [south of Slater-Marietta, see map 2]. At the age of thirteen, she gave birth to a beautiful red mulatto baby with red hair."[64] Another northern Greenville black resident knew that his "great-grandfather was a white slave owner." "I don't guess I can really call him my great-grandfather," the man reflected, "but you know that's my grandfather's pop." "Just looking at" you, a relative acknowledged, "you definitely can see that there's the strong genes from the white family that's mixed with the black race." "That's why we don't need suntans!" he joked in response.

Angela Young related that her father, James Monroe McJunkin, had always told his children that a white woman from one of the original landowning families was actually their great-grandmother. Young explained that back in the days of slavery, this white woman had owned Joseph McJunkin and also had become his "mistress" (when asked to explain, she specifically denoted both an intimate and an ownership relationship). Given this white ancestry on his side, James McJunkin had always wondered why his daughter Angela had not "blanched out" when she was born, because her mother had also been very fair-skinned. In fact, Young indicated, the physician attending her birth originally even had written "White" on her birth certificate.

Another theme about life under slavery that emerges from these family stories is more ominous. "You have to feel bitter" about the days of slavery, James Monroe McJunkin recalled. Contemporary readers from a privileged position may find it impossible to imagine the horrors of the culture of terror under enslavement: the constant fear of instant death or horrible disfigurement by torture; the ever-present knowledge that one's spouse, children, or parents could disappear forever in the back of a new owner's buggy; the omnipresent threat of rape or the fear that a "consensual" union might suddenly metamorphose into a deadly accusation; and the continual stress of constantly being watched, evaluated, and criticized for "inappropriate" behavior, an evaluation shifting like branches in the wind. Historian John Blassingame discussed the subsequent psychological stresses and necessary survival strategies for enslaved persons. "Appropriate" behavior depended solely on the judgment of whichever white was immediately present, regardless of whether a slave was owned by a "good" person or not. Walter Edgar described the feeling as "walking on eggshells," for owners "literally had life and death control over the lives of human beings subject to their caprice." "There was always the possibility of cruelty in the domination of the owner," Jane Edna Hunter had learned from her enslaved grandparents. Because of this arbitrary and unpredictable cruelty, Jane Hunter's grandparents had taught her that "beneath the trust and dependence of the slave smouldered [sic] resentment that might readily kindle into flame."[65]

Understandably, such horrific stories would not pass down through a white family's oral tradition, except in situations in which one family's ancestors might have been "better owners" than their neighbors. On the other hand, African American families do remember such incidents. "Yeah, they were quite rough" on the slaves, James McJunkin recalled hearing from his grandfather Joseph. "Some [of the old-timers] tell me they would whip them till they started bleeding; then they would put salt on their cuts, and make it hurt." Starks Adams (from northern Greenville County) provided a chilling example of humiliating torture from his own family history. Adams's grandmother, from a plantation in Travelers Rest (south of Slater-Marietta), "said that her mistress said, 'Pull off my shoe, Nancy!' And she'd pull her shoe off. [Then her mistress would] smack her in the face with it, then say, 'Put my shoe back on!' And she'd put it back on. That's slavery."[66] As the McJunkin tales illustrated, however, such episodes pervaded the lives of every enslaved (and freed) black. Even an act as mundane as a personal opinion uttered in public could result in death. Thus, as Joseph cautioned, "you zip your lips" and act benevolently, deferentially, humbly, and jovially in the presence of every white person in your life for your entire life.

Such superficial passivity, however, disguised various forms of resistance utilized by enslaved African Americans. Sociologist Bertram Doyle described slave accommodation strategies such as acting submissively, laughing, joking, singing, and quoting Scripture, and reminding potential tormentors of a slave's well-known fidelity or the master's well-known empathy. Sociologist Wilma Dunaway documented both active and passive forms of resistance, by individuals and groups, ranging from breaking tools and slowing work to physical retaliation and revenge killings. As

James Scott argued, if whites controlled the public memory, and subordinates' resistance was hidden (for their own protection), then black family histories illustrating either public forms of resistance or the hidden transcripts that circumvent that power (Scott's "infrapolitics of the powerless") become critical theoretical support for presenting a countermemory, or an alternate truth to white domination, even under slavery.[67]

For example, Furman Suddeth (a white northern Greenville County resident) recalled a story told to him by his father "about this slave that had a walking cane, and the cane was hollow." The master allowed his slave to visit "public places" on Saturday evenings and Sundays. Unknown to the master, the slave filled the cane with liquor, sold capfuls for ten cents a cup, and made enough to buy his freedom. In the stories discussed earlier, there are even more dramatic examples of Scott's breaching of the public and hidden transcript boundary: Joseph actively resisting his master and ending whipping on the Blythe Plantation; and his brother John, drowning his new master when he discovered he was being sold down to Alabama. The latter man swam across the Ohio River to freedom—flight being another form of resistance—and was never heard from again.[68]

The most effective, and least dangerous, form of resistance, however, was what Dunaway described as the development of a separate culture, religion, and social institutions, based partly on African roots, which created for the slaves an identity of strength, intelligence, and utility apart from the identity of submission and inferiority created for them by whites. Borrowing James Scott's concept, Dunaway characterized these alternate cultural identities as hidden transcripts that reflected the social world as the marginalized group saw it rather than as the dominant group defined the world. "Because it aimed at building long-term family and community solidarity," Dunaway noted, this "nonviolent covert resistance was probably the most effective strategy feasible to slaves on small plantations."[69]

Unfortunately, most of these slave-period hidden transcripts remain undocumented, for cultural details do not appear in either black or white family histories from the Oolenoy Valley. However, as will be seen in chapter 3, African American communities, families, churches, schools, and cultural traditions appeared as well-established institutions by 1865, and so it is quite reasonable to assume that similar traditions, communities, and institutions existed in previous decades.

Most of the original white settlers to the Oolenoy Valley rest peacefully in the Oolenoy Baptist Church Cemetery (see map 3). Here lies Cornelius Keith, along with his kin and those of many prominent local families, including members of the Edens, Sutherland, Hester, and Reid families. Nestled under a grove of majestic cedars lay two clusters of the oldest graves, enclosed in rectangular, coffin-shaped fieldstone constructions, with soapstone tombstones (some with hand-carved inscriptions). Local historian Bert Reece believed that the soapstone "was mined, shaped, and lettered . . . by the Negroes of Liberia with much skill and artistry" from the large slabs about two miles across the Oolenoy Valley near the present-day Soapstone Baptist Church (see map 3). On the other hand, Reid family history credits Ambrose Reid with some of these carvings, for "he had dressed, polished, shaped and carved other soap stones and made quaint markers in the Oolenoy Cemetery, but he had carved each letter of this tombstone [Elizabeth Allen Reid] with special care, giving it the studied, gentle, and creative touch. He also composed the inscription, 'When death comes, the truest loves must part.' "[70]

No one knows the purpose of these boxlike structures. One Keith descendant believed that the graves reflected the traditional structures of England and Scotland, "because there were English graves that look like that now over in England today." On the other hand, Bert Reece suggested they had been "patterned after that of an Indian chief—a mound of field rock with a small soap stone head rock."[71] A marker to the presence of Cherokee graves had been erected at Oolenoy Church Cemetery near a cluster of a few rough fieldstones—and a marker dedicated to the "faithful slaves" buried here as well. A current Oolenoy resident remembered that two of those gravestones actually bore names: "one, a man named Isham, and a woman named Agatha. Their tombstones are still there and they were slaves." Her brother added, "They were the only ones that were marked." Since most slave graves had been marked by wood, they would have rotted by the mid-twentieth century. John De Forest, the commanding officer of the Freedmen's Bureau in Greenville shortly after the Civil War, described an old cemetery: "Walking in a wood a mile or so from [Greenville], . . . I came upon a Negro cemetery of the times of slavery. A headstone of coarse white marble, five or six of brick, and forty or fifty wooden slabs, all grimed and mouldering with the dampness of the forest, constituted the sordid sepulchral pomps of the 'nameless people.' "[72]

Conclusion

By the dawn of the Civil War, family stories (whether by whites or blacks) designate only a few enslaved individuals by name. The other "nameless people," the original residents of Liberia, only became "real" persons (that is, named individuals) with the close of the war and subsequent historical documents. Until then, it is only possible to speculate about their personal lives, but readers obtain a better sense of those lives through the collected slave narratives and general histories of those times. These individuals labored in obscurity, without compensation and frequently without thanks, under constant threat of brutal physical punishment, sexual assault, torture, and death. Their children or spouses might be torn from their arms at the whim, or economic expediency, of their owners. At the same time, these enslaved individuals resisted this domination in many ways: false smiles disguising disgust and hatred; derogatory jokes and stories about their owners told in small private homes; the manipulation of white benevolence for black benefit; and active resistance to enslavement through argument, escape, and revenge killings. While it is impossible to trace all of the original inhabitants of Liberia, it is possible to follow the lives of some (see appendices 1 and 2). For Aunt Katie, Emerson the overseer, Sam/Goob, Joseph, and their families and friends, life in the Oolenoy Valley would soon change dramatically.

3 The Times Ahead Are Fearful

The Late Nineteenth Century

Between the census decades of 1860 and 1870, life for most African Americans in Upstate South Carolina, and in fact the United States, radically changed. While black farmers or blacksmiths or midwives or laundresses continued their tasks in much the same way as they always had, ownership of their labor now became contested between themselves and (for most of them) their former enslavers.[1] Historian Steven Hahn described this time as a "liminal period" (a period of transition), during which "issues of land, labor, power, and authority would be contested in good measure by means of personal confrontations, community skirmishes, and subterranean discourse." This contestation, historian Loren Schweninger added, took many forms across time and space.[2] It is during this national liminal period that the freedom colony of Liberia emerged.

Journalist Sidney Andrews, a traveler throughout the South in 1866, captured the general sentiments of the time. Contemporary whites, Andrews observed, viewed blacks as having "most of the vices and very few of the virtues of humanity. The negroes charge that the whites are revengeful, and intend to cheat the laboring class at every opportunity, and credit them with neither good purposes nor kindly hearts. . . . To dream that any of these States will voluntarily grant the ballot to the negro during this generation seems to me to qualify yourself for the insane asylum. . . . The whites seem wholly unable to comprehend that freedom for the negro means the same thing as freedom for them"[3] (lack of capitalization in original).

Reconstruction

Freedom! Immediately after the Civil War, "a millennial expectation of impending change swept the South," as blacks explored their economic and political freedom. Andrews wrote that black "souls are filled with a great but vague longing for freedom; they battle blindly with fate and circumstance for the unseen and uncomprehended, and seem to find every man's hand raised against them either for blows or reproaches."[4] The victorious North needed to crystallize immediately the malleable and juxtaposed social forces of black freedom and white domination. Reconstruction began.

One of the immediate consequences of Northern victory was the question about what to do with the former slaves, now freed as a consequence of the war but without access to the means of production. Throughout the war, Northern forces had been overwhelmed by former slaves as war refugees, and so almost from the war's beginning the North faced the ethical and practical dilemmas of providing these long-suffering human beings with the means of survival. Following his successful March to the Sea and occupation of Savannah in December 1864, Gen. William T. Sherman issued Field Order No. 15, which confiscated portions of the abandoned plantations along the South Carolina–Georgia coast and granted to all former slaves forty tillable acres of land. By April 1865, Gen. Rufus Saxon had begun implementation of the plan in South Carolina, but by September President Andrew Johnson had rescinded the order as the unconstitutional seizure of private property. However, the order entered popular culture as a "promise" by the federal government to provide all freed slaves with "forty acres and a mule," offering a message of hope for blacks and one of fear in whites.[5]

Following the general path of his predecessor, President Andrew Johnson allowed the southern states (under Presidential Reconstruction) to re-enter the Union, requiring them only to abolish slavery, repudiate secession, and abrogate the Confederate war debt in their new state constitutions. In response, however, southern whites implemented the "Black Codes" across much of the South, attempting to regain complete control over black labor by establishing extremely strict and unequal labor conditions. Angered by this southern intransigence, a Republican Congress then passed the Fourteenth Amendment (equality for all before the law, to be defended by the federal government) over Johnson's objections. The Congressional Reconstruction Acts of 1867 formalized black male suffrage and liberated black labor again (at least ideally; in reality, policies varied by state and even by community—see the following discussion of Liberia). Federal and state elections in 1868 swept black and white Republicans into office, beginning Congressional (Radical) Reconstruction. Blacks gained access to some public offices, public facilities, and public schools.[6] Historian Steven Nash described this period as a power struggle between the national government over local communities, between blacks and whites, and between upper-class and lower-class whites themselves. At least in western North Carolina (just north of Pickens County, South Carolina), Nash noted that many whites so opposed the old Confederate aristocracy that they initially supported the Republican Party's stance on civil rights.[7] With the new South Carolina state constitution of 1868, African Americans now had the rights to vote (males only), own property, and work where and how they chose.[8]

However, general forces conspired to undermine Reconstruction almost from its inception: widespread government corruption (a common national problem at the time); the lack of capital for development in the war-torn South; a declining international price for the South's principal crop (cotton); and white prejudice against the governing ability of blacks. More locally, in western North Carolina, Nash wrote that the faltering mountain economy and federal control over local alcohol production increasingly alienated many whites from the Republican Party. In response to these general trends, southern whites launched the more innocuous "home rule" movement and the more inimical Ku Klux Klan to restore local (that is, white and non-northern) control in order to "save" the South. After 1873, Reconstruction would be on the defensive.[9]

The public memories of South Carolina whites reflected this period of contestation over black and white control. "We decided that life was not worth living under the circumstances," Ben Robertson wrote in the early twentieth century, speaking for his elderly Pickens County relatives living in the late nineteenth century; "the North could send another vast army against us if it liked, it could shoot us, but we would not tolerate any longer the government the North had forced on us. So we [whites] got together and rebelled. We organized the Red Shirts. We took over. We intimidated, we hanged and shot, we voted tombstones in the election of 1876, and we won." "The evils of Negro rule was [sic] very grievous to the south," local historians Alma Lynch and Elizabeth Ellison lamented; "we turned to Wade Hampton and the 'Red Shirts' and returned the whites to places of leadership."[10]

By spring 1877, about nine months after Custer's annihilation at the Battle of the Little Bighorn, Republican presidential candidate Rutherford B. Hayes bartered a deal. Hayes and the Republicans agreed to recognize the South Carolina Democratic gubernatorial candidate Wade Hampton (a Confederate war hero backed by his paramilitary Red Shirt organization advocating "home rule") and to withdraw federal troops under Reconstruction supporting Daniel Chamberlain (the South Carolina Republican gubernatorial candidate) in exchange for South Carolina's electoral votes counting for Hayes. Even though Chamberlain actually won the election (according to modern statistical analysis and even some contemporary perspectives), federal troops were withdrawn, Hayes was declared president with the help of South Carolina's electoral college votes, and Wade Hampton and his allies occupied the statehouse in Columbia.[11]

With "home rule" (that is, white domination) reestablished, South Carolina's blacks lost most of their voting rights; lost most of their national, state, and local political positions; and faced much stricter penalties for petty crimes (thus increasing the convict labor pool for infrastructural improvements). Whites regained political control and consequently regained control of black labor. By this time northern interest had shifted from benign concern over the freed slaves to a desire to close the western frontier and to expand the Industrial Revolution. With the demise of Reconstruction and the loss of its reforms, for nearly a century afterward, most South Carolina blacks faced "a life of sharecropping, of tenancy, of poverty, of malnutrition, and of ignorance."[12]

Through the 1880s, the Republican Party in South Carolina declined in power as more African Americans lost their voting rights and no Euro-American constituency allied with them.[13] During this period, historian Glenda Gilmore noted, popular culture supported racial inequality and black male infantilism, as exemplified by the "science" of Social Darwinism. It was widely believed in white society that miscegenation, especially between black males and white females, watered down the superiority of the white race. According to Gilmore, this explained the widespread fear among whites of black male rapists. The black male rapist myth also served to pull lower-class whites away from closer populist ties with lower-class blacks and into the arms of the Democratic Party, Gilmore concluded. During this period, social custom enforced segregation, but the line was not rigid.[14]

However, with the 1890 South Carolina gubernatorial victory of Democrat "Pitchfork" Ben Tillman and the implementation of his radical racist policies, blacks fell into long-term second-class status, and the revised state constitution of 1895 enshrined that power differential into much more rigid segregation.[15] The new constitution legalized school segregation and defined racial categories—one-eighth African American ancestry equaled "black."[16] The next year, the Supreme Court's *Plessy v. Ferguson* decision legitimated southern segregation, and in short order South Carolina's mass transit systems, prisons, and the state militia all became segregated; blacks now rarely served on juries, could not work alongside whites in mills and factories, could not enter public buildings by the same door, drink from the same fountain, or use the same bathrooms.[17] In the reality of their everyday lives, African Americans thus faced much of the same antagonism, prejudice, and inequality as they had prior to 1860 within a "caste system based on race."[18] The new restrictions came to be known as "Jim Crow" legislation, named after a popular minstrel character.[19] Under these regulations, historian Glenda Gilmore noted, white males ruled; white women needed white male protection from dangerous, sexualized, uncontrollable black males to maintain racial purity; and the "best blacks" had no place in this hierarchy.[20] Significant black migration from the state began toward the end of the century.[21]

While the late nineteenth century presented blacks with many challenges, and while some whites served as critical black allies, historian Eric Foner described blacks during this time as "active agents" in improving their own lives. Foner argued that Reconstruction demonstrated the "heroism of former slaves who embraced emancipation, participated actively in politics, and struggled to consolidate their families and improve their communities."[22] "Despite the fact that blacks faced violence, segregation, and political proscription," historian George Tindall observed, African Americans were now equal under federal law (theoretically). Blacks attended free public schools (although segregated and of poorer quality), increasingly viewed literacy as a critical path to greater freedom, enrolled in segregated universities and professional programs, and established black churches as important community institutions. Labor contracts replaced permanent enslavement, and negotiable wages offered new opportunities.[23] Blacks increasingly left the exploitative labor market, using pooled household income in strategic ways to gain more economic independence and to seek power in other ways.[24] Independent black communities blossomed. The long, slow march forward, toward equality, had begun.

The Founding of Liberia

As historian Walter Edgar noted, "between February and June 1865 most black Carolinians learned that they were free"; historian W. J. Megginson specified that formal freedom arrived to the Upstate in July 1865 along with federal troops.[25] It may be impossible to imagine the complicated feelings of euphoria and shock, then followed by a mixture of confusion and rage, as former slaves found themselves free to go anywhere but with little idea of where that might be. At the same time, local civilian government had been superseded by a welcome (or despised) occupying military government. In her analysis of this epoch, sociologist Wilma Dunaway noted that newly freed mountain slaves, with no support from white neighbors, faced a challenging future—they had no education, no material resources, no farm tools or animals, no money, no homes, and no income. Reflecting back on this era through the lens of white paternalism in the 1930s, local historian Flora Keith Overman asserted that Lincoln's "freeing the slaves was the most inhuman and cruel command in the annals of any country in the world. They were like 'babes in the woods.' They had no home to shelter them; no means with which to buy bread or clothing—all these things had to be given to them by their masters and mistresses. They wandered over the country, with no bread or clothes or shelter."[26]

Throughout the summer of 1865, historian W. J. Megginson noted, "many freed people hoped for land of their own, the 'forty acres and a mule' they mistakenly believed were promised them" by the federal government, following Sherman's Field Order No. 15.[27] The landed white farmers, awash in rumors of all kinds, feared for their lives and property. For example, on July 29, 1865, Floride Clemson (granddaughter of John C. Calhoun, the prominent Upstate landowner and politician), summarized the fears of her white neighbors when she wrote in her diary that "the negroes being freed, almost everyone is turning them away by the hundreds to starve, plunder, & do worse. The times ahead a[re] fearful. All negroes have now asserted their freedom now [sic]."[28]

Labor Reorganization

Black assertions of freedom brought them new opportunities. In one of the most revolutionary moments in the history of American labor, millions of workers now had the right to negotiate with the same people who used to control their every move, and their former owners ideally no longer dictated the terms for black labor (or black life). Historian Eric Foner described this new social order as an immediate class struggle between white landowners desperate to harvest their fall crops and black laborers who now refused to help without fair compensation. The short-term solution was a labor contract, specifying the conditions under which blacks agreed to help their former masters and the conditions by which whites agreed to compensate them for their work (the longer-term solution was the passage of restrictive Black Codes).[29] As one might imagine, whites did not surrender easily their public transcript of universal domination to a group of people who had been their self-perceived social inferiors for centuries. As an example, South Carolina's Black Codes determined that "all persons of color who may contract for service or labor shall be known as servants, and those with whom they contract shall be known as masters."[30] The actual labor contracts reflect this deeply rooted reluctance by whites to surrender their traditional domination.

On October 19, 1865, Robert Scott (director of South Carolina's Freedmen's Bureau, a federal bureaucracy established after the war to regulate social conditions of freed slaves), "issued a proclamation that the expectation of getting forty acres and a mule was not going to happen, and that freedmen needed to sign 1866 labor contracts."[31] On October 30, 1865, white Pickens District landowner McElroy Jameson (or a scribe) wrote out by hand the conditions under which he consented to compensate two of his former slaves, Faith and Moses, in exchange for their harvesting Jameson's fall crop (which they had undoubtedly planted for him in spring 1865 as enslaved laborers). "For the remainder of the present year," the contract read, the former slaves agree to "reside upon and devote their labor to the cultivation of the plantation." They cannot keep "guns pistols or other offensive weapons" (lack of punctuation in original) without permission of their employer, and they "will yield all obedience to all orders" pertaining to their duties as laborers. Finally, they will be "orderly and quiet in their conduct, avoiding drunkenness and all other gross vices." In exchange, the laborers "are to be treated in a manner consistent with their freedom," and their employer will furnish "the usual [implying this had been done under slavery] notions clothing shoes and medical attendance" (lack of punctuation in original). The workers also were to get 200 pounds of pork and thirty bushels of corn from the harvest. Moses and Faith, being illiterate, left Xs next to their names at the bottom of the document. On the back was the signature of the commanding officer of the occupying Northern forces, stationed in Greenville.[32]

Handwritten with a different color of ink, implying that the clause had been added to the contract next to the description of the workers' share of the harvest, were the words "also their own crops." While these words could have been added as an afterthought by the white landowner or lawyer who drew up the contract, it is also possible to imagine the contract being read aloud to the illiterate former slaves. At the reading, the former slaves then demanded from their former master that the work of their own hands, on their own time, in their own gardens, be theirs to keep as well and that this agreement be added to the contract to make it binding. It is possible that those four words exemplify the direct agency of these former slaves, a rare "public transcript" of black empowerment, where Faith and Moses seized an opportunity to control the means of their own production and demanded and required their former owner to respect their wishes. It also demonstrates that, even before liberation, hidden transcripts had maintained black pride and dignity, which manifested as public demonstrations of power and pride as soon as possible after freedom.

Land Acquisition

Since many of the newly freed blacks had to live under such regimented working conditions, it is easy to understand why they sought to control their own destiny by obtaining their own land. Now that the Northern occupation forces offered former slaves a new world of economic and social freedom, expectations grew that the liberators might confiscate former plantation lands and redistribute them to the ex-slaves. The process had already begun on the Sea Islands along South Carolina's coast, under Sherman's Field Order No. 15. Freedmen throughout the state (and the South) began to spread rumors that the government was going to give all of them forty acres and a mule. Floride Clemson described contemporary white fears in her diary on September 2, 1865: "They say the state of things in the low country is terrible. Men, formerly wealthy, have literally not wherewithal to buy bread, & many must starve. Lands which have been abandoned by their owners during the war, are confiscated to be divided by the 'freedman's beaureau' [sic] among the negroes. An insurrection is much dreaded."[33]

"The desire to own land became an article of faith" in the slaves' description of freedom, historian George Devlin noted. " 'What's the use to give us our freedom if we can't stay where we were raised, and own our houses where we were born, and our little pieces of ground,' " blacks challenged.[34] Historian Eric Foner argued that freed slaves recognized that "whatever its limitations, land ownership ensured the freedmen a degree of control over the time and labor of themselves and their families." Land ownership equated to personal freedom, because it allowed for economic self-sufficiency independent of white control. More importantly, historian Martin Abbott noted, land ownership represented "the expression of a people's aspiration to be free in a way that they could see and feel and measure, the voicing of a dream to own the land which for so long had owned them." Historian Loren Schweninger noted that some blacks even sought the confiscation of former plantations "as punishment for holding a people in bondage." These reasons, Foner concluded, explained why blacks "sacrificed and saved in an attempt to acquire land, and those who succeeded clung to it with amazing tenacity."[35]

National movements for the confiscation and redistribution of land "climaxed in the summer and fall of 1867," but plans failed due to underestimating the class conflict and racial hatred between freed slaves and their former owners.[36] A less radical approach was taken by the South Carolina Land Commission. Created in 1869 and reformed by 1872, the Commission "purchased tracts of land and resold them to small farmers for modest sums at interest. The impetus for such an agency was the desire of freedmen to own their own land, to be independent. By 1877 some two thousand small farmers, most of them black, had purchased commission lands."[37]

According to historian Walter Edgar, blacks (like their white neighbors) felt "an attachment to the land" and "a sense of place," and so most wanted to stay near familiar fields and mountains (see chapter 8 for a theoretical discussion). Without a major urban center and thus external transportation connections via railroads, and without critical community services, former slaves in the Carolina mountains were relatively isolated and thus needed to create their own communities and social services.[38] Dunaway proposed that ex-slaves remained close to their former homes in case long-lost kin returned. But, historian Walter Edgar added, blacks also wanted to sever all ties with "the world of whites" and thus built their homes "out of sight of the white men's houses." As historian Steven Hahn observed, these enclaves also offered African Americans "some semblance of safety" from the outside world of whites. In fact, historian Loren Schweninger discovered, beyond the protection of Northern military forces or missionaries, only "in remote and infertile back-country regions, did significant numbers of former slaves acquire small tracts of land."[39]

"Black highlanders," historian Steven Nash noted, "asserted their new independence in a variety of ways," including establishing their economic independence, founding black schools, and reuniting separated families. Thus, former slaves abandoned their old slave quarters and built new cabins or moved their old homes onto new sites for a variety of reasons.[40] This desire by blacks to remain close to familiar fields and to family, but at the same time to live beyond the view of their former masters, probably explains the geographical seclusion of the Liberia community (a place Megginson termed "remote"), tucked away in a cove but not far from the main valley of the Oolenoy (see map 3).[41]

Location of Liberia

There are conflicting oral traditions about the reasons for Liberia's founding, and these alternatives relate directly to this book's theme of hidden transcripts and African American empowerment. All stories agree that the terrain eventually called "Liberia" lies outside the main fertile floodplain of the Oolenoy River, in a relatively isolated area. However, the unresolved issue is how this land was obtained. Was the land given to freed slaves out of generosity or guilt by former slave owners? Was it given to slave owners' mixed-race offspring? Was the land exchanged as compensation for labor or work? Or did former slaves purchase the land themselves? Was the "remote" location deliberately chosen by them to escape white surveillance and achieve a degree of black independence? Depending on the "truth" of the alternate versions, Liberia's founding may be seen as a white kindness or as a black protest.

According to white tradition, the establishment of the community called Liberia has been claimed by several different founders. Local historian Bert Reece, for example, credited four prominent local white families:

> Four men, James Sutherland, a Keith, a Hester, and a Hughes decided some provision of homes should be made for these freed slaves. They decided to each give five acres of land for establishing a Liberia here in America similar to that of Africa. . . . Any slave family who wanted to build a house and move there was allowed to do so and was given a few acres. They then sold them more land at 50 c[ents] or $1.00 an acre and gave them the privilege of paying for it as they could by labor or produce. Many were happy with this plan and moved in and built some sort of house, according to their means. Finally, there were 300 negro citizens living in Liberia. Most of them were loyal, honest, hard-working citizens willing to do what it took to make a living and be a good neighbor. . . . Their white folks were kind of heart, tolerant, and appreciative of the humor and pathos of this kind of negro life (lack of capitalization in original).[42]

It is interesting to observe that the first names of these generous white farmers have not been preserved, except for that of James Sutherland. Bert Reece's son Josef added his own grandfather to the donors (whom his mother did not name). Josef Reece credited his grandfather and the other white landowners with dividing up some of their land so that each black family had between fifty and seventy-five acres, with fifteen to twenty acres tillable, "and settled a black family on each parcel with basic equipment to start farming." Reece continued: "I was told by my Grandfather [sic] that they deeded the property to them but with a mortgage to pay for the farm and equipment. He said they only charged them a dollar an acre for the land, and most had paid it all off in 10 years."[43]

Donations of land by benevolent white former enslavers to their black former slaves sounds overly generous, especially given the southern white economic distress immediately after the Civil War. However, this generosity becomes more believable if the formerly enslaved recipients were the mixed-race children of their former enslavers. Multiple types of interracial relationships occurred during this period, and black family histories preserve stories of such land donations (see the Joseph McJunkin story later in this chapter as a possible example).[44]

It is also interesting to note that this generous gift occurred during the time of the statewide fears of land confiscation and redistribution following Sherman's field order. As discussed in chapter 1, subordinates use various forms of infrapolitics, including rumors, to manipulate dominant groups into actions the subordinates desire. Historian W. J. Megginson described the federal and state officials' fears in December 1865 about "major disturbances if freed people around South Carolina had a simultaneous protest or uprising against their government's failure to distribute land to them. These officials clearly recognized that a far-reaching slave communications system operated throughout the state."[45] Perhaps local Oolenoy-area blacks so worried their white neighbors with rumors of land confiscations that the owners gave them these small plots of land in "worthless" places in order to safeguard their larger holdings in the higher-quality Oolenoy Valley, should federal confiscation prove to be true.

For evidence, there exists the countermemory of differential land value, because according to Mable Owens Clarke, the whites gave the freed slaves this small side valley to the Oolenoy because they said, " 'We don't want to live in the valley. Let's put the [freed] slaves over in the valley,' because they said, 'the land over here is not worth anything.' . . . They wanted to be on the main road, you know, like . . . Highway 8 all through there."[46] Throughout the lower South, where freed blacks obtained land, "it was often of poor quality or located in remote sections." In fact, in land records of 1899, historian W. J. Megginson discovered that, in upper Pickens County around Liberia, the "land is very hilly, poor in quality, and cheap in price."[47]

As an alternative legend to the donation of land parcels from generous, guilt-ridden, or fearful whites, a countermemory of land acquisition proposed that blacks bought the land themselves or at least acquired it themselves, and situated their homes deliberately apart from white society. As discussed earlier, the significant class conflict between hundreds of local blacks, newly freed and thus "unemployed," and the white farm owners, with crops needing to be harvested but no cash to pay labor, created multiple solutions, including the direct exchange of black labor for poorer-quality white land. As local historian Bert Reece noted earlier, in addition to land gifts, Liberia's black founders also obtained the land in exchange for "labor or produce," a process paralleling land acquisition in the Low Country as well.[48] On the other hand, historian W. J. Megginson concluded that land purchases by blacks could have been possible because of income they gained as slaves, while historian Sharon Holt suggested postwar household income also made this possible through a process she described as "cooperative accumulation"—families began by selling small animal products (chickens and eggs) and progressed to larger livestock (cows and milk, for example).[49] (See chapter 2 for these slave strategies for acquiring wealth.)

On the other hand, with illiteracy rates and prejudices high, it is also possible that blacks thought they had obtained land legally, but in reality, actual deeds never may have been filed at the county courthouse. "Tax records for 1899," historian W. J. Megginson discovered, "show only two men, whose holdings totaled 630 acres, in the area considered Little Liberia; for most families supposed to have been early black owners, such as Owens, no deeds were recorded until a decade or more later." While the black-defined area of Liberia may be larger than Megginson's investigative range, historians Thad Sitton and James Conrad offered a possible explanation for Megginson's failure to discover tax records: "most freedmen's settlements existed as informal communities for years before courthouse records began to register their existence in land deeds and other legal transactions."[50]

For example, Chris Owens had told his children that *his* father, Will Owens, remembered that the whites "rang a bell, and you run around and stake off a piece of land. . . . And all you can stake off within that time while they ring the bell, . . . that was your land. No money changed hands," one of Mable's brothers recalled. Myrta Lockett Avery, a white woman raised in South Carolina during and immediately after the Civil War, supported a version of this memory, as she described corrupt agents of the Freedmen's Bureau or northern carpetbaggers who would enter African American neighborhoods and seek "private interviews with negroes [*sic*] possessing a little cash or having access to somebody else's cash; to these would be shown, with pledges of secrecy, packages of red, white, and blue sticks, four to each package. 'Get up before light on such a date, plant a stick at the four corners of any piece of land not over a mile square, and the land is yours.' Packages were five dollars each." According to historian Carol Bleser, since land titles legally never changed hands, this "staking out of property" was actually a swindle perpetrated against illiterate freed slaves.[51]

In addition to these significant and plausible reasons, it is also possible to view Liberia's founding as the deliberate attempt by a smaller-scale group to escape hegemonic state-level control and to create an independent refuge to protect and safeguard their dignity and freedom—another form of a hidden transcript. Like Scott's Southeast Asian hill tribes, black freedom colonists avoided the hegemonic surveillance of white observation and control and strategically retreated to their remote mountain communities. These refuges become places where residents could give unfettered voice to their true feelings and know those feelings were shared by those around them. Historians Sitton and Conrad described black Texan freedom colonies as "communities of avoidance and self-segregation, where black people adapted to Jim Crow restrictions not by fighting back or moving north, but by withdrawing from whites. . . . Freedmen's settlement residents watched what they said, carefully managed their interactions with whites, and stayed to themselves."[52]

Because these communities of former slaves remained (ideally) outside of white control, such freedom colonies stood as a "symbolic gesture of independence and free choice"; another way "'to throw off the badge of servitude' [and] to overturn the real and symbolic authority whites had exercised over every aspect of their lives."[53] Thus these communities were "fundamentally defiant" in that they countered the public transcript of blacks as powerless and instead these places empowered them.[54] Equally important, these spaces helped former slaves construct a sense of "blackness" by differentiating themselves from their white neighbors. As enclaves, James Scott argued, these protected social spaces have to be "won, cleared, built, and defended." The more resources and prestige a separate community gathers, Scott continued, the more likely it becomes necessary by the residents to define and defend its borders. In fact, Scott concluded, "the strongest evidence for the vital importance of autonomous social sites in generating a hidden transcript is the strenuous effort made by dominant groups to abolish or control such sites," as in his Southeast Asian hill tribe examples.[55] Likewise, strenuous efforts have been made decade after decade by dominant white society to abolish the community of Liberia, and the defense of this freedom colony as a hidden transcript site remains a recurrent theme in its countermemory.

Naming of Liberia

Written and oral sources do not agree on the origin for the name "Liberia." According to Angela McJunkin Young, her great-grandfather, Joseph

McJunkin (the slave from chapter 2), named the area that had been given to the newly freed slaves "Liberia" or "Little Liberia," after the region in Africa he had been forced to leave. Local historians Alma Lynch and Elizabeth Ellison reprint a 1979 *Pickens Sentinel* article by George Laycock (interviewing Chris and Lula McJunkin Owens [see chapter 4]); Laycock wrote that "the freedmen themselves decided to call the new community 'Little Liberia' after the newly established black nation in Africa."[56]

Another possible source for the name comes from an emigration movement to Africa, specifically Liberia, spreading rapidly through South Carolina but peaking at two different times. The West African coast long had been considered as an emigration site for freed slaves due to relatively direct access from Charleston. On November 20, 1866, the American Colonization Society paid to transport 600 black émigrés from Charleston to Cape Mount, Liberia; 300 more left on May 21, 1867.[57] It is possible that news of these departures suggested to either (or both) whites and blacks in other parts of the state that a side valley of the Oolenoy might provide an equivalent refuge and thus might be given an equivalent name.

The emigration movement gained even more strength the next decade. After Wade Hampton's restoration of southern white control in the state by 1877, historian George Tindall explained, more and more blacks began to contemplate emigration. While those in states farther west crossed the Mississippi, blacks in South Carolina focused "almost altogether on Liberia" in Africa because of the earlier colonization movement. Calls for emigration were made throughout the state, including Pickens County. The movement lasted only a few years, however.[58] It is also possible that "Liberia" got the name (either from whites or blacks) as the local, more accessible substitute for the country across the Atlantic, historian W. J. Megginson wrote. "Promised Land," in Greenwood County, and the "Kingdom of Happy Land," in northern Greenville County provide parallel examples of freedom colonies from the Upstate.[59] From whatever source, the new nation in Africa settled by freed slaves (Liberia) became the model (perhaps symbol) and place name for the new community of freed slaves in Pickens County as well.

Just to the east in northern Greenville County, according to the (black) McJunkin family history, by 1869 Joseph McJunkin "received" his first parcel of land—fifty acres, from the daughter of his former owner after the war. McJunkin land lies near the foot of Bald Rock (at the base of Caesar's Head and the Blue Ridge; see map 2). Angela McJunkin Young noted that her father, James Monroe McJunkin (Joseph's grandson), used to say that the whites probably did not want that land because "it's back in the hills." Joseph

McJunkin's granddaughter (Mable's mother) Lula Owens described the land as a "hillside up in a hollow that wasn't fit for nothing." It is interesting to note that McJunkin's land (in the South Saluda River valley) lies about eight miles from River Falls (on the Middle Saluda River), the plantation of his enslavement (see map 2). Thus, McJunkin as a free man raised his family on his own land within walking distance of his first South Carolina home, where he had been enslaved before the Civil War—perhaps an act of defiance. As indicated in chapter 2, according to black McJunkin family tradition, McJunkin's former owner also may have been his lover, and so perhaps the land had been willed to him after her death. "I'm going to put it this way," Joseph McJunkin's great-granddaughter observed: "I would like to think he must have been a pretty good 'black fella' and the people kind of liked him. And they said we've got some land for sale and we'll sell it to you. So that's how he got his first tract and then on and on" (perhaps another hidden transcript of manipulation through superficial deference). For the next three decades, reporter Jimmy Cornelison wrote, McJunkin "continued to acquire land until he had almost five hundred acres. He farmed the land, . . . [and] continued to raise his family in the shadows of Bald Rock."[60]

Liberia's Founders

The actual number of the original settlers of Liberia remains lost to time. Virtually every oral history of Liberia cites only one family as a source: Chris and Lula Owens (see chapter 4), and the number handed down through the generations by Mr. Owens has generally been 300 (sometimes 300 families, sometimes 300 people) "in through here," daughter Mable Owens Clarke quoted her father as saying. Given the actual size of the Liberia Valley itself, this number (either of families or of people) in that specific valley seems highly improbable.

However, if one examines the U.S. Census figures for the area, the number becomes a much greater possibility if Owens's phrase reflected the area he knew from his peddling route (see chapter 5), a much more likely possibility. In the Pumpkintown census district in 1870 (an area including the Liberia Valley), there were 198 blacks and "mulattos" and 521 whites (approximately 28 percent black). The Dacusville district to the south and east included 294 more black or "mulatto" individuals, and the adjoining Cleveland district in Greenville County listed seventy-eight additional African

Americans. Thus, conservatively, at least 570 African Americans lived in the northeastern areas of Pickens and Greenville Counties in 1870. Since virtually no freed blacks appeared on the 1860 Census from these areas, these residents were mostly newly freed local slaves. But there also could have been some in-migrants.

In October 1866, John De Forest (the commanding officer of occupying federal troops stationed in Greenville) observed that the primary request of freed blacks in the Upstate was for transportation: "In their eyes the work of emancipation was incomplete until the families which had been dispersed by slavery were reunited. . . . The Negroes who had been brought to the up-country during the war by white families were crazy to get back to their native flats of ague and country fever. Highland darkeys [*sic*] who had drifted down to the seashore were sending urgent requests to be 'fotched home again.'"[61]

According to historian Julie Saville, land claims in the Piedmont were less important than reclaiming kin from neighboring plantations. "'Families' in a variety of forms," historian W. J. Megginson argued, "became the strongest continuity" between slavery and freedom. "These three-generational families," Megginson continued, "testify powerfully to their ability to stay together, or keep in close touch, during slavery and in the early years of freedom." Despite the horrors of slavery, Dunaway added, "it is phenomenal that the kinship networks of about three of every five black Appalachian families persisted."[62] This urgency to consolidate households and reunite separated family members may explain some of the in-migration of African Americans to the Pumpkintown area after 1865.

Who were these people, specifically? Precise identification is challenging, because immediate family members may have been scattered (even regionally) under slavery, and thus "coordinating a [surname] choice among parents, their siblings, and their adult sons and daughters may have been difficult," historian W. J. Megginson noted.[63] Nevertheless, there are four general sources of information to help identify Liberia's original founders: family oral tradition, local (published) histories and newspapers, private documents, and government forms. At this time, regional newspapers still reported local news, primarily that from white neighborhoods or communities. Thus, by combining what is known of the lives of these former slaves from government documents with what can be learned from family traditions, printed local histories, private documents, and a few hints from local papers, it becomes possible to trace some of these people through time, and help to give voice to individuals who otherwise lived, labored, loved, and died anonymously.

One of the critical acts of the federal occupation of the state was to register male voters in order to prepare for the state constitutional convention and general elections in 1868; potential registrants included those former Confederates swearing allegiance to the United States or those newly enfranchised—the freed slaves. According to local historians Peggy Rich and Fred Holder, voter registration in Pickens County took place in early September 1867, and so there exists a list of residents (males above eighteen years old), from that specific point in time, including those from the Pumpkintown district. In 1867, there were seventy-two registered white voters and fifty-three registered black voters. From another source, local historian Bert Reece provided a separate list of the "original settlers of Liberia."[64]

There is a strong correlation between the 1867 voter registration list and Reece's list (probably obtained from Mable Clarke's father, Chris Owens). Four original settlers have already been introduced as local slaves in chapter 2: Aunt Katie (see figure 2), Samuel "Goob" Keith, Emerson Kemp (see figure 8 and cover photo), and Joseph McJunkin. To get a little more detail on these people, the census records may be utilized; then it becomes possible to trace many of them through the nineteenth century, getting a better glimpse into their lives. The story of Liberia, however, will focus on those selected individuals and their descendants whose lives entered into contemporary memory.

Census Information from 1870–1900

Historian W. J. Megginson found that many freed slaves "still lived within five or fifteen miles of their former plantations, and many bore their former owner's surname."[65] For example, in 1870 in the Pumpkintown district (which included Liberia) are listed Samuel Keith (born ca. 1814), a black farmer living with his eighteen-year-old son, also named Sam—this latter person is most likely "Goob" Keith, bought by the Keith family about a decade earlier as a young boy. Both men lived adjacent to the prominent white family of Cornelius Keith, their former owners. In the community also lived Patience Glenn, born about 1830, with two children, including son Willis (born about 1854; see appendices 1 and 2 for names and kin relationships). While Aunt Katie does not appear in the Pumpkintown or Dacusville census records at this time, in the latter district resided "Emory Camp," his wife, and an infant son (James), living near James Hester. Most likely, this is Emerson Kemp (perhaps a local mispronunciation of "Camp"), still living near his former enslaver.

Abutting the Pumpkintown census district to the east was the Cleveland district in Greenville County, and here resided seventy-eight more African Americans, including Joseph McJunkin (born about 1818; see chapter 2), with his second wife, Sarah, and six children. Virtually all of the adults listed earlier, and even some of the children, were born into slavery and gained personhood, and names, only after 1865.

Ten years later, by the 1880 Census, 845 people lived in the Pumpkintown census district, including 630 whites and 215 blacks and "mulattos," representing about 25 percent of the total population and actually an 8.5 percent increase in overall black population. Families were generally large, with lots of children to help with farm work (typical of rural families at this time). Perhaps this demographic increase also reflected the relative prosperity for African Americans under Reconstruction.

Many of the same people still lived in the area at this time. Emerson Kemp (see figure 8, book cover photo) and his wife have moved away from his former enslaver into the Liberia area; they have son, James, and five daughters. There were two Willis Glenn households, with one Willis Glenn (twenty-five years old) married to Alice with an infant daughter, Rosa (described as Chris Owens's mother; see figure 3), while the other Willis Glenn (twenty-six years old) had married Sally.[66] A decade earlier Patience Glenn had one son (Willis), who would now be twenty-six years old. Of course, it is entirely possible that the same Willis Glenn maintained both households. Since all these individuals had been born into slavery, actual dates of births never may have been recorded accurately.

As noted earlier in this chapter, Aunt Katie had not appeared in the 1870 Census in Pumpkintown or Dacusville, but in 1880 she was back in the Pumpkintown district as Katy "Tyrell" [Terrell], married to Thomas "Tyrell" (born about 1836), with four children (perhaps Thomas's from a previous relationship). The couple also lived with three other children with the surname Owens, listed as stepsons to Thomas Terrell and thus evidently from Katie (Owens's) former relationship; the youngest of these Owens boys is William (born about 1874). Emerson Kemp and his wife had six children, including son James (born about 1868). Just to the west, in the Eastatoe district, lived George "McKennie" (McKinney) with his wife and four sons, including Ansel, born about 1874. In the adjacent Cleveland district in Greenville County to the east, among others, lived the Joseph McJunkin family: the patriarch is still listed as a farmer, with his third wife, Leah, and seven children, including the youngest, "Joab" [Joseph Absalom], born about 1875.

Unfortunately, almost all the original census records for 1890 were destroyed in a fire at the Commerce Department in Washington, D.C., in 1921, so all that remain are the statistical totals reported eventually to Congress and published in the official census reports from that decade. There exists, however, some documentation of the lives of Liberia residents between these decades, and so it is possible to trace the names a little more.[67] Because of the loss of the actual census registers from 1890, those demographic changes remain unknown. By 1900, the overall population of the Pumpkintown district had increased again, to 968 people, of whom 728 were white and 240 black, still about 25 percent. However, there is another demographic increase from twenty years before, with almost a 12 percent jump in the African American population.

By this time "Binjman" [Benjamin] and Mary Terrell, the former born into slavery about 1861 while his wife was born about 1869, have a son, William. "William" (not "Willis," b. 1852) and Sallie "Glyn" [Glenn] have five resident children, including three sons (Lonzo, William Clarence, and Ernest); Willis and Alice Glenn's daughter Rosa had married William Owens in 1896. They have a young son, Christopher, born November 1896 (see figure 4). Living nearby is William Owens's mother, Katie Owens Terrell, now widowed. Emerson Kemp and his family do not appear in the district's list. In the adjacent Eastatoe census district lived a few more African American families and some boarders, but the number had diminished significantly. In Greenville County's Cleveland district, Joseph McJunkin lived with his wife and several children, including "Joab" (Absalom) McJunkin; his wife, Emma; and two children.

The census records from Upstate South Carolina support sociologist Dunaway's general analysis of ex-slave narratives and census records. She found that after the Civil War, many black households "were complex combinations of kin and nonkin, the children from several marriages, women who merged their own offspring with orphans and elderly, sometimes even multiple spouses." Families often contained two or more surnames, and households with the same last name lived near each other.[68] Local census records from upper Pickens County reflect these same trends. For example, families like that of Katie Owens, William/Willis Glenn, and Joseph McJunkin lived in joint or extended households, adjacent to kin or former fellow slaves (now with the same last name of the former owner). The result, historians Sitton and Conrad found, was that "African American families shattered and truncated by slavery reformed, extended, and attained almost clanlike complexity."[69]

Thus the core families of the Liberia community consisted of former slaves to local white families, settling and/or being settled outside of direct surveillance by their former enslavers, and owning or at least occupying significant portions of land in upper Pickens and Greenville Counties. These former slaves were surrounded by hundreds of other former local slaves, their reunited family members from elsewhere in the region, and perhaps friends and others as well who may have in-migrated. In remote mountain communities such as Liberia, archaeologist Jodi Barnes concluded, "the mountain land became a place to re-unify and build families and to enact plans to improve their lives."[70]

General Way of Life (Late Nineteenth Century)

The landscape in which these residents lived had changed little since 1865. One contemporary source (a personal memoir of resident Leroy Smith) mentioned the area during this postbellum period. At one point during the lifetime of Smith's grandfather (a local resident), the grandfather had befriended Milford Sutherland, from Pumpkintown. Smith's grandfather elaborated: "The Southerland [sic] family owned a large farm and a country store which were located on a crossroad [State Highways 8 and 288 today], with the store located diagonally across from the house and the barns across the roads between them. All of this was located almost under Table Rock Mountain, a huge loaf shaped granite dome above the trees. A creek [Oolenoy River] ran under the road to the south."[71]

Historian W. J. Megginson noted that in 1870, Upstate African American occupations fell into three major categories: agriculture (95 percent of adult men), day laborers, and (for women) domestic service—cooks, servants, or children's nurses.[72] Liberia's residents reflected these occupations. Those blacks (and whites) without land worked that of owners, with compensation either in shares of the final crop or in exchange for rent, with tremendous inequality.[73] In the county, corn was still the major cash crop, being replaced decade by decade by cotton. Black tenants and sharecroppers lived right next door to black landowners, who served as valuable role models.[74] Both large and small farms dotted the landscape up and down the Oolenoy Valley, tied together by dirt roads, dusty in the summer and muddy in all seasons. Horses and mules carried travelers and pulled buggies and wagons for people to journey between the small crossroads communities like

Pumpkintown and (especially on Saturdays) into the larger towns of Marietta or Pickens (the new county seat, a different town than Old Pickens) both about ten miles away (see map 2).

Daily life in southern unincorporated rural areas of the late nineteenth century may be reconstituted in several ways. In their study of Texas "freedom colonies," historians Thad Sitton and James Conrad described these places as "unplatted and unincorporated, individually organized only by church and school and residents' collective belief that a community existed." In an excavation of the Brown Mountain Creek site in western Virginia (also founded by a freed slave landowner), archaeologist Jodi Barnes defined this black Appalachian "community" as the social interaction between households including houses, churches, stores, cemeteries, and post offices within a specific period of time (the late nineteenth century). Her community, like Liberia, was heterogeneous, with landowners and tenants, mixed race and not mixed, with ties to the larger white community. "As a community," she observed, "the people living on the mountain land shaped and modified the landscape to provide housing, accommodate the systems of production and reproduction, facilitate communication and transportation, mark social inequalities and express aesthetics."[75]

As might be expected, finding material evidence of these cultural behaviors is challenging but not impossible.[76] For example, one excavated structure in Barnes's project (the household of a former slave of mixed ancestry) revealed a relatively low number of artifacts, reflecting "an economic strategy that favors the acquisition of land over the purchase of material objects," similar to strategies Holt outlined in North Carolina.[77] A second structure, with a wide range of recovered buttons, was the home of a laundress, who supplemented her income and broadened her connections with both the black and white communities, much as Aunt Katie did in her later years. Another resident of Brown Mountain was a midwife (like Aunt Katie), playing "an important role in community formation since she was intimately involved in the reproduction of community members." Brown Mountain, like Liberia, "emerged as the outcome of individuals negotiating their interests" within the confines of a larger white society formed by Jim Crow racism.[78] While sociologist Dunaway argued that deep poverty, debt peonage, continuing illiteracy, and racial violence plagued black families, it is also possible to view Liberia's black farmers and renters, seamstresses and midwives, peddlers and day laborers, as deliberately constructing a balancing act between state-level, white-controlled, commodity capitalism and smaller-scale, black-controlled, economic entrepreneurship, much as James Scott's Southeast Asian hill tribes have done.[79]

Personal memoirs enhance oral history and archaeology. Two autobiographies of children of former slaves described life in upper Anderson and lower Pickens Counties during the late nineteenth century. William Pickens (born in 1881) described this region as "exceedingly poor, with red hills and antiquated agriculture."[80] Jane Hunter (born in 1882) and her family lived on an antebellum plantation in a two-room frame dwelling, near a red clay road, with an old well and an apple orchard nearby. In a nearby home garden, Hunter's mother grew tomatoes, okra, and mustard and turnip greens, and her father plowed long rows of corn, cotton, and molasses cane. Typical foods were hogs, hominy, and sometimes poultry, with cows for milk and butter. Mothers worked in the fields and brought their babies with them or left them with older children. The only other labor opportunity for women was to serve as domestics.[81] According to Hunter, children swept the yard (bare dirt), drew water from the well, milked the cows, and swept the cabin. As she got older, Hunter worked in the fields, planting, hoeing, picking cotton, and pulling corn stalks for cattle fodder.[82] To supplement returns on farm production, some residents hunted game (especially opossums or raccoons), fished the upland streams, or transformed corn into moonshine. Such informal activities helped some households gradually achieve economic independence by accumulating enough wealth for land purchases.[83]

To generate this informal household income, occasionally families rode or walked several miles into towns on Saturdays to sell the extra garden produce or homemade liquor and to buy essentials like hardware, coffee, or canning jars. During this process, "vehicular" accidents were not unknown: in 1894, Soapstone's pastor died after being thrown from a mule.[84] Sundays were days of rest, spent visiting extended families, eating sumptuous midday meals, reading the Bible, and attending the numerous churches in the area.

In addition to the benefits of informal household income for black farmers in the late nineteenth century, historian Sharon Holt added "double-farming," where black farmers owned one piece of land and rented other parcels. This strategy allowed black farmers to benefit from renting additional land when farm prices exceeded rental costs, and to avoid renting additional land when prices fell below rental costs. By not investing in larger and larger land accumulations, small black farmers also avoided external scrutiny and suspicion by whites.[85] By 1900, historian Gilbert Fite found, 23 percent of black farmers throughout the South were owners or part owners, mostly of small holdings. Even into the twentieth century, double-farming, strategic credit requests, and household income characterized black Piedmont farms, Holt argued, and this strategy may explain why Megginson was unable to locate large black land holdings for Liberia's farmers in the county tax records. Even the more successful black farmers knew they would never be accepted fully into white society, but they served as role models for their poorer black neighbors and a direct counterargument against racial inferiority.[86] In this way, black farmers in remote mountain enclaves like Liberia exemplified James Scott's hidden transcripts and Southeast Asian mountain tribal strategies by deliberately manipulating economic decisions to avoid state-level economic control and to maintain a degree of economic, political, and cultural independence as well as racial pride.

Some hints of other aspects of traditional culture for Liberia's residents appear at this time, often filtered through white memories and white local histories. For example, local historian Bert Hendricks Reece described the food traditions of Burr Hill, born in 1833: "The way of living in the days immediately after slavery, of course, was very primitive. I remember going with an older brother to the hut of Burr Hill, an ex-slave. He was baking an ash cake. The method interested me. He explained that he swept the hot rock clean, patted down his hoe-cake, and then covered it with hot embers and coals to bake. When it was done, he would brush off the embers. If he didn't want to eat the crust, he would peel it off and the inside was 'moughty good.'"[87] Reece's description of Hill's "ash cake" reflects hidden cultural influences. As linguist Allison Burkette noted, that term for cornbread cooked on a flat stone (or hoe blade, thus "hoe cake"), covered in ashes, with the burned crust peeled away, preserves a Native American food preparation technique and hints at similar cultural traditions that may have been forgotten by the late nineteenth century.[88]

Local historian Reece also mentioned a story from her family's oral history about Luke Terrell. To describe the general atmosphere, Reece quoted an old minstrel song by James Bland: "In the evening by the moonlight / You could hear those darkies singing / In the evening by the moonlight / You could hear those banjos ringing." "The negroes loved to sing to the music of the banjo," Reece continued, and

> Luke Terrill [sic], a Sutherland ex-slave, picked the banjo. He would
> sit on the porch steps of Mr. Jim Sutherland's house and play for the
> young people to dance in the covered breezeway between the large

rooms of the big log house. You could hear their favorites: "Nobody Purty but Black-eyed Susan," "Shortnin' Bread," "Cripple Creek," "Turkey in De Straw," and "Git Along Home Lucindy." . . . [89] Luke Terrill, the banjo picker, also told fortunes, using the coffee cup dregs for his signs. By looking in your coffee cup, he seemed to be able to reveal much of your past as well as the future. This would add spice to their parties when they could have Luke in the kitchen telling fortunes. He might even tell you some stories about "sure enough witches," for negroes were strong believers in witchcraft.[90]

William Pickens, son of former slaves, recalled additional hints of traditional culture: "By the ruddy glow of the fire at nights the children were told of ghosts, of strange cats, dogs, voices and sounds, of the 'no-headed man,' of graveyards. . . . The Federal soldiers [during occupation] were described not as common men, but as beings from a super-world."[91] These anecdotes reveal hints of a more private level of culture, hidden transcripts of oral traditions, some perhaps even with origins in Africa—food preparation techniques, traditional music and instrumentation, folktales, and supernatural beliefs. This oral tradition served actively to preserve a sense of "blackness," to safeguard a cultural pride in heritage, and to maintain a social link between multiple generations of family members whose lives straddled slavery and freedom.

Founding of Soapstone Baptist Church

During slavery times, African Americans in the Oolenoy Valley frequently were allowed to attend white churches but sat in segregated balconies. After the war and freedom, however, blacks were strongly encouraged, or strongly desired, to create their own congregations. Historian Joel Williamson argued that "the withdrawal of Negroes from churches dominated by native whites was the most striking development in religion in South Carolina during Reconstruction." But was the withdrawal one of white exclusion or black secession, and from which group's perspective is the "true" reason documented? Williamson described various possibilities, partly influenced by denomination and partly by ante- and postbellum desires by both whites and blacks.[92]

For example, according to the Oolenoy Baptist Church records, freed slaves continued to attend this white church until February 1868, "when the church passed this resolution: 'if colored people feel that God has forgiven them of their sins, we will receive and baptize. We do not grant them the privilege of opening the door. They can set up their own meeting house. We will not grant them the privilege of holding meetings at this place.' "[93]

Historian W. J. Megginson described black churches as "that core institution of African Americans in freedom," and historian George Tindall illustrated the critical importance of these small churches for African American communities: "Religion . . . provided for the Negro church member a merciful relief from the hopeless monotony of grinding poverty and ignorance in the promise of better days to come."[94] More importantly, black church members could gain skills in community organization, financial management, self-government, and self-reliance.[95] Ultimately, black churches provided members with a medium for spiritual sustenance, a podium for leadership development, and a forum for primary education.

Supported by informal household income, black churches became "centers of community life," housing schools, social events, political gatherings, and social clubs. As historian Jennifer Lund Smith indicated for a black community in northern Georgia, "the church [became] . . . a symbol of education. Soon after the war ended, the church building began to serve as a schoolhouse."[96] Because churches remained outside of state control, they surpassed schools in becoming significant social and community centers.[97] As noted in chapter 1, these private spaces (hidden transcripts), beyond the generalized surveillance of white society, became areas for blacks to associate and communicate freely and thus provided another means to retain control over their lives.

While other denominations had different trajectories, historian Joel Williamson argued, "once freedom was achieved, exclusively Negro Baptist churches appeared everywhere, growing either out of the 'praise meetings' on the plantations or out of the secession of Negro members from churches dominated by whites." In fact, Williamson noted that Baptist "commitment to religious freedom" made such separations the norm for Baptist congregations.[98] The origins of the congregation of Soapstone Baptist Church may have come from either secession or independent development. Unfortunately, no church records exist from the early years of Liberia, because all historical records burned in the church fire of 1967. Thus, family histories, a few published versions of resident memories, and some microfilmed meeting minutes are all that remain.

"After the freed slaves had congregated in Liberia," local historian Bert Reece noted, "they attended a Negro Church" at Bald Rock, "far up in the cove of Greenville County [see map 2]; many of them walked the eight or ten miles to church." Joseph McJunkin was pastor. According to Reece, "this church became divided on some matter" and McJunkin took some of his loyal flock across the county line and organized the church at Liberia. Historian Mark Schultz noted that "many planters let the ex-slaves worship in groves on their land and sometimes contributed plots of land or even lumber for building black churches." According to Chris Owens (interviewed by local historians Ethel Edens and her coauthors), the residents first held religious observances in a brush arbor, a timber frame structure sided with brush or left open on the sides; sawdust covered the floor and wooden slabs served as benches. "People sat on split logs which had two limbs driven into each end to make legs. Sometimes backs were added," Chris Owens stated.[99]

The prominent soapstone boulder crowning the knoll in Liberia would be an obvious place to worship God—a stunning view to the north to the Blue Ridge, opening out on the Liberia Valley below. In her autobiography, Jane Hunter supported this perspective: "The Negro of those days used to betake himself to the woods when his overwrought soul felt the need of more than usually fervent prayer. . . . This practice of praying under the trees was something more than a mere belief of the colored folk. It was their intuitive knowledge of the healing strength that comes from growing things, and of the quiet of the woods where they could hear the 'still small voice'" (2 Kings 9:11–12).[100] According to Mable Owens Clarke, the congregation eventually built a permanent church at Soapstone in 1899. Most likely, this was built of logs and later weather boarded (see figure 6).[101]

Other African Americans lived across the Oolenoy River valley on the southern side, and perhaps because the river and lowlands were difficult to cross on foot during rainy or muddy Sundays, or perhaps because of the desire for a church closer to these black residents, a second black church began. Despite the fact that regional historian Pearl McFall credited the founding of Mt. Nebo Baptist Church to the "plantation owners for their slaves" before the Civil War, the official church association booklet observed that "Mt. Nebo Baptist Church was established in a Brush Arbor [sic] on the Rock Hill of Pumpkintown, South Carolina in 1866." Most likely, this brush arbor and "rock hill" actually referred to McJunkin's church in Liberia and the prominent boulders at Soapstone, since there is no equivalent rocky knoll where the present-day Mt. Nebo Church sits. In fact, local historian Bert Reece claimed that a year after Soapstone began, McJunkin also founded Mt. Nebo Church, a congregation undoubtedly enhanced by blacks expelled (or seceding) from the white Oolenoy Baptist Church. According to the church association history, "about 1873, the brush arbor was moved to the location of the present church [about a mile east of Oolenoy and about two miles southeast of Soapstone; see map 3], on land owned by Earl Edens. In 1873, Mr. Edens partly sold and partly gave land for the construction of a church."[102]

Thus Joseph McJunkin, the former enslaved laborer at the River Falls plantation, founded at least three Baptist congregations (an original one at Bald Rock, then Soapstone, and perhaps Mt. Nebo). According to his great-granddaughter Angela Young, McJunkin had no formal theological training; "I was called to preach," he always told his descendants. McJunkin's fervency and leadership fit a process described by historian Joel Williamson, who noted that the early pattern of growth for black Baptist churches "was one in which strong local leaders established numerous churches in one locale, and gradually brought other churches, founded separately, into association with them."[103]

By 1881, the African American Baptist churches in the region (including Soapstone and Mt. Nebo) were further linked together into the Oolenoy River Baptist Missionary and Educational Association; by 1885 there were twelve churches in the organization, historian W. J. Megginson reported. Associations like these "brought people together from wide areas and provided relief from the monotony of isolated existence."[104] While not every year's minutes have been preserved, those that remain revealed a complex and puzzling relationship between Soapstone and Mt. Nebo. Although the churches were only about two miles apart, apparently they served overlapping congregations, for the minutes reflect names of deacons or representatives who appear from one church but lie buried in the cemetery of the other, or who represent one church in one decade, but another later. Furthermore, the congregation numbers also fluctuated significantly from decade to decade.[105]

A few stories about these two churches also appeared in the *Pickens Sentinel* during this interactive period. On March 9, 1893, the paper reported that Martin Terrell was rebuilding Mt. Nebo Church (perhaps placing clapboards over the older log structure), while William Edens was building a church house in Liberia known as "Little Durby." The origin of the name "Little Durby" within the Liberia area is completely unknown (possibly a further slurring from "Liburry" for Liberia?). Several weeks later (March 30, 1893), the paper reported what appeared to be a schism of some kind: "There are three parties in Liberia: the Neboites, the Soapstoneites, and the Durbyites, and each party claims he is on a platform that is best. We shall see what we shall see. Ill feelings is [sic] perhaps the case." Several months later

(June 8, 1893), there is a brief mention of a legal dispute between (name unclear) Sizemore of Little Durby Church and "Judge McGowan" [sic] of Mt. Nebo Church, over possession of the "Nebo church book." The latter won the dispute.

While the *Pickens Sentinel's* slightly condescending attitude toward community dissention may be overlooked as a historical by-product, such disagreements may have been due to more subtle concerns. Historian Sharon Holt suggested that, during this period, internal discord arose between black congregations over creating or dissolving alliances with individual whites, over when to compromise over a challenging situation, when to apply pressure, and how to exploit advantages. Perhaps reflecting the personal disputes, family quarrels, or strategic differences that may have divided these small rural congregations, by 1894, the annual meeting minutes reported that Soapstone Church's membership had declined to twenty-five members, while that of Mt. Nebo Church had increased to sixty-seven.[106] Thus, the condescending or ill-informed *Pickens Sentinel* reporter may have overlooked completely an active hidden transcript of shifting church alliances for personal, family, or community economic, political, or social benefits.

Founding of Soapstone School

As early as 1866, journalist Sidney Andrews discovered in his southern travels that "the negroes . . . all seem anxious to learn to read,—many of them appearing to have a notion that thereby will come honor and happiness." "Everywhere they could snatch a free moment and a fragment of a book to work from, freedpeople began educating themselves," historian Sharon Holt observed. The Freedmen's Bureau helped a little by negotiating building rentals and soliciting northern charitable assistance, but the bureau "did not supply teachers, books, or buildings."[107] Local blacks had to initiate the process themselves, using their informal household income generated by such activities as produce or moonshine sales or laundry or midwife service.

Thus, almost simultaneously with the founding of a church in Liberia, the residents also started a school, "the first Negro school in the county," Betty Hendricks wrote in her 1949 master's thesis. Ethel Hagood, the first teacher, held classes on the large soapstone boulder outcropping near the church perhaps as early as the "late 1870s." Soon, three men built a log cabin, "very crude and small, being unceiled, with shutter-type windows and a big fireplace at one end of the building. The children wrote on slates," Hendricks noted. Once the original school building rotted, the church then functioned as a school for the next several decades.[108]

Rural schools in the late nineteenth century, regardless of race, were very simple institutions and supported only the surrounding neighborhood—extending out several miles, however.[109] William Pickens, son of former slaves from southern Pickens County, described the "characteristic Negro schoolhouse" from this period such as the one he attended before his parents moved to Arkansas: the school was "built of logs, with one door and one window, the latter having no panes and being closed by a board shutter which swung on leather hinges outward. The house was not larger than a comfortable bedroom and had a 'fire-place' opposite the door. The children faced the fireplace, so that the scant light fell through the door upon their books. There were no desks; the seats were long board benches with no backs."[110]

Typically taught by the best-educated and most available member of the community, students met in ungraded units for an uncertain period of time, depending on the necessity of planting or harvesting schedules. "School interests were secondary to farm interests," Pickens noted; "the landowner would not tolerate a tenant who put his children to school in the farming seasons." Reading, writing, and arithmetic were quite basic skills, with perhaps some geography and Bible study. Lunches were brought from home or prepared by the teacher in a small on-site kitchen from foods donated by the community or government agencies. As historian George Tindall noted, after Reconstruction, South Carolina disproportionately supported white schools at the expense of black ones. Household black income thus had to be diverted to equal out the inadequate white support, increasing black poverty. Despite this difference, however, historian Steven Hahn argued that black schools, inadequate as they were at this time, nevertheless initiated the process of African American education. Moreover, sociologist Patricia Hill Collins added, schools and churches provided black women with places to speak their minds freely and to challenge the white hegemony of the submissive "mammy" stereotype.[111]

White-Black Interactions

During the late nineteenth century, the little valley sheltering the Liberia community changed dramatically. Now home to dozens of free black farmers and their families, Liberia residents interacted with hundreds of other African Americans (relatives, friends, and neighbors), in a wide belt extending from Marietta and northern Greenville County southeastward up the Oolenoy River valley beyond Pumpkintown (see map 2). Although geographically removed, Liberia's residents were not completely isolated, nor did they deliberately avoid the surrounding white society (unlike James Scott's hill tribes, which often ignored their surrounding state-level societies). Instead, Liberia's residents needed to purchase necessities like coffee or mass-produced consumer goods, visit the post office, take products to mills, and interact with county government; these activities "were situated in 'white' culture and necessitated familiarity and a willingness to participate in it."[112] Large, intermarried white families still lived on their ancestral family lands, but by now they hired white and black farmhands to work the fields or paid them with a share of the crop. Many African Americans continued to live near and to work for their former masters for a variety of reasons: familiarity with local topography and farming techniques, loyalty to or friendship with former owners, family roots, fear of the unknown, or poverty (see earlier discussion, this chapter).

Loyalties and friendships between blacks and whites at this time are difficult to prove, and demonstrate an excellent example of "partial truths." Because her research community had disappeared, archaeologist Jodi Barnes argued that "it is difficult to know how white families living in the area surrounding Brown Mountain Creek [Virginia] may have related with . . . African American families in the area." Historian Lynwood Montell's oral narratives about Coe Ridge, Kentucky, found that "only a certain segment [of white families] resented the presence of an island of Negro culture in their midst."[113] One of the benefits of working closely with a descendant, still-existing community like Liberia is that historic white-black interactions are more easily recovered and may be documented in multiple ways, including oral history. Despite the documentation, these materials still present alternate views of "truth," as postmodernists would predict.

On the one hand, during his southern excursions in 1866, journalist Sidney Andrews concluded that "the most charitable traveler must come to the conclusion that the professed love of the whites for the blacks [before the war] was a monstrous sham."[114] Given this antagonism, why would freed blacks remain near their former masters? The public transcript by whites indicated that the primary reason for the settlement proximity by former slaves to their former masters was due to loyalty. "Some slaves were so devoted to their masters that they chose to remain near them after they were freed," local historian Bert Reece recorded. For example, a brief obituary from the March 23, 1923, *Pickens Sentinel* noted that Luke Terrill "spent all his life at Pumpkintown where he was born and reared. He belonged to the Sutherland family before freedom." In Reece's family's memory, four "mammies remained near our family," including Aunt Mariah (wife of Emerson Kemp) and Aunt Katie (wife of Tom Owen[sic]). Bert Reece's son Josef recalled in his personal memoirs that "Aunt Katie was hired by Grandfather to help my Grandmother and help her take care of the children."[115]

In her personal memoirs, Jane Hunter described working for a white family when she was a girl, and she was treated as a "member of the family; . . . I can remember no difference in the care given us children." Later, by this time a girl of ten, Hunter "cooked, cleaned, washed, and ironed for a [white] family of six; in addition, I looked after two younger children." She was so mistreated that both white and black neighborhood families protested.[116] Ideally, blacks were now free to leave for better economic opportunities elsewhere, but the strong pull of home and typical southern ties to the land kept many families, both black and white, in the area (as the census records attest; see also chapter 8). Kin ties remained strong for both black and white families, but the post-Reconstruction Jim Crow laws forbade miscegenation.

Illegal and potentially life-threatening, sexual relationships between blacks and whites, or between "mulattoes" and whites, nevertheless occurred. The general sense of disdain and stigmatization by contemporary white males toward white females who were involved with men from other ethnic groups is reflected by Freedmen's Bureau Assistant Commissioner John De Forest, who described the attitude of white Greenville society toward these women just after the Civil War: "There is little social distance at any time between the low-downer [lower-class whites] and the black. Two white women were pointed out to me as having children of mixed blood; and I heard that one rosy-cheeked girl of nineteen had taken a mulatto husband of fifty." By the end of the nineteenth century, popular culture and newspapers had sensationalized the black male rapist myth, providing "justification" for segregation, harassment, and lynching of blacks by whites.[117]

As in antebellum times, sexual relationships between white men and black women were generally ignored by white society, Tindall believed (a hidden transcript among whites); in such cases, children born from such relationships followed the race of the mother, he added. On the other hand, Patricia Hill Collins argued that black women did not, and could not, ignore these relationships, whether consensual or not. Born in 1882, Jane Hunter mentioned that both her grandparental and parental generations contained interracial relationships.[118] However, many local whites and blacks considered such historical unions to be shameful or embarrassing, since there existed a strong possibility that some (most?) of those associations were forced, given the power differential between men and women, significantly compounded by racial inequality.

For example, William and Rosa Glenn Owens were married (as the census indicated), but according to Owens family oral history, Rosa's first three children had been fathered by a white man, whose name was lost to history, her granddaughter said. "They kept them things secret," her brother added; "They didn't tell you too much."[119] Emma McJunkin (Absalom's wife) "had a big knot on her head," her grandson recalled years later, "where the white man hit her . . . because she didn't give up no 'goodies.'" Working as a waitress and chambermaid in a boarding house in southern Pickens County, Jane Hunter (a self-described "pretty mulatto" girl) faced a "constant battle against unwanted advances, . . . impudent glances, insulting questions." Such examples of resistance, whether successful or not and whether publicly viewed or not, exemplify Scott's breach of the hidden transcript into public view, allowing the insubordinates a sense of "personal authentication" and a chance "to restore a sense of self-respect and personhood."[120]

Another consequence of miscegenation was resentment and bitterness, especially for those born into one race being subjugated by another. In her autobiography, Jane Hunter observed that her parents frequently quarreled, but she did not realize why until later. "To Mother, I was the living expression" of an interracial relationship, and she "disliked and feared the characteristics of the white race in me, and she disliked and feared them in Father; but with no power to explain or rationalize her feelings."[121]

Miscegenation (especially between black or "mulatto" males and white females) was only one potentially life-threatening experience faced by blacks at this time. Sociologist Bertram Doyle described the general etiquette of race relations at this time (whites dominant, blacks publicly submissive), and historian George Tindall added that "a strain of violence has always characterized race relations in the South." Emanating from the physical force needed to maintain enslavement, and exacerbated by an impossible standard of gallantry toward white women, interracial violence increased dramatically during Reconstruction, especially with the patina of antebellum paternalism removed. Even with a slight downturn by the turn of the century, Tindall noted, lynching of blacks and overall intimidation continued: "Violence, while normally latent, was endemic. The fear of violence is a basic context in which the history of South Carolina Negroes during the period must be studied to be clearly understood." Unlike the plantation Lowlands with more rigid racial boundaries, historian W. Fitzhugh Brundage argued, whites in the Appalachian Mountains used racial violence "as a tool to define racial boundaries in a region where traditional racial lines were either vague or nonexistent." As Michael Taussig indicated (chapter 1), this culture of terror maintained both racial boundaries and inequalities by means of the "cultural elaboration of fear," even without the actual perpetration of many violent acts. But black Appalachians, sociologist Dunaway concluded, "faced a higher probability of day-to-day violence than freed people in other parts of the South, and this trend continued well into the 1930s." In fact, she discovered, "Pickens County, South Carolina exhibited a higher incidence of racial violence than most counties further [sic] south in the state."[122]

As Taussig had hypothesized, and as W. E. B. DuBois knew, threats of violence created constant stress for all African Americans. Moreover, Barnes added, "racial tensions increased significantly among lower-class whites who perceived more clearly than ever the impact of large-scale black competition for low-status jobs, as both poor whites and blacks were dependent upon the landowning class for their livelihoods as tenants and sharecroppers." For example, Jane Hunter recalled an episode where a drunken white called an older black hired hand "a bad name." In retaliation, the black threw a stone at the drunkard, which incited "a lynching party" against the black man. The plantation owner rushed the hired hand "out of the state" until the white man could be fired. Several months later, the black man returned.[123] According to the McJunkin family history, at one time Joseph's oldest son owned most of the land at the foot of Caesar's Head, now bisected by U.S. Route 276 (see map 2), but "he was ran off of it," a descendant added. She hesitated to explain at first, but continued: "If the whites told you not to come up on your land you didn't go because you knew that there would be a mob and they were going to kill you." In this way, she added, a lot of African Americans simply lost their land.[124]

In part, this "forced reallocation" of land explained the drastic decline in black farmers in the area and also demonstrated the constant threat under which even the most well-mannered African Americans lived. As summarized in chapter 1, this disciplinary power and overarching surveillance embedded themselves into every African American, so that a threat to one man's life, perhaps conveyed only as a vague reference not to visit his own property, then reminded a black farmer of every story he had ever heard of beatings, torture, lynching, and murders. Domination, inequality, and property theft then persisted without the necessity of any white actually doing any evil act at all.

Because of this constant tension from the culture of terror felt in personalized form by every black (including those in Liberia), many residents felt, as Jane Hunter came to feel as a young woman, "a desire to escape racial heritage as a Negro." As a lot of Liberia's residents did, Jane Hunter escaped "the curse of being a Negro—poverty, contempt, subjection, the badge of sufferance which my people had worn for many years." Hunter moved to Cleveland, Ohio, for better economic and social opportunities. Her contemporary, William Pickens, moved with his family to Arkansas. But some Liberia residents, like Hunter herself, later came to realize "that I was, above and beyond all, my mother's child—a Negro; that I was proud of the blood of my black ancestors."[125] Hunter's eventual acknowledgment and recognition of her own African heritage reflected the more general pride that many of Liberia's residents took in their own heritage; in turn, that pride strengthened their resolve to remain on their lands and to persevere through difficult times.

Historians disagreed on the overall gains for blacks during the late nineteenth century. "The story was still a complicated, multifaceted one," W. J. Megginson concluded. On the one hand, Loren Schweninger offered a rather pessimistic view: "Despite slavery, racism, war, emigration, colonization, lynchings, and brutal murders, most blacks continued to view the South as their home and clung to the values and attitudes that they had grown to accept: that acquiring land and property would somehow free them from the burdens of the past. Their tragedy, and the region's tragedy, was that it never would."[126] On the other hand, historian Eric Foner noted the significant gains blacks had made during this period: "In stabilizing their families, seizing control of their churches, greatly expanding their schools and benevolent societies, staking a claim to economic independence, and forging a distinctive political culture, blacks during Reconstruction laid the foundation for the modern black community, whose roots lay deep in slavery, but whose structure and values reflected the consequences of emancipation."[127] "Long after they had been stripped of the franchise, blacks would recall the act of voting as a defiance of inherited norms of white superiority," Foner added. Ultimately, emancipation "had brought rights and privileges that would never again be taken away," historian George Tindall concluded. This foundation of freedom helped establish the rise of blacks toward equality during the twentieth century.[128]

Conclusion

Inequalities remained for Liberia's blacks and even increased toward the opening of the twentieth century. Jim Crow laws guaranteed that African Americans could not work alongside whites in the developing mill villages, already draining many white mountain and Piedmont farmers to the cities. Schools and churches remained segregated, and blacks had to enter the rear doors of shops in towns like Marietta and Pickens. Some whites enjoyed and socialized with their black neighbors (although segregation prevented complete equality), while other whites looked with condescension, disdain, pity, or even hatred on the former slaves. Juries in the Upstate were virtually all white, as was the entire judicial system, from judges to police officers and sheriffs, thus creating a legal system that held every black in suspense. Under Foucault's system of the normalizing gaze of overarching surveillance, one black illegal activity, one accident, one inadvertent glance, one raised voice, and the "perpetrators" might find themselves cheated, beaten, jailed, tortured, exiled, or executed by whites. Consequently, all African Americans, including those in the Liberia area, tried to live in a protective shell, a hidden transcript, within their own secluded freedom colony of like individuals. But beyond that enclave blacks entered a public stage of generalized and constant observation: scrutinized, corrected, ridiculed, and harassed. This overarching white surveillance did not yield black docility and resignation, however. Whenever they could, blacks resisted white domination through myriad forms of hidden and (sometimes) public retaliation.

In this ironically still segregated world of newly acquired freedom, former slaves like Joseph McJunkin, Emerson Kemp, and Katie Owens raised their children and grandchildren. By this time, Katie Owens's youngest son, William, living near his mother and married to Rosa Glenn, had recently welcomed to the world a baby named Christopher, Rosa's firstborn son. During Chris Owens's lifetime, which spanned the entire next century, he would see enormous, unimaginable transformations in the nation, in the state, in the Oolenoy Valley, to his neighbors and friends in Liberia, and to his own family.

4 The Whites Got the Best

The Early Twentieth Century

. . . .

The community into which Katie Owens's new grandson, Christopher, was born underwent significant demographic transformations within both their adult lives. As the new century opened, much of the South remained very rural, historian Gilbert Fite observed: "many families never traveled out of their home county or beyond the nearby village." Rural roads remained largely unpaved until the 1920s, and rural mail service was poor. Most people still traveled by wagon, by horse, or on foot. Most general store community discussions centered on crop conditions, the weather, commodity prices, and other farming issues. Tenants and sharecroppers lived in substandard housing, ate inadequate diets, had little education or health care, and faced a bleak future.[1] The South remained "the land of cotton" with a white-controlled economy; because of the racial inequality, in fact, historian Theodore Hemmingway described the South as an "internal colony" of the United States.[2]

As the United States entered the global community of nations through participation in a world war, the national economy diversified, especially in the northern and eastern states. Immigrants seeking a better life continued to flood into the northern cities. Coal mines powered factories, organized labor operated them, and that labor produced automobiles and other consumer products. Radios and newspapers brought news of the world beyond the Oolenoy Valley. Telephones, automobiles, tractors, and electricity altered southern lives.[3] A national network of rail lines now made the new economic opportunities more accessible, and African Americans already working in northern cities told their relatives on Pickens County farms about the (legally but not residentially) integrated public schools, restaurants, parks, and public transportation. A better life became attainable once again, a generation after Reconstruction.[4] The South lost tens of thousands of the grandchildren of former slaves to segregated neighborhoods but integrated factories in the exploding northern cities.

Immigration, industrialization, and unionization created a national back-lash among many whites, especially in the South, who saw the United States as undergoing rapid social and cultural changes. In response, many southern whites launched a propaganda campaign to promote white supremacy. To reinforce inequality, whites transformed black institutions of higher education into industrial arts and training schools, especially targeting black females for primarily domestic activities.[5] Contemporary American historians redefined the collapse of Reconstruction and African American civil rights as due to the ascendancy of legitimate and appropriate white rule over corrupt and inept black and northern political control; hundreds of thousands of black and white schoolchildren learned their southern states' histories based on this revision.[6] North Carolinian Thomas Dixon penned the novel *The Clansman*, which became the film *Birth of a Nation*. The film sparked a resurrection of the Ku Klux Klan, reigniting its culture of terror from a generation earlier.[7]

Nevertheless, despite terrorism, disenfranchisement, segregation, and "systematic pauperization through tenancy," southern blacks overcame these obstacles with myriad responses.[8] By this time, regional cities like Greenville and Easley drew some black laborers for the expanding (but seg-regated) textile mills, especially for lower-paying jobs as teamsters for un-loading and loading trucks or janitors for cleaning bathrooms. White mill families, often with both parents working, needed black women as maids or nurses for white children. Timber and lumbering replaced cotton and corn for many farmers, but "blacks traditionally labored at dirty, arduous, menial jobs that few whites wanted." Even professional positions such as doctors, nurses, and ministers were differentially paid.[9] Despite the in-creased racism, economic opportunities for blacks improved.

However, historian Walter Edgar continued, as the nation enjoyed the economic boom of the Roaring Twenties, South Carolina cotton agriculture collapsed due to the predations of the boll weevil and soil exhaustion (and erosion). "Our trying time came between 1910 and 1930," Pickens County journalist Ben Robertson recalled; "those were the years that bled us and nearly dried the well of our faith." Black high school and college graduates sought better opportunities elsewhere, especially in the North. Over 50,000 black farmers abandoned the state in 1922 alone. Less than a decade later came the Great Depression, hitting South Carolina especially hard.[10]

Because of these disasters, farmers who remained on the land learned to rotate crops and diversify agricultural production. New Deal policies in the 1930s initially improved economic conditions and fostered black activism, organizations, and political awareness. Consequently, as the United States stood on the brink of a second world war by 1940, the descendants of former slaves remaining in Liberia had faced tremendous economic and political challenges. Far fewer of them remained on family farms, but those who stayed saw a brighter horizon.[11]

Census Information from 1910–1940

As historian Adrienne Petty noted, communities like Liberia (or Promised Land, farther downstate) were unusual in that some local black farmers owned land, whereas "the vast majority of black farmers in the South remained landless."[12] In a sense, then, the continuing presence of Liberia constituted a hidden transcript, providing an example of black resistance to overall white domination. Simultaneously, Liberia's residents continued to seek refuge in this physically remote place, much as Scott's Southeast Asian hill tribes, relatively secure from the generalized observation and domination by whites.

In 1900, 240 people described as blacks or "mulattoes" (as indicated on the census) lived in the Pumpkintown census district (about 25 percent of the population of that district), with hundreds of others living in adjacent areas. Within a decade, seventy-three African Americans had departed, a 43 percent decline that transformed the district to about 80 percent white. In comparison, white numbers declined from 728 to 696, a net loss of thirty-two people, for about a 4.5 percent decline during that same decade. These numbers may be explained by the forces pulling African Americans toward better economic opportunities elsewhere, and also by push factors propelling them out of the Oolenoy Valley in particular and upstate South Carolina more generally (discussed more completely later in this chapter).

One of the first African Americans (see appendices 1 and 2 for relationships) listed in the 1910 census rolls for the Pumpkintown district was Willis Glenn, now widowed but living with his oldest daughter, Rosa (Rosie) Glenn Owens, also widowed (see figure 3). Residing with father and daughter were Rosie's three "mulatto" children: sons Christopher (see figure 4) and Esley, and daughter Willie Mae. Emerson Kemp (see figure 8 and book cover photo), back in the area, was married but with no resident children. William Terrell and Sam "Goob" Keith were widowed. Nearby was Katie Owens Terrell (see figure 2), listed as the head of her household, a laundress unable to read or write. Nearby was a household of two brothers, Clarence and Ernest Glenn, probably younger half brothers of Rosie Glenn Owens (see chapter 3). Lonzo Glenn, an older brother, no longer appeared in the district's census (see his story later in this chapter).

In the adjacent Dacusville district dwelt a few more black families, with several more (including some listed as servants in white households) in the Eastatoe district to the west of Pumpkintown, but very few overall. In the opposite direction, across the line in Greenville County, lived Joseph A[bsalom] McJunkin; his wife, "Emmer" (Emma); and six children, including their second child, a daughter Lula, and their youngest son, James.

The African American exodus that began in the previous decade accelerated (or at least did not abate) during the next decade. By 1920, ninety-four more blacks had left the district, a 56 percent decline from the previous decade. This left only seventy-three black or "mulatto" residents in the district, along with 709 whites, who saw a net gain of thirteen people. The district was now 91 percent white. Socioeconomic forces compelling blacks to leave the area continued.

In the Pumpkintown district in 1920, Ernest Glenn had married; living near the couple was Katie Owens, still listed as a laundress. Rosie Glenn Owens (Katie's former daughter-in-law) had now married Thomas Gowans; the couple had eight children (the children bore the surname McGowens); also living with them was Rosie's daughter from her previous marriage. William Terrell had remarried (Minnie), and the couple had two daughters and a son. Emerson Kemp and Sam "Goob" Keith lived by themselves, Keith surrounded by the (white) Chastain family. Chris Owens, Katie Owens's grandson, boarded in Ward 1, Greenville (the largest proximal city), and worked as a laborer in a cotton "compress," (a device to squeeze cotton bales for easier shipping) while his (probable) mother's brother Clarence Glenn also boarded in Ward 1 and worked as a laborer in a government camp. They maintained strong ties to their home community of Liberia.

In an adjacent district, James Kemp reappeared. Back in 1880, James was the eleven-year-old son of Emerson "Empse" Kemp, and he had not appeared in a Pumpkintown census for forty years, probably because he had moved away for employment opportunities elsewhere. By 1920 James had returned, along with his wife, Hattie, probably to care for his aging father. James Kemp worked as a laborer for a cotton mill. In the next district lived Ansel McKinney, widower, with two daughters, one son, and two stepsons. The (black) McKinney family in earlier decades had resided in the upper Keowee Valley (descended from slaves owned by the [white] McKinney family), but had been displaced by the Toxaway Flood of 1916 (a North Carolina dam burst) and eventually settled in Liberia.[13] By this time, few blacks remained in the Dacusville district or in Greenville County's Cleveland district. Among the names in the latter district were "Abraham" McJunkin; his wife, Emma; and their seven children, including their daughter Lula and son James.

By 1930, the exodus of African Americans from the Liberia area continued, and the demographic increase of whites did as well, further altering the racial character of the region. By this time, eighteen more blacks had left, leaving only fifty-five, for another 25 percent loss. In contrast, white residents increased by eighty-seven people, for a total of 798. As African American numbers dwindled, intermarriages between residents in this district and nearby ones increased, " 'cause they didn't have too many people to go around to get married to," Mable Clarke joked. The Pumpkintown district was now about 94 percent white. A few of the oldest original inhabitants had died, and more and more frequently younger people abandoned the farm for a better life in Greenville or regions farther away, reflecting the overall exodus of blacks from the southern states (discussed more completely later in this chapter).

On the other hand, some aging residents remained, wishing to spend their final years in a familiar place. Rosie Glenn Owens Gowens still resided with her five children from her most recent marriage, and she also continued to live with her daughter from her previous marriage. Nearby resided William Terrell and his wife, "Minnie," with three adult children in their early twenties. Clarence "Glynn" [Glenn], a farmer, lived alone, but near his (probable) nephew (Rosie's oldest son) Christopher Owens and his family. A perfect example of community intermarriages, Christopher Owens from Liberia had married Absalom McJunkin's oldest daughter, Lula (see figure 4), from the Cleveland district in Greenville County, and they have three children. Ansel McKinney dwelt with his wife, "Mima," in the district, but all of their children had left. Samuel "Goob" Keith, a farmer, resided alone. In a nearby district (Pickens 23) lived James Kemp and his wife, Hattie, while in Greenville County's Cleveland district, "Ab" McJunkin and his wife, Emma, still had five resident children, including youngest son "Jim."

By the 1940 U.S. Census, the story of Liberia entered the memory of living people and also reached the limits of publicly released census forms. By 1940, census districts had become much smaller, and so the overall population fluctuations are much more difficult to compare. On the other hand, the census now asked for grades of education, so one can get a better glimpse into the class divisions fostered by the relative lack of education for Liberia's residents. Within the Pleasant Grove census district (containing Liberia but no longer Pumpkintown), there were 302 whites but only thirty-six "Negroes" (no longer differentiated by ancestry as "black" or "mulatto"). No African Americans at all lived in the adjacent Oolenoy district, which now included Pumpkintown. Pleasant Grove district was just over 89 percent white.

By 1940, the remaining names listed in the Liberia area were almost precisely those recalled by still-living residents. Rosie Glenn Owens Gowens lived with one son, while her oldest son Christopher Owens's growing family supplied one-quarter of Liberia's population. Mr. Owens was forty-three, a farmer with three grades of schooling, and his wife, Lula, also had three grades; the couple now had seven children. Nearby lived Ansel McKinney, a farmer, and his wife, Mina. Their children had returned to help take care of their aging parents (a pattern repeated often). Clarence Glenn, Chris Owens's (probable) mother's brother, was a single farmer. Will Terrell lived with his wife and two daughters. Both of these women were single, but one woman had a son. Across the county line in Greenville County, Cleveland district, Emma McJunkin, now widowed, resided with her youngest daughter, Lilly.

One of the more poignant stories revealed in the 1940 Census was that of one other resident in Liberia: Hattie Kemp. Listed as a sixty-seven-year-old widow, she had been married to James Kemp, who in turn had returned to Liberia about a decade earlier to care for his aging father, Emerson Kemp, a man born into slavery (see figure 8 and photo on book cover). In the older slave Soapstone Cemetery, very few graves are actually marked with legible stones. One grave bears a tiny, white metal funeral home marker (a white post with a four-inch rectangle on top) holding a barely legible printed card underneath a glass panel. The card reads: "Mr. James Kemp," with a death date of July 19, 1938. Just to the right of Kemp's grave is another grave, a depression in the ground parallel to him, but unmarked—except for a white metal post that most likely had held another rectangular funeral home marker, now long gone. Since the posts of the markers are very similar, and since Christian customs recommend adjacent spousal interment unless mitigating circumstances cause other arrangements (for example, divorce and remarriage), it is very likely that Hattie Kemp lies next to her husband in this unmarked grave in the old Soapstone Cemetery.

Another prominent resident of Soapstone at this time was Katie Owens. She lived her entire (documented) life in the Oolenoy Valley and Liberia community, near the farms of her daughter-in-law Rosie Glenn Owens (later

Gowens) and Rosie's oldest son, Chris Owens (Katie's grandson). Katie's great-grandson added: "She used to go to work for Amos [Sutherland] over here at Pumpkintown. And she didn't want to be free from slavery, because she said I'm too old to try to go anyplace else. I remember her saying that. . . . She couldn't see going out on her own, 'cause she had done give so much to white folks." Addie Sutherland, a congregant at Oolenoy Baptist Church, recalled that for baptisms, the women "wore mittie [sic] blouse dresses and Katie Owen [sic] . . . helped them at the pool. She pinned their dresses very tight so they would stay in place in the water."[14] Current Soapstone Church members had heard stories of Katie Owens as they visited older relatives in the Liberia community. One woman stated that she "was something like a midwife. When the whites would have babies they would always call her because she was the one that would stay with them and . . . deliver their kids. . . . She was well-known with whites."

In a testament to her regional notoriety, Katie Owens comes to life in a detailed sketch about her that appeared on the front page of the *Easley Progress* on January 13, 1927; her obituary in the *Pickens Sentinel* of February 23, 1928 (p. 8) provided additional information. As noted in chapter 1, in the early twentieth century, virtually all newspaper obituaries were those of prominent people, and almost exclusively of whites. For African Americans to break the "color barrier" of segregated news stories, even if only with their deaths, reflected the extraordinarily high position of the few who actually crossed that barrier. Katie Owens, a woman born into slavery about 1840, was one such prominent black.

Front and center of page one of the *Easley Progress* was a two-column article entitled "Aunt Katie," describing "one of the oldest and most interesting of the few remaining inhabitants of Liberia, . . . a genuine Southern Mammy" and "an interesting character of the hills." She was "perhaps one of the most widely known and respected colored women of the county," the *Pickens Sentinel* added. According to the *Progress* writer, "Aunt Katie . . . still wears the old time spencer-waist dress, . . . a tight fitting bodice to the waist line, buttoned up in front, to which is gathered a full skirt, with deep [next word unclear] and with ample pockets. . . . She always wears a large apron and a snow white kerchief, neatly hemmed by her own fingers, is twined about her head in that coronet style of the old mammy, binding back the wavy locks, scarcely less white than the folds that confine them."

"One acre of land and a small log cabin of one room constitute Aunt Katie's home," the writer observed, and she farmed corn and potatoes "as long as she was able to work." Aunt Katie earned additional income by helping whites in neighboring communities by cleaning houses and baking cakes for weddings, cooking meals at the Table Rock Hotel, and preparing meat at hog killing time, where she was "always well paid for her services," including "nice, crisp 'cracklings,' for the little pone of 'fatty-bread,' so dear to all the old time darkies." She also had cared for numerous children in the Oolenoy Valley, "dandled to sleep on her knee or rocked in the old time box cradle, while she crooned some plaintive melody peculiar to her race, or told witch tales to the older children as they huddled near the big kitchen fire . . . lighting up the room in a fanciful way."[15]

By the winter of 1927, the writer noted, Katie Owens suffered from "serious organic heart trouble," and so she "sleeps at the home of a grandson [Chris Owens], just opposite her little cabin." "In the little cabin are two trunks[,] one containing her most treasured belongings, carefully packed away and marked as to whom they are to go at her death." The other trunk holds "the entire outfit to be used at her burial. These garments are made by herself, and have been ready for a long time, so when the boatman calls for her to embark, she can do so with but little extra trouble to those about her." The article concluded that Aunt Katie's life has been "a sermon to all who know her. It has truly been a life of service." Perhaps even weaving her own burial shroud was an unselfish act, for contemporary Appalachian folklore dictated that "if you weave a shroud for a dead person, you will be the next one to die."[16]

Katie Owens (like her neighbor Hattie Kemp) might be expected to lie in her carefully prepared burial shroud in the old Soapstone Cemetery, just up the hill from her home site. If she had, no one would ever know, for almost all of the graves are marked only with rough fieldstones. Fortunately, her obituary in the *Pickens Sentinel* of February 23, 1928 (p. 8), revealed a little more about the circumstances of her death and interment. According to the obituary, Katie Owens died at the home of her grandson, Chris Owens, late the previous Friday night:

> "Aunt Katie," as she was known to people of both white and black races, . . . made her home with some of the best families before the 60's. These people were always "my folks" to her. Her loyalty grew stronger as the years went by. Soon after the war she married and to her were born three children. But the companion and the children passed away and for some thirty years she lived alone on her own little farm. It was during this period of her life that she was useful to the greatest number of people. She was much sought after in cases of

sickness, and in all times when extra help was needed. Many of her "white folks" friends braved the cold winds and weather on Sunday when she was laid to rest in the church yard of the Mt. Nebo church. Beautiful flowers were placed by them on her casket. A prominent woman of the community made a brief but feeling talk on the useful life of the departed. In appreciation of this the audience reverently applauded.

According to this obituary, Katie Owens was not buried in the old Soapstone Cemetery near Soapstone Baptist Church, even though she lived just down the hill from that church. Instead, she was interred in Mt. Nebo Baptist Church Cemetery, about two miles away. Why? One possibility is that the Mt. Nebo Cemetery was also that of the Terrell family (based on other graves there), and since at one time she had married into the Terrell family, it would make sense that she would be buried near them. According to Andy Gowans's [sic] obituary (see later in this chapter), the old Soapstone Cemetery may have been associated traditionally with the Gowens family. Still another possibility, Katie's oldest great-grandson thought, was that she may have been baptized at Mt. Nebo and thus would have been buried at her baptismal home. It is also possible that her burial reflected some family and/or congregational conflicts between Soapstone and Mt. Nebo (discussed in chapter 3).

In the Mt. Nebo Cemetery, off from the left rear of the church, lies a small headstone, about eighteen inches high, with the simple inscription "Our Aunt Katie 1840–1928." This is the final resting place of "Aunt" Katie Owens, a woman born into slavery, at one time owned by "some of the best families" in the Oolenoy Valley, a mother, grandmother, midwife, cook, and laundress, a woman well respected in her community by both blacks and whites, and the founding matriarch of the last remaining family in Liberia.

Not only has her grave been identified, but her image has also been preserved. In the *History of Pumpkintown-Oolenoy*, local historian Bert Reece published two photos of African Americans; one is of "Mammy Katie Owens." The photo (see figure 2) shows a tall woman, bent slightly at the waist, standing in front of a large frame house with a full-length front porch. Chickens scurry by her feet. The caption reads: "After slavery she continued to be a wonderful helper of the Hendricks, Edens, and Sutherlands. She was faithful in helping with Church [sic] dinners and never failed to see that children were well fed."[17]

While most of Katie Owens's life remained undocumented, from the scraps of information linked in the preceding narrative, one discovers a very prominent black woman, "one of the most widely known and respected colored women of the county," the *Pickens Sentinel* reported. Based on this information, it is possible to view Katie Owens as an example of what sociologist Patricia Hill Collins described as an othermother—a black woman who cared for her own children (and grandchildren such as Chris Owens) and by doing so influenced the lives of all the children in the Liberia area (as well as many white children in the Oolenoy Valley), for several generations.[18] "Aunt Katie" may have wanted to stay in Liberia due to "loyalty" to her white employers (some of whom were also her former owners), but it is equally possible that she continued to reside in the area as a deliberate act of defiance, consciously protecting and securing her legacy—the land and community of her children, her grandchildren, and her black neighbors.

As historian Glenda Gilmore observed, since black males were disenfranchised and feared during this time, black women "discovered fresh approaches to serving their communities and crafted new tactics designed to dull the blade of white supremacy."[19] It is impossible to guess what impact Katie Owens may have had during her eighty-something years of life: encouraging her black male relatives and neighbors to vote during Reconstruction, offering emotional support during the oppressive Jim Crow era, or encouraging neighborhood children and adults to seek an education at every opportunity. Given the fact that blacks were excluded from most hospitals, Katie Owens's knowledge of folk medicine and midwifery served to protect and (literally) to reproduce the community.[20] Grandmothers during this time, sociologist Jillian Jimenez documented, "maintained their status through storytelling, continuing these [slavery] narratives of resisting oppression, and turning whites' power against them in family histories, folktales, and songs."[21] Katie Owens's fireside stories presented oral traditions to generations of enraptured children. Even weaving her own burial shroud protected her survivors, she may have believed. Whatever actions she may have taken to implement self-reliance and resistance among her black neighbors, the actions remained a hidden transcript for her, because simultaneously she maintained the protection and admiration of her white employers by acting with the deference toward them that they expected. Whatever her motivations, Katie Owens's energy as an othermother for the Liberia community established a foundation for her children, grandchildren, and great-grandchildren to emulate and expand.

The few other extant obituaries of African Americans from this same period represented the passing of men and women born into slavery and now departing a society still divided by race. Five years before Katie Owens Terrell's death, Lewis (Luke) Terrell also passed away (*Pickens Sentinel*, March 23, 1923, p. 4). Described by the writer as a "good old-time darkey," he was "able to do actual labor until his death." "Quite a number of white people attended his funeral," and he "will be greatly missed by both black and white," the writer noted. "He spent all his life at Pumpkintown where he was born and reared," and before freedom he had "belonged to the Sutherland family," the obituary observed. Terrell's body "was laid to rest in Nebo churchyard the day following his death," most likely because Mt. Nebo Cemetery was the family graveyard of the Terrell family.

Four years later, the *Pickens Sentinel* of December 29, 1927, ran a front-page headline: "Former Slave Dies at Home of Son." "Throngs of relatives and friends attended the funeral and burial of Emerson K. Kemps [sic], one of the best known and most popular former negro [sic] slaves of this section." The article provided a brief glimpse into Kemp's life: "He was 83 years old. For the past fifteen years he had made his home with a son, James Kemps [sic] of Pickens, but his early life and manhood was [sic] spent in and around the Oolenoy section of the county. In slavery time he was owned by J. Hester and was considered a valuable person. After the war he settled on a farm of his own in the settlement of Liberia in which all of the people belonged to his race. He was carried back to his old home church for burial." What did the writer mean by "old home church?" As already seen, people who had spent their entire lives in Liberia might have been buried at Mt. Nebo, across the river, rather than at the top of the hill near the closest church, Soapstone. Nevertheless, as the barely marked grave in the older slave Soapstone Cemetery attests, James Kemp lies in that cemetery; most likely his wife does as well. Emerson Kemp's mother, Chaney (a woman born into slavery; see chapter 2) is also buried there. Is it possible that one of the reasons James Kemp was buried in the old Soapstone Cemetery is because his father and paternal grandmother were as well? If former slave Emerson ("Empse") Kemp was indeed buried in the old cemetery, his grave remains unknown and unmarked beneath one of the many rough fieldstones dotting the peaceful hillside.

While the final resting place of Emerson Kemp remains unknown, his image does not. Beneath Katie Owens's photo in Bert Reece's book is another one—that of a well-dressed African American gentleman in a three-piece suit, sporting a long white moustache, leaning on a post in front of a small clapboard cabin. The photo (book cover) has no title, but the caption reads: "Empse [*sic*] Kemp at his home in Liberia. He was Boss of James Benjamin Hester." Local historians Alma Lynch and Elizabeth Ellison published the same photo, provided Kemp's full first name (Emerson), and described him as "J. B. Hester's Boss [foreman] Slave."[22] Emerson Kemp's importance as "boss slave" to James Hester has been described in chapter 2.

A fourth intriguing obituary appeared in the *Pickens Sentinel* on May 31, 1928 (p. 5). The headline reads: "Andy Gowans (Col[ored].) Dead." Perhaps reflecting the need to differentiate between the white and black Gowans families, the reporter twice indicated the race of the deceased. Gowans was described as the "oldest resident" of Liberia, "this once popular negro settlement," reflecting the general exodus taking place by this time. The obituary offered a few other clues about his life: "He held the esteem and respect of neighbors, both white and black. By meager earnings he had accumulated some property. It had been his policy to save something of what he made. A few weeks before his death he willed his property, a little farm, personal property, and some savings to his son-in-law, Ansel McKinney, the husband of a deceased daughter. In this respect he proved that his love not only took in his children but also the 'in-law.' Funeral services and interment took place the day following his death at the family graveyard near his home."

As noted earlier, very few tombstones in the older slave Soapstone Cemetery bear legible inscriptions, but there is a relatively elaborate marker for Rev. A. R. Gowans and his daughter Charlota [*sic*], the wife of A. P. McKinney. Gowans's first wife died the previous century, and lies in that cemetery as well (see chapter 3 and note 67 to that chapter). According to the census lists mentioned earlier, by 1930 Ansel McKinney had remarried and still lived in Liberia (see also appendix 1).

One additional clue may be obtained from this obituary. Andy Gowans is buried in the old Soapstone Cemetery; in the obituary, his grave is described as being in "the family graveyard." Perhaps this explains the differential burials of Liberia residents between Mt. Nebo and Soapstone Cemeteries. In addition to the doctrinal and/or personal quarrels between these two congregations (as documented in the church records from the late nineteenth century), it is also possible that those buried in the Mt. Nebo Cemetery were related somehow to the Terrell family and baptized at that church, while those in the old Soapstone Cemetery may have been related to the Gowans family and baptized there.

In her excavation of the Brown Mountain Creek community in Virginia's mountains, anthropologist Jodi Barnes discovered that in this community, "prior to 1929, African Americans were buried in family cemeteries on mountain land."[23] After that date, families used church cemeteries. This trend seems to reflect burials in the old Soapstone Cemetery as well. That cemetery is located about 200 yards from the church, back in the woods. The most recent identifiable date from the older cemetery is that of James Kemp, from 1938, who may have been buried there because his paternal grandmother (and perhaps also his father) is buried there as well.

On April 17, 1930, the *Pickens Sentinel* ran a front-page story announcing the death of "Uncle John Miles." As indicated in census information, John Miles had at one time been a resident of the Pumpkintown census district, but at the time of his death, Miles lived "a few miles north of town" (Pickens) with his son-in-law. The obituary continued: "His passing came quietly and unknown to a wide circle of friends, both white and colored. This circle included all of his acquaintances for his was a character that held the respect and the esteem of all with whom he came in contact. Uncle John, as he was called, belonged to the family of Doctor Miles, of the Greenville vicinity. Later, he belonged to the Hagood family. He belonged to that class that represented the highest type of citizenship—law abiding, cheerful, a good neighbor to both whites and blacks. He is survived by nine children, fifty-six grand children and sixty-nine great grand children." Local journalist Coy Bayne, in a personal recollection, provided one additional fact about Mr. Miles: "Another ex-slave with a great deal of respect was John Miles. How many people recall John's favorite past-time? He would walk up and down the streets in Pickens, playing a flute. The children would fall in behind and up and down the streets the procession would go, everyone laughing and clapping their hands."[24] The document gives his death date as April 2, 1930.

Perhaps the most curious obituary from this rare collection of African American memorials is that of Sam "Goob" Keith, who died in 1935. Keith first appeared before the Civil War in documented local history as the small boy begging to be purchased by the Keith family (described in chapter 2). Throughout the nineteenth- and twentieth-century census lists, Keith continued to appear as a resident of the Liberia area, but his age did not increase by ten each decade. This is undoubtedly because he had no idea of his actual birth year or day (being born into slavery), and so either he or the census taker simply estimated his age.

On August 30, 1967, the *Easley Progress* carried a story by John McCravy titled "The Historical Trail," about the life of Samuel "Goob" Keith. The article repeated the story about little Sam being bought by the Keiths, but then added some very interesting details:

He bought and paid for his home and farm which overlooked the Oolenoy bottoms. He was resourceful and independent, honest and completely trustworthy. . . . At one time he produced the finest peaches and apples grown in the valley. He understood erosion and he built rock fills in washes which soon filled up with topsoil and was put into production. Some may have a tendency to call "Goob" an "Uncle Tom" . . . but this is not the case at all. Goob was respected and admired by everyone and he was resourceful and frugal. His high morals elevated him in the eyes of most white men. . . . He had the greatest faith in prayer and he prayed constantly. . . . Goob was a natural entertainer, [sic] he sang many songs as he played the accordion. He knew folk songs and the ones popular in his day. At times he would surprise his listeners with excerpts from light opera and songs of deep feeling. . . . Goob was the only Negro man to live in that particular section of the county. He had very little to do with other members of his race. He said he was Indian and not a Negro. He said Indians did not have hairy chests, [sic] he would then pull open his shirt neck to show a smooth chest. A smile went over his face each time he did this. . . . Goob married once and had a son. His wife had died many years ago and his son went away a half century ago and never returned. Goob Keith lived on in the old place he had bought and developed. . . . His one request was to be carried and buried in front of the rock boulder near his home.

The author claimed that several neighbors, along with his own wife and granddaughter, climbed up the knoll upon which the grave sat and chiseled the words "Sam 'Goob' Keith, 90 yrs. 1935" on the boulder tombstone. Today the grave rests on private property, about five miles up the Oolenoy Valley from Liberia and Pumpkintown, but the owners have photographed the grave.

The reasons for Goob Keith's geographical isolation from the core of the African American community in the Liberia area may never be known. Taking him at his word that he had Native American ancestry, it is possible that Keith may have been related to some of the last Cherokee in the area, or to others across the border in North Carolina (see his origin story from chapter 2). On the other hand, some contemporary informants mentioned that the designation "Indian" had been used by past generations to disguise the parentage of mixed race (black and white) children due to forced or consensual (often discrete) sexual relationships (see chapter 1). Perhaps Keith had been the offspring of such an interracial relationship during slavery times and thus did not identify with the "blacks" in the Liberia area.

General Way of Life (1900–1940)

Country Life

Henry Fulmer, a researcher for the South Carolina Agricultural Extension Service, described southwestern Pickens County in 1939. Mostly white and "descended entirely from pioneer American stock," they are "a peace-loving, church-going, law-abiding folk." Residents of the Oolenoy Valley and the small crossroads community of Pumpkintown, about twelve miles away from Fulmer's study area, reflected those same values, with the addition of, and recognition of, the strategically remote Liberia community. According to local historian Josef Reece, twelve large white landowning families (with roots back to the early nineteenth century) dominated the "sparsely populated" valley: Edens, Southerlands [sic], Keiths, and a few others. Family farms still dotted the landscape, and fields of corn and cotton (along with home gardens) provided much-needed cash to support families.[25]

The sketch of Katie Owens from the front page of the *Easley Progress* (January 13, 1927) provided a somewhat romanticized view of the Liberia area: "Hidden away in a remote and rugged section of Pickens county lies a scope of land owned exclusively by negroes, and in the midst of which is [a] quaint and unique settlement which is inhabited solely by negroes, which bears the name of Liberia. . . . Liberia is located in a very secluded portion of this county. . . . [Other than biweekly mail delivery or an occasional car], the echo of the wood-chopper's axe by day and the howl of the big owl on a winter's night are about the most that disturb the silence of this secluded spot, which reminds one of some of those hills described by Washington Irving" (lack of capitalization in original).

Here, the paper continued, families tended "their rugged red fields, . . . eking out a very meager existence." After an exhaustive search of tax records, historian W. J. Megginson located twenty black landowners in the area, and only seven black families owned homes (see census figures earlier in this chapter).[26] Aunt Katie Owens, the focus of the *Progress* article, farmed "corn and potatoes," the writer observed. "We growed corn for the animals and for ourselves, too," Katie Owens's great-grandson recalled.[27] He also remembered his family raising hogs, calves, and chickens when he was young, with the meat larder enhanced by wild game, especially squirrels, rabbits, and possums (baked with "candy yams around it"). Other favorite foods from his mother's kitchen included peach cobbler, sweet potato pie, egg custard, and "good, good biscuits" and gravy.

During the Depression, however, "times was tough," Philip Owens conceded. Government workers "used to have a truck, and they [would] have soup on the truck," he continued. Lula Owens used to meet the truck with a foot tub, and the government workers would fill the tub with soup, " 'cause there wasn't nothing to eat," Owens recollected. "Good white folks" might also provide "baked potatoes, sometimes corn, [to] feed us," he added. Extension agent Henry Fulmer described Pickens County farm life as challenging, even for the whites of his study group: tenant farmers especially suffered from poor nutrition, and mothers needed to work in the fields for vital family income and thus were unable to prepare nourishing meals for their families.[28]

In addition to farming, the older Owens brothers helped their father, Chris, bury six-foot logs with leaves and dirt and then slowly burn them, to make charcoal to sell. Philip Owens recalled tramping into the woods before daylight to help drag limbs and then trudging up the hill to the little Soapstone School every day. Michael Owens came home from school and cut cordwood to stack along the road for whites to drive by and purchase. He also caught rabbits, squirrels, and possums and sold the meat at the Edens Store (see map 3). Additional family income came from Mrs. Owens selling butter, eggs, milk, and her preserves, while other family members "had a hand in" helping local white farmers transform some corn into moonshine, an Owens son noted.[29]

Besides working on their own farms, Liberia's residents also labored on the farms of their white neighbors. Sometimes, juveniles or young adults hired themselves out as well. For example, a long-term white resident of the Oolenoy Valley (and a direct descendant of Cornelius Keith) remembered a few black families across the valley in Liberia, including "Uncle Jim Kemp." "Now he did a lot of work for my Daddy," the resident continued; "he would help him. He'd come and help him get his cane ready to make molasses and all that."

As in the past century, Liberia's farmers, including the Owens family, grew more than cotton and corn for a market economy controlled and enforced by white hegemony. By continuing to utilize a varied range of economic activities, the Owens family and their neighbors exemplified what anthropologist Rhoda Halperin described for more recent decades as "the Kentucky way": "homeplace ties, loyalty and generosity to kin, commitment to versatility, self-sufficiency, and self-reliance." Generalizable to many parts of the world and to many centuries, this strategy allowed rural people to maintain dignity and self-sufficiency and to resist a dependency upon state-level capitalism, in precisely the same ways that James Scott's Southeast Asian hill tribes resisted domination by their state-level neighbors.[30] The strategy combined the growing of market crops (corn and cotton), peddling barnyard products (milk and eggs), selling assorted commodities (charcoal, firewood, and moonshine), and "truck" (or wagon) selling of homegrown vegetables. For their own subsistence, families also gardened, canned, hunted, fished, foraged for berries and medicinal plants, and shared food and labor throughout extensive kin networks. Some of this "underground food economy" could be done by children or the elderly.[31] In this way, Liberia's residents (like other peoples) purposefully and strategically distanced themselves as much as possible from white economic and social control and reinforced the existence, and persistence, of Liberia as a social and economic "freedom colony."[32]

Houses in the sanctuary of Liberia were of log or wood frame with no indoor plumbing, no running water, and no electricity (like most rural houses at this time).[33] One of Katie Owens's great-grandsons remembered that she "used to live in a little shack on a hill over here," just below the church. "We called it the little hut," he continued, because it was only one room, about the size of the kitchen in his parents' house (about fifteen by twenty-five feet).[34] Michael Owens remembered his own place of birth as having only four rooms, with a separate kitchen. "Some [children] had to sleep at the foot of the bed, some at the head of the bed," he added. "In that old house," his sister Mable recalled, "you could look straight down through the floor and [see] the chickens running underneath the house." Several photos of Liberia houses exist. Local historian Bert Hendricks Reece published a photo (book cover photo) of Emerson Kemp "at his home in Liberia." Regional historian Pearl McFall also published a photo of a "Negro Home in Liberia." The clapboarded home, about thirty feet long and about ten feet wide, has a gabled end, one story tall, with a porch covering about a third of the front, and no visible chimney, perhaps indicating stove heating in some homes by this time (see also figure 8).[35]

Because of distance, cost, and segregated facilities, most communities also supported traditional healers, such as Katie Owens and her daughter-in-law Rosie Glenn Owens, both of whom served as midwives for the community (helping deliver their own grandchildren, in fact, the grandchildren recalled).[36] Will Terrell, another neighbor, could "talk fire out of you," a resident recalled. For this effect, the healer whispered a secret verse from the Bible over the affected area, and very soon thereafter the pain disappeared.[37] "My brother got burnt" as a child, Michael Owens offered, and his brother Philip continued the story. While tamping down the covering on his family's smoldering charcoal pile one day, Philip accidentally drove his leg into the pile and burned himself "up to my midsection." He raced to the nearby creek to soak, and his mother came to the rescue, smothering his leg with Vaseline and wrapping it in a tow sack, " 'cause it was really hurting." They carried him up to Will Terrell, and "he was telling me that it was going to be all right; I'm talking the fire out of you." The Owens siblings also remembered "Grandma Rosie" Glenn Owens using yellow root, black snake root (soaked in some bootleg whiskey), boar hog root, and other concoctions containing turpentine for healing purposes.[38] "My mother [Lula McJunkin Owens] knowed something about it, you know," Michael Owens explained. According to baby sister Mable, her mother acquired her knowledge of medicinal plants from her father, Absalom McJunkin, over in Bald Rock: "My mother used to follow her father around every place he went, . . . and she learned all her wisdom from him," Mable Clarke observed.[39]

Most roads remained dirt, impassable for many weeks during the year, and transportation was frequently by foot, by horse or mule, or by wagon. "The roads are narrow, winding trails, with but little outside travel," the *Easley Progress* reported in the front-page story on Katie Owens (January 13, 1927). J. L. Burgess, the white store owner in Pumpkintown, offered to purchase a wood heater for the new Soapstone schoolhouse (see later in this chapter) but admitted "the roads are so bad I cannot come myself" to pay for it.[40] Michael Owens recalled that the old dirt road through Liberia mired people all the time. A few families owned automobiles by the 1920s, but these were relatively rare.[41] For example, James McJunkin (Absalom McJunkin's son) purchased his first car, a Ford, in 1931, just before starting his teaching career in Central, South Carolina, according to his youngest daughter.

Curiously, Liberia and the surrounding farmsteads supported two crossroads stores within a mile or so of each other; Michael Owens speculated that the Edens Store existed first, and later the Sutherland/Burgess Store developed as competition (see map 3). As mentioned in chapter 3, the Sutherland home sat diagonally across the highway intersection from their country store, owned and operated by the Burgess family after 1941. According to local historian Bert Reece, "the Sutherlands kept a general merchandise store through the years," and managed the post office in the store as well.[42] Philip Owens remembered taking his mother's farm products to the store to trade, "and she [Mrs. Burgess] give me a little . . . peppermint candy" with the admonition to take the butter and egg money back to his mother.

About a half mile to the south and across the Oolenoy River, on the same side of the road but at the junction of a highway connecting with Dacusville to the south and east, sat the store of Sid Edens. Local historian Ruth Hendricks described the store: "S. B. Edens [sic] store was a popular gathering place for the men of the community to gather and talk politics and news of county and state. . . . Food, feed for animals, coffee, sugar, tea, candy, and ice could be purchased here, on shelves were gingham, percale, and muslin, along with dry goods. Mr. Edens was a kind and humorous store keeper. His wife, Emma, helped him run the store."[43] As part of the underground food economy, and to supplement their family's income, Michael Owens remembered picking scrap cotton in the fields of the Sutherland place and then taking it to the Edens Store to trade for "whatever we'd need." His brother Philip added skinned squirrels and possums as items exchanged at the store for necessities. Michael Owens even traded blackberries at the store "so we'd have clothes to wear to school."[44]

Church Activities

Sometime between 1899 and 1905, the old brush arbor structure at Soapstone had been replaced by a wooden, framed building. A black-and-white photograph of this building exists in private hands (see figure 6), while a second photo, taken from the opposite side, appeared in print.[45] Estimating from both photos, the unpainted frame structure was rectangular, about fifty feet long and about eighteen feet high, with a gabled, steep-sided roof (tin covered, since it appeared smooth in both photos; the second showed alternate rusting on separate panels). Two doors, about five feet apart, opened on the front, with what appeared to be wooden stairs leading to both; there was no porch. "Men used to go in one door [the left side] and the ladies had to enter through the second door," Mable Clarke noted. Four windows filled each visible side, with a chimney pipe protruding about three-fourths of the way on the lower right side of the roof (not visible in the McFall photo). A square bell tower rose about another six feet above the gable, while the foundation appeared to be rough fieldstones upon which the frame sat.

As in previous decades, the church remained an important meeting place for the community.[46] Black churches provided locations for public speakers, sites for homecomings to maintain familial and generational ties, and places for social interaction and the exchange of community news. Sunday schools assisted with adult literacy and supported local and regional charity work.[47] Led especially by black women, social movements in black churches also promoted personal hygiene, prevention of teen pregnancy, and temperance.[48] In anthropologist Barnes's Virginia mountain community, the church "created a sense of 'blackness' as a place to worship and a place to socialize with friends and neighbors."[49] Largely out of sight and thus beyond direct white control, black churches served as another hidden transcript to promote black pride and assertiveness within the boundaries of a protected community cocoon.

While Soapstone church records were destroyed in the fire of 1967, some documents had been filed with the regional Oolenoy River Baptist Association, and these reports provide a few more names and some attendance statistics from the first decade of the twentieth century.[50] At least one other church-related document remains. Angela McJunkin Young had saved a lined white paper, dated 1928–29, with figures written in ornate penciled script; Mable Owens Clarke immediately recognized her mother's handwriting. Lula McJunkin Owens had been treasurer of Soapstone Baptist Church's Sunday school class in the late 1920s, and the bimonthly notations suggest the relative amount of "disposable" income available in the community at this time. "Somebody gave twenty-eight cents on a Sunday, eighty-one cents, then they went up to a dollar and thirteen cents," Mable Clarke noted. "After all the classes reported that was their grand total, I guess," Mrs. Young added. Her husband observed: "Most days all they took up was thirty-eight cents."

As noted in chapter 3, the relationship between the sister churches of Mt. Nebo and Soapstone has been socially complex. Living congregants of Soapstone felt there may have been "a split" at some time in the past, but later in the century the churches alternated Sunday services, and members of both attended the others' churches. During this time, the Rev. Henry Cureton served as Soapstone's pastor.[51] Cureton came from Easley, indicating the relatively small size of the congregation at Soapstone (unable to support a full-time pastor) as well as demonstrating the growing regional influence of Easley as a railroad and mill town.

Since pastors visited on Sundays, families very often invited them to their homes for the afternoon dinner. While the parents considered the visit an honor, children invariably suffered, because the preacher was served the best food; since adults typically ate first, children received only scraps. "I remember the time the preacher used to come," Michael Owens grumbled; and they would "feed the preacher before they'd feed us. . . . We'd get the wings—I called it scrap parts, and the preacher they'd save them the best part of the chicken. So we used to go around hollering . . . 'Don't eat up all the chicken!' "

School Activities

Children in the area in the early twentieth century went to segregated (and not equal) schools. Near the Oolenoy Baptist Church and historic cemetery, about two miles away from Liberia, was the multiple-room Oolenoy School, now a two-storied frame structure on State Highway 135, a main road between Dacusville and the Edens Store on Highway 8 (see map 3). County extension agent Henry Fulmer described rural white Pickens County schools as having "badly-used double desks," poor lighting, inadequate wood stove heating, "and on cold days the children spend too much of their time grouped" around the stoves. Drinking water was drawn from a well or nearby stream, with a common drinking cup for all students.[52]

Segregated black schools were even worse. After the original log cabin (described in chapter 3) had rotted, Liberia's pupils met in the Soapstone Church. By 1913, school enrollment was twenty students with a school session of forty days; average attendance was seventeen pupils. "The teacher, who held a second grade certificate, received an annual salary of sixty dollars."[53] In an interview late in his life, Chris Owens recalled his classmates from his childhood; he attended school from 1904 (when he was eight years old) until he left Liberia about 1917 to work in Greenville as a cook on the Southern Railway. Lula McJunkin (later Chris Owens's wife), attended South Saluda School (the same school her father had attended) for five years, and then attended Bailey View Academy in Greer, a boarding school.[54]

The couple's oldest son, Michael, attended school at first in Soapstone Baptist Church, but, he continued, "that [was] before they built the new schoolhouse over there.[55] And it was built I think in 1928 [or 1929]. Then I transferred over there. And we used to have old buck heaters—only way we could heat the schoolhouse was by wood. We had to go out and pick up some kindling, hope it would dry, so we could start the fire the next day. But it was a one-room school. They used to serve us hot lunch—old [government] commodities [such as] . . . cheese, powdered milk, peanut butter, and powdered eggs."

When Michael Owens first went to school in the tiny, one-room building (see figure 7), it had no heat. On January 9, 1931, J. L. Burgess, the clerk at the Pumpkintown Store, wrote a letter to the Pickens County school superintendent, requesting him to "please let these colored people of Soapstone school have a wood heater for their school house" (lack of capitalization in original).[56] Burgess also offered to pay for the stove, illustrating the benefits for blacks of having white patrons (see later in this chapter). It is also interesting to note that the schoolhouse at Soapstone was built about 1928 or 1929. According to researcher George Devlin, whites so feared the loss of black (thus cheap) labor in this decade (see the following discussion) that South Carolina poured funds into the construction of black schools in order to demonstrate white commitment to improving the lives of blacks through education.[57] Perhaps the Soapstone schoolhouse is an artifact of this movement, and another demonstration of Scott's infrapolitics of the powerless, who can manipulate the public transcript of white benevolence for their own advantage.

Due to separate and not equal education in the early decades of the twentieth century, Michael Owens also recalled that "the white got the best book and we gots the old book, what they used. That's the only thing we could get. They wouldn't give us, you know, up-to-date book[s] like they would [give] themselves. Some of the books [were] way outdated, so that's what we had to learn out of." "But it is a notorious fact," sociologist Bertram Doyle confirmed, "that Negro schools are generally inferior in structure and equipment in most of the South, . . . occasionally furnished with equipment discarded by the white schools."[58] By the Great Depression, rural white schools (let alone black schools) had deteriorated even more.[59] Black parents did their best to maintain and support community schools, using any income they could spare.[60] One of the logical consequences of unequal education was subsequent unequal employment opportunities, exacerbated by Jim Crow segregation.

By recognizing the inequality in South Carolina's school system even as a young child, Michael Owens highlighted a second lesson of Jim Crow education: a racially divided society. As Owens talked with his white playmates, he realized his own schoolbooks were outdated and deficient. Moreover, he also realized he could not attend the same institution where his white friends went. The subtle lesson was that the schools "demonstrated to each child his or her [racial] place in a public, institutionalized society."[61] In addition to arithmetic and spelling, black schools taught black children "how to negotiate their harsh and oppressive reality, even as they caught a glimpse of how to overcome second-class citizenship."[62] In this example, Foucault's theoretical description of power achieves another capillary form of existence, where inequality penetrates every black child and reminds all black children of their apparently inescapable place in society.

A subtler lesson presented in school exemplifies the ability of those in power to control those without power through the manipulation of historical "truth." In an analysis of South Carolina's school history texts, education scholar Alan Wieder found that even as recently as 1995, required texts were "written as white racial therapy," and had been even worse in past decades. In fact, this manipulation of truth had been deliberate. Historian Theodore Hemmingway cited a South Carolina State Superintendent of Education report from 1900 that argued that whites should not only "'dominate . . . the educational machinery which is already done, but [also] shape the educational thought and the educational atmosphere.'" Consistently, at this period black (and white) pupils read the historical "truth" that the Civil War had been about "states' rights" and not about slavery, that slavery had beneficial consequences for the enslaved, and that Reconstruction nearly destroyed the state under illiterate, inept black leaders and corrupt, invasive northern sympathizers. Such "truths," Hemmingway concluded, affected black dropout rates and lowered self-esteem.[63] On the other hand, black families preserved in their freedom colonies a countermemory of black successes and voter empowerment from this same period.

White-Black Interaction

Much of the rural South during this period reflected what historian Mark Schultz described as an interracial social world.[64] Black and white children frequently played together; adults hunted and fished together, talked on the porches of homes and stores, occasionally attended religious services together, and assisted each other in times of sickness, injury, or death. In the Oolenoy Valley, the public white transcript presented perfect racial harmony: "In no other land could there be any more congenial cooperation between a negro [sic] and a white community than here in this original American Liberia," local historian Bert Reece elegized about this time. Local historian Pearl McFall noted that the "Liberia Negroes spend their lives happily and peaceably on their little farms still showing friendliness and affection for their former masters in the Oolenoy area." Historian W. J. Megginson echoed these sentiments, concluding that the Liberia community "seems to have functioned harmoniously with local whites most of the time. Post–World War books and newspaper articles by whites have stressed this harmony."[65] The "contented population" of Liberia included a public transcript of many "good old time darkeys" and "southern mammies" such as Uncle John Miles or Aunt Katie, as described by whites in published obituaries.

As discussed in more theoretical terms in chapter 1, the white public memory disguised the countermemory of Liberia's own story, the alternate truth of the difficulties and joys experienced by blacks during this period. Historian Mark Schultz cautioned that the appearance of a "Solid South," whether contented or contested, in actuality varied by region, by class, by race, and by residence. "We might do better," he concluded, "to examine it [this perception] in local places . . . to detail how it was observed and suspended in actual experience." The "Behind the Veil" project used oral histories from this period to describe the "rich, complicated, heroic, and ultimately ambiguous texture of African American lives during the end of segregation."[66]

Two themes pervaded the Piedmont Georgia county studied by Schultz: a "culture of personalism," where local white elites dominated politics and other forms of social life, and a "culture of localism," where urban, strict racial segregation blurred during the course of daily rural activities. These themes explained why "powerful whites sometimes tolerated a surprising degree of interracial intimacy and black assertiveness"; blacks could use retaliatory violence occasionally as long as such retaliations were personal and did not challenge hegemonic white domination. On the other hand, landowning blacks needed to profess a public transcript of humility and not rise above their position. Historian Jack Hayes argued that a constant barrage of white propaganda reminded blacks of their subservient position: the racist school texts, racist newspaper comments, racist jokes by public officials, and the term "nigra" rather than "Negro" were all designed to "stunt self-concepts, blunt aspirations, curtail ambitions, produce apathy, and promote a sense of powerlessness."[67]

Historian Theodore Hemmingway elaborated on the social details of early-twentieth-century Jim Crow South Carolina. Blacks and whites legally could not work together in mills or factories, could not enter stores by the same door, could not drink from the same fountain or use the same bathrooms. Social custom further prevented blacks from entering white homes by the front door (whites could enter black homes by the front door). In stores, "blacks were not allowed to try on the merchandise, were forced to wait until after all whites were served, and encountered, more often than not, a hostile clerk." "Blacks made no laws, enforced no laws, and interpreted no laws."[68] Even walking down the street required blacks to be careful not to brush a white person and to step off the sidewalk for whites. "In short," historian Jack Hayes concluded, "this inferior-superior relationship required that blacks be subservient, deferential, and cognizant of all whites as society's natural leaders."[69]

By examining the countermemory of Liberia's residents in more detail, it is possible to recover examples of hidden transcripts and to examine the strategies by which African Americans sometimes neutralized the generalized domination of white surveillance and actively resisted white control on a local and personal level, as Schultz suggested. Like the residents in Schultz's Georgia study, Liberia's blacks "refused to surrender" to white supremacy. Instead, they used "religious faith, the love of family, the support of community, retaliatory physical violence, reputations as valued workers, force of character, or even ties to local whites who some named as personal allies." Likewise, contributors to the "Behind the Veil" project used the strength of the family and community to persist and assist each other, as well as the art of resistance—"sustaining a delicate balance between appearing to comply with prescribed norms, on the one hand, and finding ways to subvert those norms on the other."[70] The Jim Crow era faced by the small group of Liberia's residents serves as a test case for greater theoretical issues.

In the "late modern period," sociologist Bertram Doyle wrote, the South still "shows a society divided into halves, with the white people on one side of an imaginary line and the Negroes on the other." Contemporary Pickens County journalist Ben Robertson described his white family's relationship with their black cook and farm laborer as "intimate and personal, and at the same time strict—on both sides they were strict, old-fashioned, and Southern. The standards of behavior for both sides were established and we knew it, and we knew why it was so, we knew what had happened to make it so. Memory with all of us, white and black, was long. All of us remembered." At this period in the South, historian Mark Schultz argued that whites valued the social hierarchy more than they feared interracial propinquity.[71]

Robertson summarized (perhaps a bit apologetically) the process by which whites in his grandparents' generation (during Reconstruction; see chapter 3 for a historical overview explaining this southern white perspective) had reasserted their domination over blacks and had achieved contemporary satisfaction: "They had fought a gigantic devastating war and had lost it; they had seen the country stripped and looted, had lived under the unreasoning despotism of soldiers, under a radical black government; almost starving, they had taken the law into their own hands, . . . they had nullified an amendment to the Constitution, had reconstructed a state, and in their old age their strength was firm; they were stoic in repose."[72]

Writing a generation later, theologian Howard Thurman summarized the process by which Robertson's relatives, and other whites, had achieved their old-age satisfaction by dominating an entire group of human beings. In order to control blacks as a group, a dominant white society "must array all the forces of legislation and law enforcement; it must falsify the facts of history, tamper with the insights of religion and religious doctrine, editorialize and slant news and the printed word. On top of that it must keep separate schools, separate churches, separate graveyards, and separate public accommodations—all this in order to freeze the place of the Negro in society and guarantee his basic immobility."[73]

One consequence of this power differential, political scientist James Scott observed, is that "the power of the dominant thus ordinarily elicits—in the public transcript—a continuous stream of performances of deference, respect, reverence, admiration, esteem, and even adoration that serve to further convince ruling elites that their claims [of legitimate inequality] are in fact validated by the social evidence they see before their very eyes."[74]

The public transcript and dominant white attitude were characterized by Myrta Avery, a white South Carolina belle who witnessed the Civil War and Reconstruction. She reflected on the "good old days" in comparison to the early twentieth century: "But I must say my affection is for the negro of the old order. . . . The real negro I like, . . . the tiller of the soil, the shepherd of the flocks, the herdsman of the cattle, the happy, soft-voiced, light-footed servitor. The negro who is a half-cut white man is not a negro; . . . he is unattractive when compared to the dear old darkey of Dixie who was worth a million of him! . . . The one true plane of equalization is that of mutual service, each race doing for the other all it can" (lack of capitalization in original).[75] The writer of Luke Terrell's obituary (*Pickens Sentinel*, March 23, 1923, p. 4) also described him as a "good old-time darkey." To elaborate on that public transcript, the reporter then editorialized: "We sometimes think how much the old time colored people of latter days out strips [*sic*] the colored people of today in many ways," apparently longing for the days of greater black submissiveness.

Also reminiscing about this period, white journalist Ben Robertson (b. 1903) described his own childhood and young adulthood in Pickens County: "We live like Job of old in our country, with cooks to do our cooking and washwomen to do our washing." In fact, Robertson admitted, "we were among the poorest folks in the United States, but in South Carolina our hundred and ninety-seven thousand white families were waited upon by seventy thousand colored servants; we had nineteen thousand washwomen, thirty-two thousand cooks, which meant that too many of the women in our households sat on the piazzas and hymn-sang and rocked."[76]

These contemporary white attitudes also appeared in the Katie Owens articles as well. First of all, both the sketch and the obituary called Katie Owens "Aunt," a pseudo-honorific title for many middle-aged or elderly African American women. The more formal titles of "Miss" and "Mistress" (Mrs.) along with surnames were virtually always reserved exclusively for white women, historian George Tindall observed.[77] Second, the obituary emphasized Katie Owens's "loyalty" and devotion to her "white folks," describing her like a favored pet or perpetual servant rather than (for example) describing her as a devoted wife, mother, and grandmother. She was twice honored for being "useful" (like an instrument or tool) and for leading a "life of service" (matching Avery's recollections) rather than being commemorated as a human being whose utility could have been measured in other ways, such as by a well-lived, virtuous, or honorable life. Whether deliberate or accidental, the obituary also obscured the parentage of Katie Owens's first three children, describing them as born "to her" rather than "to this union" or "to them" (to her and her unnamed "companion" [not spouse]; see the following family stories). Finally, the "prominent woman of the community" who delivered the oration remained anonymous in the news story, reflecting the social division between blacks and whites in the early twentieth century. Even though the burial ceremony contained people from both races, the article did not name individuals of both races in the same story. In early-twentieth-century South Carolina, even news stories were segregated.

Despite the racial divide, it was certainly true that "you get some good white folks," Philip Owens acknowledged. As noted earlier in this chapter, J. L. Burgess petitioned the county on behalf of the Liberia community for a wood heater for the Soapstone schoolhouse.[78] In Adamsville (northern Greenville County), Starks Adams grew up socially interacting with his white peers: "'We was raised up here with them [whites], and we used to fight [like kids do]. . . . We never did have any trouble. I didn't know anything about separation of races when I was coming up. We'd play together, we'd eat together, and we'd fight. Only thing, we just didn't go to school together.'"[79] Philip Valentine also remembered playing and fighting with the white children of his father's farm laborers and visitors, "but I was bigger than they was, so I could handle it." Alice Jackson, an Oolenoy Valley white, remarked that her mother, Alma, played and worked "in the field" with the Owens children, and that Chris and Lula Owens had named their oldest daughter Alma after her. An older Owens relative mentioned that her brother was taught to read informally by Inez Edens, a white teacher and wife of the landowner whose property he worked; because of that and other kindnesses, the female narrator of the story was named Inez, after Mrs. Edens. Michael Owens recalled that whites would "come by around here and eat dinner [the noon meal], sit down and eat with us." Brother Philip observed that the whites loved to hear his father, Chris, sing "and he sang to them, the white folk, and the white folk was happy." In the late 1920s, Josef Reece reminisced about his Oolenoy Valley childhood; he recalled that he would "hear a fife being played coming up the road to the house, and it would be Chris [Owens] in his Buggy [sic] drawn by a Pinto horse. He had come from his house to give me, 'Mr. Joe,' a ride in his buggy. He would take me for about an hours [sic] ride with Chris playing or talking telling me about things and stories."[80]

Everybody knew everybody else, both white and black, and everyone "recognized a well-established social and economic hierarchy." Regardless of race, neighbors depended on each other for assistance as well as friendship. In fact, sometimes white and black friends were actually relatives (see the following discussion). Whites purchased garden vegetables, milk, butter, canned fruits, charcoal and stove wood, and even an occasional jar of moonshine from their Liberia neighbors.[81]

Simultaneously to this enveloping blanket of apparent (and genuine) friendship, African Americans also lived in a constant state of uncertainty and caution (Foucault's generalized observation), under constant surveillance by whites, and knowing that the slightest misstep might escalate into a deadly confrontation.[82] The researchers for the "Behind the Veil" project summarized this concern: "Just as any stretch of ocean might offer smooth sailing on any given day, individual white southerners might be friendly and even helpful at times. However, they might also be unaccountably hostile and prejudiced. Thus, blacks had to remain ever vigilant in case storms of white fury should suddenly begin to blow."[83]

Especially for the old-timers, those born into slavery, "people kind of stayed to their self," Philip Owens explained, "'cause the white man have them scared. They couldn't talk too much. . . . They was scared for their life—they [were] lucky to be living." "What I can truthfully speak of," Angela McJunkin Young acknowledged, "is that back in the day, if a white person liked you, they'd go to the bat for you, but if they didn't like you it was just trouble. I can contest [attest] to that and I guess as today you had some people that were trustworthy (and I don't want to name) and you had some that just weren't. But then I think as you went through life you got to the point where you knew who you could trust or at least think who you could trust and those that you knew that you couldn't."

Young's comment illustrated the complex and nuanced social interactions required of African Americans at this time.[84] Historian Mark Schultz described white supremacy during this time not as physical separation between the races "but by paternalism and racial etiquette backed by the regular, physical threat that white bodies posed to black bodies." Moreover, Schultz continued, whites benefited from that fear because blacks were then more subservient, accepted bad deals, and didn't challenge economic inequality. Informants for the "Behind the Veil" project vividly described "the dailiness of the terror blacks experienced at the hands of capricious whites . . . the ubiquitous, arbitrary, and cruel reality of senseless white power." Theologian Howard Thurman observed that "the measure of a man's estimate of your strength is the kind of weapons he feels that he must use in order to hold you fast in a prescribed place."[85] Stepping outside of the protective shell of Liberia (the hidden transcript of a defended black social space) meant that black residents would then face a larger white world, requiring a public transcript of deference and submission enacted with humor and humility, while masking one's true feelings as best as possible—under the normalizing gaze of disciplinary power and the constant threat of torture or death.

For example, Edgar Smith repeated a story he had heard from Chris Owens when a younger man. Owens had been working with white friends on a team threshing wheat, an exhausting job in the hot and humid Upstate summers. The landowner's wife had just prepared the noon meal and invited the crew inside. Chris Owens related that the woman stated, "'All you can eat, except for that man [indicating Owens].' Says, 'He's not allowed to.' He had to sit there without anything to eat because he was black."

Whites acknowledged the boundaries and sometimes (perhaps with the wisdom of hindsight) now recalled with melancholy and guilt some past episodes that manifested these boundaries. For example, an elderly white woman described the neighborly interactions between the Oolenoy whites and Liberia blacks. "They were about as close a neighbors as we had," she fondly recalled. "Uncle Jim" Kemp helped her father on his farm, working side by side. And yet, she added: "We would have—Momma would cook dinner [noonday meal]. . . . Uncle Jim Kemp would sit on the door step on the outside before we all got through eating and then she called him in and let him eat. I never understood, 'well, why don't he come on in here and eat with us?' And it was not right that he didn't."

Liberia's adult African American population recognized the visible and invisible barriers of the segregated South, but those barriers had to be learned by children. Philip Owens recalled taking his mother's farm products (milk and butter) to the Pumpkintown store to trade. Along the dusty road, occasionally cars of white teenagers would "run you in the ditch. . . . You got to get down in the ditch sometimes and lay down so they don't see you, so they won't bother you. Then they holler at you and call you little names and stuff." Even his white playmates would be prejudiced, Philip Owens noted; "they'd run around the house, then they [would] start wanting to call you names, beat up on you. They love to beat on black folk. . . . [In fact], they treat us worse than they treat a dog." As a child at the Edens Store one time, Michael Owens stood at the counter: "And I was ahead of a lot of white people, . . . and I had to wait and wait 'til they took care of all the white people. So my mother—I told her what happened. So my mother had to go and get on them, get that straightened out. So every time you see me come in after that, it's 'Take care of him.'"[86]

Hidden transcripts offer the powerless various forms of resistance, including cultural separation, face-saving behaviors, and actual retaliation (Scott's infrapolitics). In his study of rural Georgia, historian Mark Schultz documented stories of black retaliation in his study area, but then "wonders how often other African Americans were able to assert their dignity in the face of white oppression in the rural South. The written sources are largely silent on the matter."[87] Liberia's oral history provides examples.

One form of resisting the humiliation of the public transcript of docility, Wilma Dunaway observed, was the creation by blacks of separate social worlds, where "cultural specialists" could perform and preserve traditions out of the generalized surveillance of white observation, allowing former slaves their social privacy and the agency to develop their own cultural identities.[88] The *Easley Progress* sketch of Katie Owens (January 13, 1927) hinted at some of these oral traditions, perhaps even with an origin in Africa or from African exiles. For example, Aunt Katie was said to have enjoyed certain recipes such as "'fatty bread,'" apparently popular with older African Americans (with ties to European cultural influences as well). To the children in her care she sang "some plaintive melody peculiar to her race." She told "witch tales" to older children around flickering hearths in dimly lit rooms (as did Luke Terrell in chapter 3). While it is now impossible to determine the origins of Katie Owens's plaintive melodies, her witch tales, or her fireside recipes, it is certainly possible that traditions "peculiar to her race" existed in Liberia, relatively unknown and underdocumented by neighboring whites.[89]

Liberia and similar freedom colonies allowed the residents to create a secure cultural space, where not only folk traditions could be preserved, but also other forms of oral tradition. As in the "Behind the Veil" project, memories "served as powerful teaching tools for black survival." Black stories of resistance to slavery and black activism during Reconstruction functioned as countermemories for the next generation in order to maintain dignity and hope in the face of Jim Crow segregation.[90] Black elders like Katie Owens or Absalom McJunkin reminded their grandchildren about ancestors who purchased and defended land, who voted in elections, and who struggled against the odds to obtain an education and pursue a livelihood. They identified whites who could be trusted and warned of those who should be avoided. They narrated stories of courage and tragedy (such as those that follow), and each tale provided a lesson for the next generation.

Another strategy available to the (apparently) powerless is the manipulation of elites by "calling them out" on their public transcripts of asserted benevolence and paternalism. Historian Mark Schultz linked these strategies to the themes of "personalism" and "localism": "at the back step of white homes and courthouses, hats in hands, blacks could solicit paternalistic consideration, but they could not invoke any rights at the more formal door of citizenship."[91] Thus, Liberia's residents appealed to patrons like J. L. Burgess in order to purchase a wood stove for their schoolhouse. However, this humiliation because of apparent powerlessness burned deeply into black hidden transcripts, and that ensuing bitterness could manifest occasionally as explosions of direct resistance on a personal level.

Direct resistance helped maintain black dignity, and family stories in the area preserve such examples. One time, Chris Owens had mortgaged the family's milk cow without telling his wife, Lula, about it. Chris was unable to pay the note, and the new owner came to collect the cow. Philip Owens (the couple's son) continued: "My Momma said, 'No, you're not going to take it, 'cause I'm going to feed my boy one way or the other.' . . . She got a shotgun, throwed it across the front porch out there . . . and the guy got out of the yard, boy. We had no more problems." As generations of whites would discover, Lula Owens (granddaughter of Joseph McJunkin, the former slave) and wife of Chris Owens (grandson of Katie Owens, also a former slave), would not be denied respect.[92] As discussed in chapters 5 and 6, Lula McJunkin Owens represented the next generation's othermother for the Liberia community.

Chris Owens, as the spokesperson for the community to the outside world, also commanded respect. During the Great Depression, the Agricultural Adjustment Act allowed farmers to limit acreage for crops in order to keep farm prices stable.[93] In order to calculate payments for underproduction, county agents needed to measure farmers' lands. According to former Oolenoy resident Josef Reece, the black farmers in Liberia ran off the county agents "with shotguns at the ready when they tried to measure their acreage." As the seventh generation descended from Cornelius Keith, Reece and his mother (Bert Hendricks Reece) were well known in both Pumpkintown and Liberia. So the county hired Josef Reece to talk to the Liberia farmers and explain the program. Reece and his mother approached the best-known man in Liberia, Chris Owens, and they "spent about two hours talking and explaining, and also what the consequences would be if they didn't conform. Chris perused a few minutes, then asked my Mother [sic] if she was doing it on her farm, and with her 'yes' reply, he said he would let me measure his land, but they better not send anyone else up there to do it."[94] Reece made enough money from this job to pay for a year's tuition at Clemson College, located on Floride Clemson's old homeplace and the former plantation of John C. Calhoun (see chapters 2 and 3).

The Liberia farmers felt the need to defend their land because of unscrupulous practices by a few local whites to drive them off their lands, a relatively common occurrence in the southern Appalachian border region.[95] These attempts at expulsion may be understood by conceiving of Liberia itself as a hidden transcript (remote and distant like Scott's mountain tribes of Southeast Asia or the freedom colonies of Texas), and knowing that elites perceive such places as dangerous because they lie outside of the normalizing gaze of dominant surveillance. Furthermore, conflicts between the public transcript of white benevolence contradicted by private transcripts of white racism or greed exacerbated the frustration of African Americans.

For example, Philip Owens bitterly described how his grandmother Rosie Glenn Owens Gowens lost her expansive peach and apple orchard to a deceitful (but prominent) white landowner. "He told my grandmother to sign some piece of paper [a loan agreement], after five years, and then he foreclosed on the property and took it away from her." Mable Clarke later added that the ploy was that the man would not accept payment when initially offered, later would claim in court that the (often undereducated) owner had failed to repay the loan, and then would foreclose on the property, a process historians Thad Sitton and James Conrad discovered in Texas freedom colonies as well. Several white neighbors of Mable Clarke described this same man as a "scoundrel," tricking both white and black landowners equally. Josef Reece claimed that the man "accumulated some very large number of farms and their acreage in the late 20s and 30s doing this."[96]

Preserved in the McGowens family history is a copy of a legal document filed by W. E. Edens Jr. against Rosie Gowens and twelve of her children.[97] According to the document, on April 30, 1912, E. T. Gowens (Rosa's then husband) borrowed $270.10 from A. and J. Gilreath, promising to pay the loan back at 8 percent per year plus thirty dollars in legal fees. As collateral, Gowens offered twenty-six acres "on branch waters of Oolenoy River" (and formerly owned by A. L. Edens) and a second tract of fifty acres (formerly owned by Martin Terrell). On March 2, 1922, the Gilreaths transferred the note to W. E. Edens, the plaintiff, and sometime in 1927, Mr. Gowens died, leaving his widow with an overdue bill of $66.68, plus the attorney's fees. Unable to read or write, unable to pay, and with four dependent children under the age of fourteen, the daughter of former slaves was forced to surrender the deed and thus lost her land, at the cost of about a dollar an acre.

In addition to losing their land, Liberia's blacks might lose their lives. As historian George Tindall observed, "the question of miscegenation always created the tensest issue of race relations where the intimacy involved a Negro man and a white woman."[98] Most frequently, this tension manifested in exaggerated white fears of the black male rapist, vague apprehensions stemming from contemporary assumptions of white superiority, fears of racial impurity, white female submissiveness, and perhaps even as a response to the Women's Rights movement (the Nineteenth Amendment, in effect by 1920).[99] The black male rapist myth contributed significantly to the culture of terror under Jim Crow segregation, and even impacted the Oolenoy Valley.

For example, when Chris Owens was a younger man (his son Philip explained), he was working at a saw mill in a nearby town when a white man stormed up to the mill and demanded that Chris "come on out of there," accusing him of having impregnated his daughter. Now a direct target of the black male rapist charge, Chris Owens (and the white mill owner) knew full well that Owens probably would face a de facto death sentence by mob violence. Chris Owens wisely manipulated his white antagonist by appealing again to the dominant public transcript of white benevolence and paternalism. Philip Owens continued: "So the white guy that . . . run the saw mill, he said, 'No, he ain't going nowhere. Y'all get out of here now.' They opened shots up on him, there on the highway; they took off. They come to find out later on . . . the white guy impregnated his own daughter and tried to lay it on my father. . . . He said, 'I'm lucky to be around, boys. I could not have been here if it wasn't for that white man he had stood up for me.'"

African Americans in the segregated South had to be prepared for welcoming situations that later might turn deadly, especially when feeding the fears of the black male rapist myth. Philip Owens illustrated this point with another story about an older Liberia resident. As a young man, this black resident once worked for a white man absent for long periods of time. One morning, during the man's absence, his wife appeared on the porch, "and she had one of these big old frill dress[es] on with a bonnet." She called out to the black worker and threw her dress over his head. "She said, "'If you won't, I'm gonna call rape!' I said, '[Name], what happened?' Said, 'I'm living, ain't I?'"

Because of the power of the myth as a method of white hegemony, even less interracial interaction between black males and white females still might mean death. Philip Owens told a story originally from his father about a cousin who "winked his eye at a white girl." A white mob captured him and told the surrounding community they were "going to hang this guy—this 'N' guy." The mob sat him on a horse, tied a rope around his neck and suspended it from a tree branch. Just as they sent the horse off, "this guy ran up—let me shoot him! . . . He said they shot and they shot." When black neighbors went to retrieve the body for a funeral, Chris Owens "said there wasn't a piece of meat bigger than a dime." Owens concluded with this caution to his sons: "'Boy, you seen a white girl,' he said, 'you go the other way.'"

This story, passed from father to sons and persisting in oral tradition for over a century, most likely described the lynching of Brooks Gordon, a seventeen-year-old black male from a neighborhood about seven miles south of Pumpkintown. Sometime on the morning of June 29, 1912, according to white witnesses, Gordon allegedly "assaulted" a local white woman near Dacusville. A mob of 300 to 500 white citizens formed, including the sheriff; everyone assumed Gordon would head for the mountains to escape and so warning phone calls were made to crossroads stores along the way. Gordon took refuge in the Pumpkintown General Store, where he was captured after a countryside search of four or five hours. While the sheriff served as judge, a "jury" on site convicted him, a local physician tied the hangman's noose, Gordon was hanged from a nearby tree, and his body riddled with bullets. Gordon's parents cut their son's body down from the tree. Chris Owens would have been about nineteen years old at the time (just slightly older than the victim), and this event served as a reminder of white power and as a hidden memory of warning, passed eventually to his sons.[100]

Leaving Liberia

While rural South Carolinians had been leaving the state since the late nineteenth century, several related trends in the early twentieth century significantly accelerated this out-migration. During and after the war in Europe, with the subsequent loss of immigrant labor, northern factories with unionized jobs drew tens of thousands of southern blacks in the "Great Migration."[101] By the 1920s, the grandchildren of former slaves had no memories of the institution and "were ready to take their place in society," historian George Devlin observed. "The years of political, social, and economic oppression . . . finally had taken their toll on enough of them that the migration became epidemic," he continued. But, as historians noted, the boll weevil continued to devastate southern farming during the 1920s, and tens of thousands of black farmers surrendered their lands and livelihoods and went north as well. The resurgence of the Ku Klux Klan and the Great Depression drove even more blacks from the state.[102]

These national and regional trends in out-migration directly affected Pickens County. As discussed earlier in this chapter, the Pumpkintown area transformed from about 75 percent white at the turn of the twentieth century to about 90 percent white at the eve of World War II. Just in one rural area,

African Americans declined in number from 240 to about thirty-six, with about one-fourth of that remaining number in one nuclear family (that of Chris and Lula Owens). Much of this out-migration was due to the increasing realization by black farmers that better wages, better social conditions, and better living conditions lay in the factory neighborhoods of the northern states; the North in effect was a safety valve to escape both poverty and (overt) racism. By the fall of 1921, the boll weevil had infested the entire state, and by 1923 the cotton harvest in South Carolina plummeted.[103] "I come up and I know what it was like," Michael Owens recalled; "it was hard back then. They [black neighbors] moved to the city where they could get a job or something." Mr. Owens remembered plowing all day for the Edens family "above Pumpkintown." "Plow all day, make about five dollars; they would feed me for dinner. Come home. I'd bring it to my Daddy. He give me about two dollars out of it. I said, 'Oh, Lord, no way.' I said, 'I'll be glad when I get [to] where I won't have to do that.'"

Not only did racial antagonism make life challenging for all African Americans in the area, but violence, social pressure, and fear drove many away permanently—flight being another form of opposition to oppression. "Lynchings conceptualized as no other factor the powerlessness and accompanying hopelessness of blacks in South Carolina," historian George Devlin observed. On the other hand, Michel Foucault had hypothesized (chapter 1) that inequality creates resistance, and historian W. Fitzhugh Brundage documented examples of black defiance toward white racialized violence. Despite some resistance to domination (even in Liberia), Tindall noted that racial segregation and intolerance increased dramatically in South Carolina after the turn of the century.[104]

For example, in the 1880 Census, William Owens, the youngest son of Katie Owens, was listed as "black," but his grandchildren had always heard that he was "white" in appearance. "That's why you see our color," Philip Owens explained (see the ambiguous statement about their parentage in Katie Owens's obituary, described earlier in this chapter). The 1910 Census listed three children from the relationship of William Owens and Rosie Glenn Owens: sons Christopher and Esley, and daughter Willie Mae (see appendix 2). According to Owens family history, at least one of these three (and possibly all) had been fathered by a white man. By 1920, Esley had disappeared from Liberia, and Owens family history revealed the reason. Jessie Owens explained: "He had to leave here because he didn't know whether he was black or white. Tall man, looked like any white guy." Owens continued: "They had the bloodhounds on him because a young white girl was liking him. . . . He had to jump in the Oolenoy River . . . and swam underneath the water until he got out of range of the sheriffs and the Ku Klux Klan shooting at him. Said he came up about two hundred feet down the river, came out to the bank and . . . he ran 'til he got out of their sight, 'til he could hitch a ride into Greenville." He disappeared from family knowledge somewhere up north.

A second story involved a personal dispute that escalated into panic and desperation—or a public display of Scott's hidden transcript, allowing for "personal authentication" and a chance "to restore a sense of self-respect and personhood."[105] Lonzo Glenn (brother to Clarence, Ernest, and perhaps Rosie; see appendix 2) got involved in a scuffle in a store at a tiny crossroads called Wildcat in northern Greenville County, between Bald Rock and Cleveland (see map 2). A local deputy (perhaps more of a vigilante) intervened, and (according to a relative), Lonzo "bit the white guy's nose all the way off, bit his ears off, [and] bit a chunk out of his face." Glenn then fled for his life and sought refuge with Chris Owens (his nephew) in Liberia, who hid him in his hayloft for a month. To foil the search party's dogs by eliminating the scent, Owens poured kerosene and turpentine around the barn. As a child, Philip Owens remembered his mother giving him a bucket of food and instructing him to take it out to the barn, bang on the bucket four times, and leave it there. "That was the signal," he explained. After thirty days, Chris Owens felt Lonzo had to leave, and so he loaded his wagon with hay and drove it to Bald Rock on three consecutive days; no one stopped him. On the fourth day, he again loaded up with hay, hid Lonzo under the stack, and carried him to safety to the home of his father-in-law, Absalom McJunkin, in Bald Rock. "He stayed over there three days," Philip Owens continued, and then McJunkin "went through the woods up through Caesar's Head Mountain into North Carolina. He trimmed a little walk through the woods, left all these markers. He said he told him [Lonzo], 'You get out there on these markers, and don't come back.' Gave him some money and some food and they ain't seen him since." Of course, the story also exemplifies the infrapolitics of the powerless, as Chris Owens tricked his uncle's pursuers by hiding behind a mask of innocence as he apparently transported only hay while surreptitiously transporting a wanted fugitive.

For those wishing to remain in state, cotton mills opened in neighboring cities like Greenville, pulling whites into the segregated factories and blacks onto the loading docks.[106] Mable Owens Clarke recalled her father telling stories about trucks driving through the Liberia area with a man on the back with a bullhorn: "'You folks, come on out of that cotton field. Got running water in the city. Throw the cotton sacks down and jump on the truck!' . . . And they said, you know, people'd just throw down them sacks and walk off and left their land." As the census records indicated, in the 1920s Chris Owens and his (probable) mother's brother Clarence Glenn worked as laborers in Greenville; James Kemp worked for a mill, and other residents did as well. Increasing white household wealth, especially in the towns, drew black women as maids or nannies, and railroads employed their brothers and spouses (reflected in the census). Railroads also led out of South Carolina, and many followed the rails northward for better employment and less racism.[107]

Disease also took a toll. While no oral or written source has mentioned the influenza pandemic of 1918–19, local historian Bert Reece instead identified "the dreaded disease of that period" as tuberculosis.[108] The "bare living" of subsistence farming in Liberia, a writer for the *Easley Progress* (January 13, 1927) noted, "invited the ravages of diseases, mainly tuberculosis and typhoid fever until now not more than a half dozen families remain." In fact, through the first few decades of the twentieth century, tuberculosis was a leading cause of death in the South, killing African Americans three times more frequently than whites; poverty, malnutrition, overcrowding, and a segregated and unequal health care system all contributed as causes.[109] A member of Soapstone Church commented on that disease specifically in the Liberia area, based on what she had been told by the elders in the community: "And a lot of [church] members died from that disease [tuberculosis], and that's why a lot of people left from here. Because that disease—everybody, they was afraid of getting it and those that had it, they didn't have doctors and stuff in the area and no known cure for it. . . . But after the disease got really bad up in here in the area, a lot of people died."

Of course, downsides to the out-migration included not only the net loss of the local black population but often the loss of their hard-won lands as well. "The large migration created a barren countryside in some areas," historian George Devlin wrote.[110] As blacks left for better economic or social opportunities, Mable Owens Clarke explained, "eventually what happened, they never came back and paid the taxes or anything on the land, and all of a sudden, you know, the whites came back and picked up and paid the taxes and got the land back."[111] But, given the difficulty of farm labor and the horrors of life under intense segregation and the threat of violence or death, Mable understood why many had left the lands of their ancestors. "But I'm grateful that my parents stayed," she concluded.

Returning Home to Liberia

Despite the tremendous factors pushing residents out of the Liberia area in particular and the South in general, and the equally powerful forces pulling residents out, a strong centripetal force drew former residents back to Liberia, to live their final days in a familiar rural setting.[112] As in Texan freedom colonies, people always had returned home to the Upstate periodically to visit relatives, attend church homecomings, or participate in family reunions.[113] These visits maintained generational kinship links that eventually pulled former residents back home permanently, especially as parents aged, as fortunes improved, or as nostalgia developed. For example, Katie Owens had lived in the area for decades, and her grandson Christopher returned from Greenville to work the farm and to care for her; as her obituary stated, she lived near him until her death in 1928. Clarence Glenn, (probably) Chris Owens's mother's brother, also returned from working in Greenville to labor on Liberian lands. James Kemp and his wife, Hattie, returned to care for his aging father (Emerson Kemp), and father, son, and daughter-in-law spent their last years in Liberia. And by 1940, Ansel McKinney's children had returned to care for him as well. As will be seen, this pattern of kin returning to care for aging parents continued decade after decade, and may be related to a deeper association with the land discussed in chapter 8.

Conclusion

On the eve of America's entry into World War II, three-fourths of South Carolinians still lived on farms or in communities of fewer than 2,500.[114] But life in the United States, in South Carolina, and in Pickens County continued to change. Decade by decade, entrenched racism pushed and economic opportunities pulled more and more blacks from the valley. Insularity decreased as remaining residents gathered around stoves and radios in the country stores to discuss international and national events, and the mail brought catalogs from national businesses and newspapers with national news. Rural roads were still muddy and rutted, but they led to towns and cities with railroads to transport people much greater distances, including away forever. By 1940, virtually all of those originally born into slavery had passed away, and their grandchildren faced a world still emerging from the hard times of the Great Depression. Within a few years, events in faraway places pulled the residents of Liberia and the nation into another world war and the economic and social transformations from those events. During the middle of these war years, Chris and Lula Owens, the largest black family left in Liberia, welcomed to the world their last child, a daughter, Mable, in 1943 (see figure 5). In many ways, Mable's childhood in Liberia would be not much different from that of her older brothers and sisters, and she would follow a very similar social trajectory to seek a better life as she matured. But Liberia and her ancestors would always be close in her heart.

FIGURE 1 Soapstone Church and Table Rock Mountain. Photo by the author.

FIGURE 2 Katie Owens. Reprinted by permission of Joseph Reece.

FIGURE 3
Rosa Glenn Owens.
Photo courtesy of
Odessa Williams.

FIGURE 4 Chris and Lula McJunkin Owens. Photo courtesy of Mable Owens Clarke.

Mable Owens Clarke.
Photo courtesy of
Brian Kelley.

FIGURE 6 Old Soapstone Church. Photo courtesy of Mable Owens Clarke.

FIGURE 7 Soapstone Schoolhouse. Photo by the author.

FIGURE 8 "Empse Kemp at his home in Liberia." Photo courtesy of the Pickens County Library.

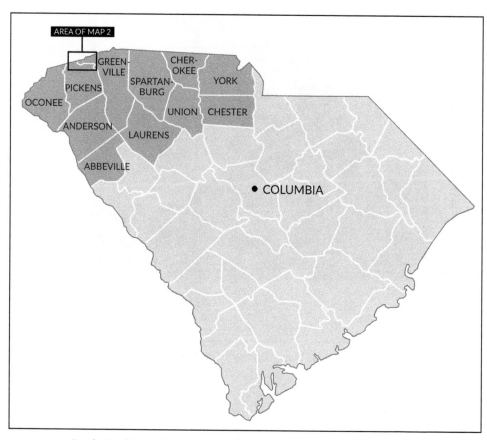

MAP 1 South Carolina and upstate counties
Map by Sarah Moore.

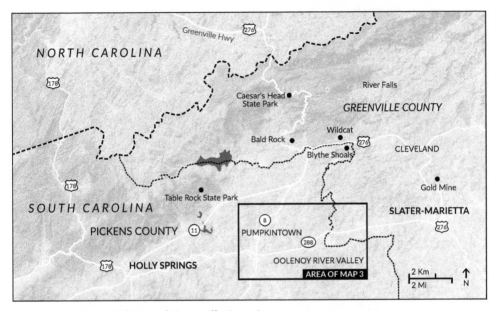

MAP 2 Upper Pickens and Greenville Counties

Map by Sarah Moore.

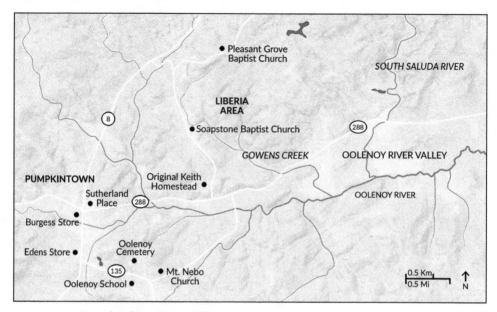

MAP 3 Central Oolenoy River Valley

Map by Sarah Moore.

5 It Really Wasn't a Bad Life

The Mid-Twentieth Century

By the birth of Mable Owens almost exactly a century after her great-grandmother Katie Owens, life in the Oolenoy Valley had improved dramatically in many ways, and yet a lingering cloud of oppression still polluted the social atmosphere. While no longer in legal servitude, African Americans in northern Pickens and Greenville Counties (as elsewhere in the nation) labored long, hard hours for generally less pay, and with greater social restrictions, than their white neighbors. Automobiles carried people farther afield on macadam or concrete roads, and larger cities like Greenville offered greater occupational and recreational opportunities. Yet these same cities presented only segregated facilities governed and protected by an all-white political and criminal justice system. While still segregated and unequal, rural black schools brought more standardized and graded education and thus greater opportunities for better jobs for African Americans.[1]

A combination of New Deal policies (from earlier decades) and wartime production "began to break the bonds that had stifled agricultural change and held so many people in poverty."[2] Agricultural labor on small family farms seemed even more difficult and less appealing; mechanization, diversification, and technology had undermined cotton and corn mule-powered agriculture in the South, while globalization and chemistry (for example, rayon) undermined American cotton overall.[3] Northern factories with better union wages and less overt racism drew many blacks out of the area (even to distant California), while others moved to expanding southern urban centers like Memphis or Atlanta.[4] Radios, telephones, and print media brought news of distant wars in Europe and Asia and amazing discoveries of atomic power and televised pictures. Electricity eventually trickled into the valley, turning sunset-timed repose into mass media family time.

Having fought for freedom overseas, black veterans returning from World War II demanded greater equality from a still-segregated South. South Carolina's blacks formally regained the right to vote in 1948, and the doors for desegregation slowly began to open.[5] The 1950s brought the national discussion of civil rights to the Oolenoy Valley, and the Supreme Court decision of *Brown v. Board of Education* in 1954 demonstrated that separate was not equal, shocking most southern whites. During this time, South Carolina's governor, James Byrnes, postponed integration by supporting an "educational revival" in the state, under which rural schools consolidated, buses transported more black pupils, and new separate black grade and high schools opened. Few adult white politicians or pastors dared to challenge the obvious inequalities between races (new bricks and mortar for black schools did not mean new books and buses, for example), and the South saw a resurgence of Lost Cause rhetoric and the black male rapist myth. On the other hand, southern working-class white and black teens pushed racial boundaries through sharing popular culture, and daring white teenagers began to adopt black musical and dance traditions.[6]

Faced with northern sentiments arriving with newcomers to southern cities, with increasing black protests over segregation and civil rights, and with the potential loss of industry (and associated taxes), by 1961 white business leaders in South Carolina decided that segregation had to end soon—and yet it still took almost a decade longer to implement. As in the South in general, integration in South Carolina came with "reluctant compliance."[7]

Whether folks welcomed or feared it, South Carolina was modernizing. As historian Walter Edgar observed, "The old South Carolina, a world of small towns in which everyone knew one another and everyone knew his or her place, was dying." Children of black farmers abandoned "the sinking wreck of southern agriculture."[8] The farm life and the social status that Chris and Lula Owens knew so well in previous decades had made them anachronisms on the landscape. And yet, they and their aging black neighbors remained planted in the same soil their ancestors had fought so hard to obtain and protect. As Liberia's residents would discover, retaining that same land continued to be a challenge that almost, but not quite, drove them off forever.

The Residents

As discussed in chapter 4, by the 1940 Census the black population of the Liberia area had dwindled to only thirty-six people, approximately a third of that number in the immediate Owens family alone (see appendices 1 and 2 for names and relationships). By 1943, Chris and Lula Owens welcomed their youngest child, a girl (Mable; see figure 5), into the world, expanding their family to eight children. The community had only recently lost "Grandma

Rosie" Glenn Owens (Mc)Gowans (d. 1941); Rosie's (probable) brother Clarence "Clance" Glenn remained. Still resident were Will Terrell; his wife, Minnie; their two daughters; and a small (grand)son; and Ansel "Anse" McKinney and his wife, Mina. Three of the McKinney children had returned to help take care of their aging parents (a pattern repeated often). Across the county line in Greenville County, Cleveland district, Emma McJunkin, now widowed, resided with her youngest daughter, Lilly.

The loss of Rosie Glenn Owens (Mc)Gowans, mother of Chris Owens, marked the passing of a very prominent Liberia resident, representing the first generation born in freedom. The grave of "Grandma Rosie" is unmarked, but her final resting place reflects the deep ties to land and kin so characteristic of this mountain region in general (see chapter 8).[9] A Death Certificate (obtained through Ancestry.com) indicated that Rosa McGowans died November 19, 1941, from a cerebral hemorrhage in September, later complicated by bronchitis. The certificate listed "Soapstone" as her final resting place, but no grave bears her name. According to granddaughter Judith White, Grandma Rosie lies at the foot of her oldest daughter, Willa Mae Owens Hagood, next to her second husband, Tom McGowans, and at the head of her first husband, William Owens. The graves of Hagood and Owens are marked today with prominent gravestones, and in between them is a gray, concrete block–lined plot, wide enough for two graves, unmarked except for a small bush sprouting from the left-hand grave. Most likely, this is the final resting place of "Grandma" Rosie Glenn McGowans.

Current residents of northern Pickens and Greenville Counties have provided anecdotes about most of these people that help readers visualize them as real human beings. For example, a former county extension agent remembered that Chris Owens was "kind of the leader in the community" (see figure 4). When Mr. Owens shook a hand on a business deal, a retired Pickens County law officer declared, "That was it. He wasn't going to change his mind." Several of Chris's sons recalled that whites and blacks nicknamed Chris "Hard Times," because he always seemed to be down on his luck (thereby conniving a better price on another sale and representing another form of Scott's infrapolitics of the powerless). But he was also a "real comical man," the county agent added; "everybody liked him. He didn't meet no strangers." He always had a "smile on his face," a white county law officer reminisced. "One thing I always enjoyed about him was his singing," the retiree noted; "he knew I loved to hear him sing, and he would pat his feet and clap his hands 'til he got his rhythm, then he'd come out with an old hymn." Few had a keener eye than Chris Owens, too. With one shot, he could "light a match stem at fifty yards," a family friend asserted. "What I remember about Chris the most," a white county official acknowledged, "is how proud he was that he had kept that land."

Lula McJunkin Owens (see figure 4), granddaughter of former slaves, "always wore a dress," a Burgess daughter recalled, and when she would enter the Burgess General Store, "she'd have her hat on." Carl French, a black county official, ate at the Owens home many times, and "Miss Lula" would always keep the plates on the table turned upside down, to prevent flies from alighting. "You could eat off the floor if you wanted to," French added; "it was that clean." Lula's daughter Mable recalled sweeping the yard clean as well (a common tradition).[10] Elaine Parker, one of Mable's cousins, remembered visiting "Aunt Lula" just to taste the fresh buttermilk from her old churn. "That was some good buttermilk!" she exclaimed.

Most of the other remaining Liberia residents were related to the Owens family in some way through kinship, and current residents recalled stories about them as well. Chris Owens's mother's brother, Clarence Glenn, "always dressed spiffy," a local white woman observed, "but he rattled his teeth all the time," an African American resident added. A white neighbor once gave Glenn an extra pair of dress pants, and he appeared one day wearing the new pants under his button-fly work overalls. When asked why, Glenn explained that he "just didn't trust the zipper." Mable Clarke remembered that Glenn "had nub fingers that was cut off in a sawmill or something. Like he always kept it [his hand] up in the air when he talked because we usually saw it." Glenn, grandson of freed slaves, also typically still cooked his food in the fireplace; "he wouldn't cook on no stove," a man observed. "Granny Minnie," Anse McKinney's wife, kept her milk in the springhouse, and her grandchildren visiting from the city (with refrigerators or ice boxes) "always wanted to go down there and bring the milk up for her" because it was such a novelty, a granddaughter recalled. Everyone remembered that Will Terrell, a community-recognized traditional healer, could talk fire out of burns (see the description later in this chapter and in chapter 4).

Mable Clarke remembered her mother's mother, Emma McJunkin, over in the Bald Rock area of northern Greenville County as having a large knot on her head, "like a golf ball." In chapter 3, one of Mable's older brothers had attributed that knot to a resisted sexual assault in her younger years, but Mable (the youngest daughter) had been told her grandmother had suffered an accident on her porch. Grandma Emma lived with her youngest daughter, Lilly, and Mable loved to visit them because of "all this great food, all these pies cooked up, peach cobbler; oh, it'd just be so good!" Grandma

Emma also kept a key around her neck, which opened a trunk filled with cookies, candy, and gum for her grandchildren.

At least one of Emma McJunkin's sons, James, lived nearby, first in Cleveland (at one time called Venus) and then (after 1947) in Marietta; he and his wife had five children, including the youngest, whose middle name was "Jamesa"—"spelled just like James but you put a 'A' after," she explained. She also remembered her father as "a man of many talents and gifts." Pamela Williams, a daughter-in-law, asserted that "there was always food" at the house. Mrs. Williams visited frequently while courting her late husband (James McJunkin's son), because "they were looking me over and I was looking them over!"

Eventually, the couple eloped when they were both in high school. "It was on my birthday," Mrs. Williams continued: "he told my mother that he was taking me up to his house to celebrate my birthday. He told his parents he was going down to my house to celebrate my birthday. We went and got married! So, naturally we couldn't stay together because it was a secret. So we got this big watermelon and went up to Bald Rock. Then we forgot a knife. . . . So he just dropped the watermelon, broke the watermelon, and we sat there and ate watermelon. We stayed out there for a while and then he took me home, and then he went home. . . . But that was our honeymoon, on Bald Rock."

As suggested in chapters 3 and 4, the kinship ties linking the Liberia residents to both their black and white neighbors created an interwoven network of blended and intermarried families. For example, Judith White and her brother came to live with the recently widowed "Grandma Rosie" as children to help care for her. As Robert and Elaine Parker struggled to remember the parentage of older Liberia residents, they discovered that a married neighborhood man had fathered a child with an unmarried daughter of "Anse" McKinney. Mrs. Parker concluded: "That's the reason I say nowadays we don't know who we [are] kin to, 'cause a bit back, you know years ago, people just lived together."

While in some ways this complicated kin network resembled that of other (white) mountain communities or rural communities in general, an added layer of forbidden miscegenation complicated the network even more, in part because some relationships had to be clandestine, by law or custom.[11] For example, Robert Parker (grandson of Rosie Glenn Owens) remembered a white coworker who had claimed they were cousins. Parker's wife added: "So see, his Daddy and the Burgesses was kin . . . Burgesses, the Owens, McGowans and all was cousins; they was kinfolk . . . white and black."

General Way of Life (Mid-Twentieth Century)

Country Life

Much as sociologist Wilma Dunaway described in chapters 3 and 4, the Liberia community of Mable Owens Clarke's childhood created a social cocoon beyond the overarching surveillance of whites, a hidden transcript of family relationships, local institutions, and cultural traditions, planted securely in the soil of her ancestors' lands.[12] Elaine Parker and other relatives visiting from more urbanized areas viewed their trips to the Liberia area as "just like going to Caesar's Head or somewhere like that, you know—really going up in the *mountains* [to] see the beautiful sceneries."

Most of the surrounding area was planted in various crops, including corn, cotton, and garden vegetables to feed the family and to be sold by peddling to surrounding communities for additional income. "This is a lot of land," Mable Clarke admitted. "And they would cover all the land . . . a field with something planted in it." Each field had a name, an Owens man recalled, so that when sent to fetch a particular item, everyone knew exactly where to go—for example, Low Bottom, Lee Bottom, or New Ground.

"As I recollect growing up on a farm" in the 1940s and 1950s, Mable Clarke reflected, "it really wasn't a bad life," especially when compared with that of her oldest brother, raised during the Depression (see chapter 4). On the other hand, she also admitted that as a young girl she had sworn "I'm *never* coming back to this place again!" As a farm girl, Mable envied the easier life of her city cousins (although they also envied her life) because farm work was "never ending." "I finally learned how to milk with both hands so I could finish up fast," Mable Clarke admitted. During the school year, Lula Owens always left an after-school snack for her children in the kitchen, but then they had to put on their work clothes "and you hit the field," Mable stated. Once it got dark, "you had to come home, . . . milk the cows and feed the horses, the pigs, and chickens, gather the eggs, wash the eggs, go to the spring and bring up the night water. Get the night pots in" in case somebody had to use them at night. Then, after the chores were done, Mable continued, "we'd sit by the fireplace and have a kerosene lamp where we would . . . do our homework. . . . And sometimes that would take up 'til 9, 9:30, 10 o'clock at night." Of course, Mable admitted, her exhausted mother stayed up even later, checking their homework. Then, that next morning, Mable explained, "you [got] up pretty early because you had to go out and . . . get the morning things done up before . . . you were off to school."

On weekends, Pickens city resident Allen Hill (a boyhood friend of Mable's nephew Don) stayed with the Owens family, and he remembered many cold winter mornings, snuggled under warm quilts, when Chris Owens entered the bedroom and announced, "'All right, boys'; that's all he'd say and go in the kitchen. But her mother [Lula] would be up and eggs would be fixed. Everything all [made] from the wood stove. You would want to get up, it would be smelling so good," Hill confessed.

Gathering fresh eggs from the family's laying hens presented some frightful moments. One time, Philip Owens remembered, his mother sent him out to the hen house (one of his usual chores) to bring in eggs. "So this particular day," Owens continued, "I went down there, . . . put my hand in and I felt something cold. And I looked up there and I saw this thing lick its tongue out at me. Oh, man! I jumped down, I ran to Momma and my heart was beating fast." Lula Owens grabbed a washtub and beat it with a plow shoe, the agreed-upon signal for emergencies. Chris Owens, plowing a field "across the branch," jumped on a horse and raced to the house. "'Get me the shotgun!'" Mr. Owens shouted as his horse reared back in fright at the snake. "Boom!" Philip Owens concluded—"eggs all over the place!"

Philip Owens also kept bees for his father. One of his most vivid memories involved a swarm of bees passing overhead and the excitement that ensued. The Owens children started banging loudly on a washtub, preventing the passing bees from hearing the queen and thus from flying farther onward. Instead, Mable Owens continued, "you started seeing them coming down out of the sky," and then someone could catch the queen and put her in a secure place, such as a beehive. Then "we would get them" for ourselves, Mable explained. Philip Owens had learned how to handle bees—"if you start fighting them, they all give a gang on you." Don Owens held the smoker one time while Grandfather Chris removed the honey, and "them bees all come out and got me! Boy, I run all the way through the woods. I come in the house, hollering for Grandma, had bees all over me! . . . I mean, it just 'swulled' up, I mean, just all over."

The Owens boys helped their father, hoeing and picking cotton in their family's fields. Ginning frequently took place at the Holder Brothers Cotton Gin in Pickens. Farmers still planted crops (and slaughtered hogs and cut human hair) by "the signs" of the Zodiac found in almanacs, a common European-based tradition.[13] Farm work required an arduous regimen. One Owens man remembered, "I'm used to [working from] 7:00 to 12:00 to get a half hour for dinner [southern lunch], and back out, work again about 12:30 or 1:00, to dark, you know. Then come and do your night things."

When Mr. Owens finally obtained a nonagricultural job, he exclaimed, "Man! This is how they work? No sweat? You know, like twenty-minute breaks every two hours?" Although another of Chris Owens's sons did not like the "backbreaking" work of picking cotton, his father left him no choice: "If you put your foot under my table, you gonna work. That was his motto."

The Owens girls were expected to help their mother in the kitchen so the family would "have a nice hot meal" when workers came in from the fields; the girls also prepared fruits and vegetables for canning. Mable Clarke recalled: "We'd sit out on the porch and it was like a family thing. . . . You'd get you a little bucket of peaches, and everybody'd sit there and peel the peaches and slice them. And my mother pretty much . . . even though I would watch her—she would do the sealing 'cause she wanted to make sure that [with] all this work, they [the canning jars] were sealed tight. . . . So pretty much she and us children helped to do the prep work. . . . We had to help string the green beans, pop them, wash them, [and] cook them."

Children had to be monitored during this prep work, however. During a family gathering on the porch one afternoon, Don Owens (then a small child) was helping his relatives shell "butter peas." No one was looking, Mable Clarke continued: "and he thought, well, it'd be nice just to pluck one up in there [up his nose]. And we didn't know; we didn't see him do it. So about three or four days later we saw this little stem coming out his nose! So, we had to take him to the doctor . . .'cause it had already implanted." "They couldn't hold me," the nephew admitted, but "they give me a lollipop and I settled down then. He got it out."

As teenagers, Mable Clarke and her cousin Judith White earned extra income for their high school clothes by picking beans on farms near Hendersonville, North Carolina. White's parents dropped Judith off at her cousin Mable's house before 4:30 A.M., and the bean truck rattled through the neighborhood and took both girls up to work all day. "And we would . . . go up there and everybody would pick beans at six cents a bushel," Mable remembered. Cousin Judith added: "I wasn't afraid to learn how to do hard work. . . . We had fun crawling on our knees picking those beans and squash, cucumbers and all that, in order to make the money." The girls earned enough money that summer "to buy us some clothes. . . . We ended up being the best little dressed children, better dressed than the city kids," Mable acknowledged.

The Fourth of July offered a welcome respite from work in the fields. Judith White remembered her family coming to Liberia to visit Uncle Chris, "and he'd cut up all of the big watermelons and . . . have peanuts and stuff."

"I remember Aunt Lula busting that watermelon," Elaine Parker recalled; "give this kid a piece and that kid a piece. And we would take it, you know, go out there and wash our faces in that watermelon, it'd taste so good!" Uncle Clarence Glenn had been nurturing a prize watermelon for company one time, but Mable Clarke admitted that she and one of her brothers snuck into his patch and "we busted this big old watermelon and just ate the heart out—the biggest part, the good part." They got caught, of course.

By November, "it was like a vacation" because most of the crops had been gathered, Mable Clarke recollected. Corn from the fields needed to be "pulled" (harvested) and taken to a nearby Oolenoy Valley mill to be ground for cornmeal as well as for livestock feed. "And they would mix that [corn] with molasses or something, but it would have the sweetest smell, you know, when you open up a sack of it," Mable reminisced. She also remembered her father growing and milling his own crops to make the molasses, "so we would have molasses and hot biscuits."

Of course, in winter also came the time to slaughter hogs and preserve the meat. The day before Thanksgiving, Mable Clarke recalled, her family would slaughter a hog and prepare "all the good pork chops and the pork round" for their Thanksgiving celebration. The men slaughtered the hog, set out a large drum full of water to scald the hog (to remove the hair), gutted and bled it, and then divided the hog into portions. The girls carried pans of meat to the women, processing inside. Mable and her nephew remembered helping to cut hog meat in her mother's kitchen, "right here on this table," and grinding the meat, adding pepper and salt and sage, and then wrapping it in wax paper. "The smokehouse would be full of just hams, just lined up," Mable observed; "they would cure them out with the salt, . . . and then after I guess a few weeks, . . . you would go out and take the ones that's been there the longest and you would just slice your ham, . . . bring it inside and make you a ham sandwich."

Thanksgiving yielded a cornucopia of food. In addition to the freshly slaughtered pork, Lula Owens would kill and fry "a couple of big old fat hens that's been wobbling around on the yard," Mable Clarke fondly recalled. "And we'd bake a big old long pan of the sweet potatoes" that had "just come up out of the field," she continued. "Good old fresh" homemade butter covered the potatoes, and the family also served collard greens, turnip greens, turnips, and cornbread. Mable admitted that they would struggle to "try to find space to fit the next bowl in."

Christmas brought special foods, Mable Owens remembered. Her parents would buy "these big old bags of oranges . . . and that's the only time of the year that we saw the oranges." Chris and Lula Owens would hide the oranges, and Mable and her siblings smelled those tantalizing scents for weeks. "Just oh, if I could just get one; I can't hardly wait!" Mable exclaimed. Finally the day arrived. The children seized their oranges, rolled them to get the juice up, plunged peppermint candy through the rinds, "and you could suck the juice up through that candy just like a straw. And to me," Mable concluded, "that was the most beautiful Christmas."

On New Year's Day, the regional custom was that families served black-eyed peas, collard greens, and sometimes pork.[14] Mable Clarke explained: "The peas was for so you can have some pennies in your pocket. The collard greens, so you have some green bucks in your pockets. . . . And then . . . it was always some kind of pork meat they would cook." Firecrackers marked both Christmas and New Year's, with gunshots highlighting the latter as well.

While the holidays provided justification for special foods, ordinary farm labor offered a wide variety of wonderful foods as well. All the labor created "a pretty good appetite once you put in about ten hours out there," Mable Clarke admitted. "Yeah, Momma could cook!" an Owens relative noted. "There was always food there to eat," Mable added; "you never grew up feeling like you was going to go to bed hungry or wake up that morning thinking there was no food." "We enjoyed just knowing . . . what was coming in the field," Mable recalled; "when the corn came in, oh, wow! . . . If the green beans was in season, we were happy for the green beans. . . . There was just vegetables after vegetables after vegetables." On cooler evenings, Chris Owens would parch (roast) homegrown peanuts, and the children would gather and shell them. Other times, Mr. Owens popped homegrown corn, and daughter Mable remembered how she and her siblings would "get so excited" as they heard the corn popping; then all eight children would rush in to grab themselves a handful. In the summertime they grew "the watermelon, the cantaloupes, all the apples on the trees," Mable Clarke noted. "You'd go down there [to the watermelon patch] and eat 'til you're sick," Allen Hill recalled. "When the peach trees would come in," Mable reflected, "we'd know then we're going to get a good old peach cobbler." Lula Owens would also always have a "nice cake . . . baked up," her daughter Mable remembered, "and she would make like a blackberry cobbler, a yield of that. Sometime it'd be a sweet potato cobbler, and it would be . . . delicious!"

In addition to consuming meat from domesticated animals, Liberia residents also hunted. Philip Owens proudly noted that his father, Chris, had numerous white friends who hunted with him, and his father owned several types of dogs used specifically to hunt different types of animals. For example, Chris Owens had a bird dog who spotted and dispersed birds so that hunters could shoot them (Philip as a boy retrieved the dead birds). Allen Hill, a friend of Mable's nephew Don, remembered "Sue," a remarkable Red Bone/Blue Tick hound also owned by Chris Owens. "And people don't believe it, but . . . early in the morning, he'd tree squirrels. About noontime, he'd start running rabbits. In the evening, he'd start treeing squirrels again. And then at night, we'd tree opossums. That one dog did all that." Hill spent numerous weekends in the country with his friend Don Owens, and the boys loved to go squirrel hunting. In fact, if the dog discovered a squirrel in a tree, it sat at the base and looked up. So the boys knew to look up on the other side of where the dog gazed. If the squirrel jumped to another tree, the dog moved to sit at the second tree and looked up. "Very smart dog," Allen Hill admitted. Grandpa Chris would issue the boys just five bullets, and they had to bring back five squirrels. Thus, the boys and Sue needed to coordinate actions very carefully. Mr. Owens trained dogs like Sue with his voice, Hill observed; "something with his voice" allowed the dogs to understand that "if they didn't do what he wanted them to do, he didn't mess with them. He said ain't no use to waste his time and money."

For hunting possums, Sue the dog would tree the animal, usually in a persimmon tree. The boys would then climb the tree with a burlap sack, Allen Hill recalled, "and we'd shake the possum off, in that sack. And then we'd bring him back to the house, and he'd [Chris Owens] put him in a cage." Then the family would feed the possum buttermilk and corn for about thirty days, to clean it out. Since possums sometimes ate carrion, cleaning them out for about a month was a common practice.[15]

Turtles also added to the larder. Allen Hill remembered catching "mud turtles" or snapping turtles as big as foot tubs, and being cautioned not to get bitten. In fact, he recalled a time Chris Owens placed a stick in front of a huge snapping turtle and the turtle bit the stick; Mr. Owens then cut his head off but the turtle still gripped the stick. " 'That's what he'll do to your finger if you stick your finger down there,' " Owens had warned. A white neighbor listening to this story added that she had heard that the turtle would continue biting until thunder rolled and lightning flashed. Both whites and blacks concurred that turtle meat contained the flavors of seven different meats, another common folk tradition.[16]

The adult Liberia children acknowledged their mothers and grandmothers taking great care in cooking this game. For example, Elaine Parker remembered her "Granny Minnie" (wife of Ansel "Anse" McKinney) cooking a big pot of squirrel and dumplings on her wood stove. "And you could smell it . . . about three miles away from the house," she added. Mable Clarke's mother cooked squirrels, possum, and raccoons, but "she had . . . such a way to fixing it 'til it didn't taste like wild meat." With the latter two, Mrs. Owens might add sweet potatoes, white (or "Irish") potatoes, carrots, green beans, "with a nice laced gravy," daughter Mable stated. "And her presentation on the table would just . . . make you want to eat," Mable concluded; "I mean, it was like rainbows of colors!"

While the Owens family consumed much of the vegetables and meats from their farm, Chris Owens also "peddled" the extra produce, first in a wagon, then a truck. Children and grandchildren assisted. Allen Hill remembered preparing all the vegetables, buttermilk, milk, and eggs for Saturday mornings; Bernard Quinn added Mrs. Owens's jelly and preserves to the list. The Owens family would travel at various times to Pickens, Greenville, Marietta, or Travelers Rest (south of Marietta). Hill added that frequently, "Mr. Chris" peddled in the poorer sections of these communities, and often accepted credit from week to week if a family did not have the needed cash. "Toward the end of his route, he gave away to the poor what he had not sold. And I'm pretty sure, you know, he didn't get all his money back, but he was blessed with a long life," Hill admitted.

Additional income came from moonshining, quite common in the Upstate.[17] One Liberia man remembered a relative sprouting corn, grinding the sprouts in a meat grinder, and carrying the material into the woods, to be distilled into alcohol. "It kind of put food on the table" for the family, a woman added. A county law officer recalled an older white woman in the Oolenoy Valley who "made more liquor than anybody up there." While the stills were hidden, occasionally hunters or "little devilish boys" stumbled upon them, Allen Hill conceded (having been a self-professed "devilish boy" himself). According to local legend, one man sought to avoid capture by revenue agents, county sheriffs, and their tracking dogs by swimming a great distance underwater in a creek. Eventually the lawmen caught on and just waited for him to reappear downstream. Another time, Allen Hill's uncle mixed Ne-Hi orange soda with bootleg whiskey, and gave it to him and his cousin to drink. Hill continued: "So, we drunk and it took our breath. I mean, hoo, that was some nasty stuff. . . . We couldn't even get in the car after about twenty minutes. They had to pick us up (we were just kids), put us in the car, and he [uncle] brought us over to my grandma's house. . . . We woke up about a *day* later!"

By the time of Mable Clarke's childhood, Liberia's farmers fully incorporated anthropologist Rhoda Halperin's "Kentucky way," maintaining family income and social connections within their remote enclave while remaining on the margins of the external market-based capitalistic system. Corn and cotton, milled in nearby towns, linked Liberia's farmers to that external system, while simultaneously farmers were nearly self-sufficient, growing what they needed in gardens or livestock pens, hunting in nearby woods, fishing in nearby streams, and foraging for medicinal or edible plants in an "underground food economy."[18] As in other rural areas, every family member helped in some way—girls prepared food for cooking or canning while boys assisted with butchering or hunting. Additional cash (for taxes, shoes, school books, or other necessary items) was obtained through peddling farm produce, selling canned or preserved materials, or (surreptitiously) dispensing distilled alcohol. In this way, Liberia's farmers controlled as best as possible their interaction with a potentially dangerous (or at least unpredictable) white-dominated world and remained, as Scott's Southeast Asian hill tribes, relatively protected in their remote mountain community. As with previous generations, Liberia's farmers utilized a variety of economic "folkway" strategies in their physical environment as another hidden transcript to secure their relative independence and security from white hegemony.[19]

By this time, very few children remained in Liberia, but Mable Clarke and her same-aged cousin Judith White had a few playmates—mostly the other Owens children and another cousin, Furman (grandson to "Anse" McKinney). With no toys—"we didn't even have a rope to jump rope," Mrs. White admitted—much recreation came simply from exploring the lands. Mable remembered climbing and jumping off the large soapstone boulders exposed near the church, the same rock her father Chris had played on as a child at the turn of the century, and his mother before him. "It's really a tradition," Mrs. White added. Cousin Furman raced and jumped the tired plow horse over ditches, to the consternation of his elderly relatives. Elaine Parker, another slightly older relative, visited frequently and would "gang up" with Mable's older brothers and sisters to walk across the countryside talking and having fun. "We covered miles and miles," she admitted. "We were some dirty little kids when the day was over because we always played hard," Judith White acknowledged.

Partly because of cost, partly because of distance, and partly because of racial segregation, emergency medical care in the Liberia community was provided by midwives and other gifted residents.[20] Mable Clarke claimed that she was the last in her family to be delivered by a midwife. "Some of the babies back then were just born in the field," Mable noted; "you know, they didn't make it home and they would just spread out on I guess . . . sheets." "I think my mother worked up in the field and that evening I was born," Mable remarked. Once a baby was born, "you would have to stay in a dark room for I believe two weeks with no lights. . . . No light on the baby's eyes or anything. They would pull the shades down and everything," Mable added.[21]

Home remedies protected children from typical illnesses such as colds. For example, Mable Clarke remembered her mother gathering mullein leaves and broom sage, breaking the material up and boiling it as a tea. Then she would rub Vick's salve on her children "and put a flannel cloth to it. And then you would drink this hot tea," perhaps mixed with commercial whiskey or moonshine, and "you would just sweat this cold out." Allen Hill had his colds cured by Mrs. Owens's homemade cough syrup, consisting of a half gallon of moonshine and horehound candy from the neighborhood store. Mable also recalled her mother making a poultice of cornmeal, turpentine, and kerosene, putting the mixture in a flour sack, warming it, and placing it on the patient's chest. "Smell like onions and garlic," Mable conceded. "And do you know," Mable continued, "that next morning you'd wake up, your whole chest would be completely open. Amazing!" Mable's mother also cleansed her children with castor oil mixed with coffee; "so to this day, I do not drink coffee," Mable admitted. Once, in defiance, an Owens brother spit his dose of coffee and castor oil back in his mother's face: "I thought she was gonna kill me!" he reflected.

Another time, this brother recalled, he had injured his leg and it "swolled up" so bad he could not walk. His mother made a poultice out of cow urine, moonshine, vinegar, and turpentine, tied it to his leg, and sent him to bed. "Momma, that don't smell good," he complained. But, when he got up the next morning, the swelling had gone down and he could walk again.

Rural emergencies required quick thinking as well as trusted home remedies. One time, Mable Clarke and her brother Jessie had to move the family goat from one field to another. While Jessie pulled, Mable pushed, but to no avail. Finally, Jessie suggested pulling the goat's tail, which his younger sister obligingly did quite vigorously. Immediately the goat whirled around and gored Mable in the leg; he "picked me straight up from the ground and took me back down. I mean like, blood was going everywhere!" The horn had broken off in the wound. Chris Owens pulled the horn fragment out with a pliers and then Lula poured kerosene and turpentine in the open wound. "And wow!" Mable recalled about the pain. But the wound healed with no further infection.

On two separate occasions, Mable and her nephew Don Owens had been playing around the fireplace and had gotten burned. The family took them to Will Terrell, who was recognized in the community as a traditional healer. Mable remembered that he kept shelves of jars, with "different roots" in them, and he would drink from these jars periodically. Terrell also could talk fire out of burns.[22] Although both victims were young children at the time and could not recall Terrell's precise ritual, Mable did remember that he blew on the wound and muttered something, "but I don't think he was really speaking words." "He was mumbling," Don Owens recalled, "like he was talking to himself, and [I] couldn't understand what he was saying." After Terrell blew on the wound, both patients noted, their pain disappeared. "Or you *thought* it did," a younger and more skeptical relative speculated.

Since some people could harness the power of the supernatural for beneficial outcomes, logically then, others might manipulate the supernatural for evil. This idea, common in many cultures (including European, African, and Native American), nevertheless typically remained secretive and difficult to discover, perhaps because of the hint of Satanic influences and thus a strong non-Christian perspective. Only a few suggestions of these ideas lingered in the distant memory of Liberia's residents. For example, as a young girl Mable Clarke overheard adult conversations about mysterious deaths, illnesses, or an unfortunate run of bad luck besetting a neighbor. Rumors in the community were that "somebody may had cast a evil spell upon them. And then they would try to figure out how they could get rid of this evil spirit," Mable added. While she did not recall a specific person having the ability to either cast or relieve spells, she did have vague recollections of traditional healers dispensing a "prayer cloth" to be worn, or "some kind of ivory . . . tooth." When prompted, she thought perhaps the wearing of silver dimes also might have been important.[23]

Social Life in the Liberia Community

Small but comfortable farm homes were where Liberia's black residents resided. "There wasn't many of them," an African American county agent recalled, and they did not have indoor plumbing. "I didn't like to go up there on a cold day," he added, because the houses themselves were cold. Michael Owens remembered that he and his siblings had to sleep "three or four" to a bed in his birth home. That house eventually was replaced by the current

Owens family homeplace, built sometime during this period. The one-story concrete block and frame house had an expansive front porch with comfortable chairs for the Owens parents to sit and survey their lands, a living room with a fireplace, a second front bedroom, a large kitchen with a long sink and extensive counter space, and a small screened porch to the side, through which one entered the home. Behind the house were the necessary outbuildings, with the domestic-related structures (hen house and smoke house) closer to the kitchen while the livestock barn would be farther away.[24] The house and remaining outbuildings are still in the Owens family today.

Like many other parts of the rural United States, electricity penetrated the Liberia area sometime in the mid-1950s. Mable Clarke recalled listening as a young girl to a battery-powered radio and playing records on a hand-cranked phonograph. She did her homework by kerosene lamps or firelight. Clarke and her cousin Judith White also remembered the ice man selling a 100-pound block of ice for the ice box, which would keep their food cool for a week. For a special treat, Chris Owens would chip off the old block and give his children a piece of ice.

The arrival of electric power meant the addition of labor-saving appliances, such as a washing machine instead of a washboard or the creek, a refrigerator instead of the ice box or spring house, electric lights instead of kerosene lamps or firelight, and a television instead of storytellers. Mable Clarke "used to hate" the old washboard, especially when ordered by her mother to rub the clothes vigorously. Angela Young's father (James Monroe McJunkin) in Marietta first got all three major appliances (TV, refrigerator, and washing machine) in 1955. Young's oldest brother had married and had a daughter by then, and the new grandmother convinced her husband to "get a refrigerator so the baby's milk can stay good" (would not spoil).

Indoor plumbing meant no more buckets lowered into the well for water and no more "whore's baths" (as one woman described them)—the nightly cleansing of "three parts: head, feet, hands, and in between." Once a week on Saturday nights, to be ready for church on Sunday, almost everyone took a complete bath in a tub of water that had been heated on the stove. Now people could wash every day. Indoor plumbing also meant the elimination of chamber pots and the outhouse, and a northern city relative remembered her first visit to her grandparents' home, when she was told she would have to use a chamber pot. She recalled, "I'm like, 'I have to do what?'" But she decided she would rather use the pot than risk a meeting with a snake on the way to the outhouse at night.

Travel at that time remained primarily by horse or by foot, and people commonly walked long distances. For example, in order to visit her mother, Emma, Lula McJunkin Owens hiked with her children the ten miles or so to Bald Rock (see map 2). The family cut through the woods in order to save miles and to avoid the roads and potential harassment from white travelers. Each child carried a stick to ward off snakes, and the distance did not matter, Mable Clarke recalled, because "we skipped and hopped [and] picked flowers along the way." Mable's older brother Philip made that journey as well, but cautioned that "you got to watch the clock, look at the sun," in order to be home by nightfall to complete the night chores or "you'll get your butt whupped." Judith White walked with her grandmother and some of her cousins about two miles to the Pumpkintown Store, and they had a "very educational" time, "walking for that distance and you looking around and seeing everything." "They got in their exercise," Mable Clarke noted, "just going [from field to field] and checking to see what's in." Carrying harvested vegetables back to the house in sacks on shoulders required additional energy.

Travel by foot enhanced more than muscles. Walking or playing throughout the countryside allowed people to observe their surroundings—to remain intimately connected to their physical environment much more closely than suburban residents in air conditioned (or heated) artificial environments might do today. As families walked through the countryside, parents could instruct children about the identification of medicinal herbs or telltale signs of wildlife. Patches of ripening berries or savory mushrooms could be identified and returned to for later harvesting. Neighbors waved to passersby from behind heavy plows or from shaded porches. Walking tied people to the landscape in intimate detail, a connection explored more completely in chapter 8.[25]

Trucks and automobiles replaced virtually all horse-drawn vehicles on the roads by the 1950s, although horses and mules still helped around the farms. Allen Hill remembered that Chris Owens's mules would "mind just like children. He'd tell them what to do, and all they got to do is hear his voice. The cows did the same thing when it was evening." By this time, Chris Owens had a truck for peddling vegetables across the counties, and with an empty truck headed back to the farm, "he didn't have but one speed—you know, about ninety miles an hour," Allen Hill admitted. Hill and Mr. Owens's grandson were returning with Chris and Lula Owens one Saturday evening after peddling, and Mr. Owens had warned the boys to sit pressed against the cab. This one time, though, Hill suggested they ride in the middle of the truck. Chris Owens "was running about ninety miles an hour," Hill continued, and "he hit a pothole. . . . And . . . when he hit the pothole, the whole truck jumped up off the ground, and he was running so fast, the truck looked like it was running out from under us while we was in the air! . . . And I heard Miss Lula say, 'Chris, you gonna kill all of us!' From then on, he didn't have to tell us to sit up by the front of the truck anymore."

Even if people owned motorized vehicles, most of the secondary roads were unpaved. "And when it rained," Mable Clarke acknowledged, "you know you was gonna get stuck coming in with the car." Pamela Williams and her late husband "lost our transmission trying to get back in" to Bald Rock to visit her father-in-law, James McJunkin. Elaine Parker's father used to come up to Liberia on Sundays to visit relatives; without his wife along, he would sometimes get intoxicated. "And I think a lot of times that's why we got stuck up there," Parker admitted; "he'd drive off in the ditch or something like that 'cause he [was] about half high!" The children had to remove their Sunday shoes and walk barefoot through the mud. Mules or tractors pulled out stuck drivers. One time, Chris Owens ran off Liberia Road and asked one of his sons to pull him out with a mule. The mule was recalcitrant, so the son was resourceful—he lit a fire under the mule's tail, which jolted the mule and extracted the car, but then Chris Owens wanted to know why his mule's rear end was blistered. Before Liberia Road was paved in the 1960s, Mable Clarke remembered sitting on her parents' front porch on a Sunday afternoon and "boy, we see a car go by, like, 'Oh! There go somebody by!' We'd be so excited. . . . Because it was just like . . . nobody out here but you."

Adults fondly recalled walking or riding to the Pumpkintown General Store, at the crossroads across from the old Sutherland homeplace. "Ever since I can remember," Mable Clarke reminisced, the Burgess family has owned that store, "down from generation to generation." By this time, Liberia's residents did their "trading" at that store because the Burgess family was trustworthy and honest, Mable continued; she would trade her mother's chickens' eggs for sugar or flour. Mable Clarke and a friend both listed the items available in the store: gasoline for cars or trucks, farming tools, automotive parts, clothing like socks and work gloves—a general store, both agreed. Large barrels held bulk commodities such as lima beans or black-eyed peas. Judith White mostly remembered the candy counter. Don Owens carried empty bottles to the store for a refund and then bought more soft drinks or candy with his money. Sometimes his grandfather Chris would take him, and Chris could empty a sixteen-ounce "dope" (Coca-Cola) in one swig; then he would berate his grandson for drinking slower, having to take the bottle with him, and thus having to pay the deposit.

City Employment

Liberia residents seeking greater economic opportunities and mercantile variety moved to, or traded in, the nearby towns. In a sense, many African Americans left the farm but re-created close-knit communities in neighborhoods and suburbs of these larger towns. Of course, residential segregation also compelled such settlements. One such neighborhood was an area called the "Gold Mine." About a block off U.S. Highway 276 just north of Marietta (and about ten miles east of Pumpkintown; see map 2), today a narrow road leads off the main highway through some small bungalows into a narrow, steep-sided valley lined with small homes on both sides. Because the hillsides were so steep, Judith White acknowledged that "when you'd look at the houses [in there], . . . you'd say, 'What was on their mind?'" Mable Clarke believed that the land was so poor that whites did not want it and thus sold it to blacks. Never an actual mine (as far as current residents recalled), the area received its name from Spann Cruell Sr., according to Angela Young. A small road still bears that family name, and Cruells also lie in the Mt. Pilgrim Baptist Church cemetery (the "Gold Mine's" local church). Mrs. Young thought that Mr. Cruell and his wife longed to buy a home of their own rather than continue to pay rent, and "when they learned that some of the property in here was for sale he would tell his wife Miss Nancy, 'Let's go up to the Gold Mine and look at the land. . . . I guess it was sort of like a gold mine for him." James McJunkin moved there about 1940, "when there were but two houses. He came as an educator and taught school there for fourteen years."[26] McJunkin's youngest daughter still lives there, next to the site of her father's home.

Increasingly, too, these same towns provided better employment opportunities, especially compared with the challenges of farming. Despite the improvement, however, segregated work spaces still relegated African Americans to the lowest-paying or worst jobs.[27] For example, upon graduation from Easley's Clearview High School in the early 1960s, Mable Clarke recognized that her principal employment options were to "clean the white people's house and cook for them." Stephen Young's father and uncles worked in the textile mills, but primarily as laborers loading and unloading trucks with hand carts or cleaning the bathrooms; the actual higher-paying weaving jobs "was just strictly white." Even when he started at the mill after desegregation, Young was not permitted to weave but instead he "doffed cloth"—taking off giant spools and replacing them. "We more or less did the kind of dirty work," he explained. Sam McGowens (Rosie Glenn Owens's son from a third marriage) worked as a "fireman" in the boiler room of a mill, shoveling coal into a furnace for heat and power—with no air conditioning and little ventilation, the job was exhausting during warmer months. Michael Owens worked for a time in a bleachery (a cloth-whitening factory), but slipped in some water and broke his knee. After his knee healed, he quit rather than be fired for failing to perform adequately. Other jobs were even more dangerous. Elaine Parker's father, in Marietta, worked at a nearby rock quarry on the "dynamite crew." "That's where he lost one of his eyes over there," she explained, " 'cause he got blowed up one time when they was doing the dynamite."

Many blacks worked as cooks or bellhops in hotels or restaurants. James McJunkin's teaching position did not pay enough "to educate, clothe, and feed five children," his daughter recalled, and so he worked for Caesar's Head Hotel (atop the mountain) and Poinsett Hotel (in downtown Greenville) for twenty-nine years. To go to work at Caesar's Head, McJunkin "walked seven miles up the mountain" just to carry bags to the rooms.[28] Once her youngest daughter had entered school, McJunkin's wife went to work "at the white school—she made fifteen dollars every two weeks as a cook," her daughter recalled. Philip Owens made enough money at the Varsity Restaurant in Greenville "doing curb hop" to buy a car, a '39 Buick, "and I give the guy five dollars a week" to pay it off.

Angela Young began her work experience as a cook, following in her mother's and mother's sister's footsteps, until she got her first "real job," as a ward secretary at Greenville General Hospital. Proudly, she continued: "I was one of the first black ward secretaries, and . . . I started off with eighty-five cents an hour! . . . I think I stayed there maybe two years, . . . and I had gotten married, and I needed to make a little bit more money. . . . I left there and I went to the Fouke [Fur] Company. I was then making a dollar and twenty-five cent an hour. Oh, I was making big money then, I thought. . . . We could go to Winn-Dixie grocery store and get thirteen canned goods for a dollar!"

Angela Young's father, James McJunkin, taught school in "two class-rooms and a kitchen," she recalled. "Back then the children all knew each other," McJunkin recalled in a newspaper interview in 1983; "they played together. . . . You knew their parents, and if they gave you a problem you would go to the parents."[29] As noted, McJunkin also needed to work at area hotels in order to supplement his meager income.

Probably one of the worst jobs recalled from this time belonged to Philip Owens. His father, Chris Owens, contracted his son to clean the outhouses at a recreational park in Wildcat, in northern Greenville County (see map 2). A sewer pipe extended from a house, emptying into a trench lined with rocks, and Owens had to "open all that up." Furious at his father for assigning him that horrible job, nevertheless Owens was required to give his father his earnings when he got home. In return, his father gave him a piece of candy and a nickel—and some advice. " 'Save this, son,' " Owens said, " 'you gonna be rich one day!' "

Intercommunity Visits

Despite the migration of families from farms to towns and cities during this period, former residents and relatives of current residents continued to maintain strong social ties with their ancestral community in Liberia and with Soapstone Baptist Church. As will be discussed later in this chapter and in chapter 8, powerful forces of memory and kinship kept people tied to that place, even generations later.[30] As country cousins visited their kin in the "big city," and as sophisticated urban residents ventured into the "wild" countryside, visitors to both areas noticed interesting contrasts and experienced cultural clashes.

Mable Clarke and her cousin Judith White, virtually the same age, spent their girlhoods almost like sisters, with Mable in Liberia and Judith in Slater-Marietta, in northern Greenville County (see map 2). Every Friday afternoon in school, Mable and her cousin would discuss where they would ask their parents to drop them off for the weekend, and Mable loved spending time off the farm. "It was like a vacation!" she exclaimed. "And then her [Judith's] mother . . . would just spoil me. She used to bake this delicious carrot cake and . . . I would just eat and eat and eat that carrot cake." Judith added that their only chores were to make their beds, wash the dishes, and "then sit out on the porch and walk up the street and come back." "Wave at whoever [was] passing by," Mable added. "And just sit and run our mouth," Judith continued. Even after spending all day together, they admitted, they would continue to talk until after midnight, and with the houses small and walls thin, Judith's mother had to intervene, she recalled: " 'I'll bet you two little hens'd better go to sleep in there!' "

As children, the ladies swore they never talked about boys; instead, they talked about clothes. They would take Sears or Spiegel's department store catalogs and pore through the pages, and, Mable recollected, "just look through and then we'd look at the shoes and say, " 'You like this pair of shoes?' 'Yeah.' 'I do, too.' You know, we was just shopping in the books." "It was just a wish book," Mable added, "because we couldn't afford to get nothing out of there, and your parents you know better than to ask them because they couldn't afford nothing." As they both got a little older and started singing in Soapstone Church, they talked about what they would wear on Sundays, and by the tenth grade or so, Judith admitted, "then we start getting the little guys on our minds."

Whenever adults visited their relatives in Liberia, they always returned with fresh vegetables from the fields, sometimes after helping to pick their own. Mable Clarke elaborated: "After church was over they'd come on down to the house and they'd load the cars up with whatever Daddy had, watermelons . . . and vegetables and stuff and they head on back down the hill." Bernard Quinn, a county farm agent, enjoyed his visits with Chris Owens and his neighbors. "We'd all get together and talk about anything and everything. . . . They was kind of up on the news, too. . . . They'd talk about all the churches [in the area], and they would talk about their children, their family and what they were doing and all."

When city children visited their relatives in Liberia, they entered a land of adventure. As Elaine Parker's father pulled into the driveway of his parents' home in Liberia, she remembered, "all us kids—we would scatter. Some going one way and some go another. And we had fun!" Judith White also loved to visit her country cousin Mable and her Aunt Lula and Uncle Chris. "I got a chance to do some things on the farm," Mrs. White recalled, and above all else she loved the animals. "There was enough of them out there," Cousin Mable added wryly. In fact, Judith White attributed her love of animals to having received "a good spanking" one time as a child. She explained: "When a stray dog came in our yard I wasn't afraid. I took my winter coat off, put it on the dog, buttoned it up. Took my little cap off, put it on the dog, tied it around his little head and he went strolling on down the street. Never saw my coat nor the dog anymore!" Once Judith got home, of course, her mother was furious at her for befriending a strange dog and for losing her winter coat at the same time.

"I always wanted to try to learn something even though I didn't know what I was doing," Judith White continued. For example, she always pinched the cow when milking, causing the cow to kick and spill the milk; she worried Aunt Lula would be upset over spilled milk. A granddaughter from Boston once watched Lula Owens milk her cow and then churn the milk for butter. "It was just all new to us because we never saw this before. . . . I'm like, 'What is she doing?' . . . 'We go to the *store* and buy our milk!' But it was good, you know."

"But you definitely need a car to get anywhere you wanted to go," the cousin continued, "and we used to always rely on 'Big Cuz' to take us to the store. And I tell you we used to stock up, . . .'cause we knew that that was only coming once a month, maybe! . . . See, in Boston, we used to have a store right on the corner. So you know, we want to go to the candy store we'd walk up the street."

These visiting northerners teased their country cousins about their rustic vocabulary. For example, Don Owens plowed mules with "Gee" and "Haw," called the cows with "Su-kay!" and ordered a "dope" from the Pumpkintown store like his grandfather, instead of a soft drink. On the other hand, the country residents teased their city relatives because "we spoke proper," a cousin observed; "but we thought they were funny just because of how they pronounced their words."

Allen Hill, visiting his friend Don Owens on weekends from Pickens, especially loved "the freedom," as the boys roamed the countryside, hunting and helping on the farm and getting into mischief. After plowing, the boys sometimes rode "John" and "Henry," the Owens mules, but "when it was evening time coming," Don added, "they knowed they's supposed to be in the barn. Once you turned them around, it was one speed!" Elaine Parker remembered her grandfather's "big old big footed horse like the Budweiser horse," named "Pat," but she was afraid to ride him. Other dangers lurked in the woods, Judith White remembered. From the Owens house to her grandmother's house was a large rock outcropping, and the children had been warned about the snakes there. "So when we would be approaching," Judith White narrated, "we'd stop, we'd look, and then we'd run!"

Soapstone Baptist Church and the Community

The "main inspiration" for the Liberia community, Bernard Quinn observed, "was the church." The small, wooden building (described in chapter 4; see figure 6) still sat near the soapstone boulders for which it was named. The church belonged to the Oolenoy River Baptist Association (see chapters 3 and 4), a network of small black churches across two counties that offered all congregants an opportunity to attend members' churches and (as with previous generations), provided a mechanism to develop wider social ties, to exchange important information, and to develop leadership abilities.[31] Younger people also enjoyed the chance to meet a wider network of potential friends and future spouses. For example, Elaine Parker admitted that she and her husband "grew up in the same church. . . . Back years ago, that's [church] where you would get your boyfriend, your husband, wife . . .'cause that was the only place we got to go, really, was the church." Another woman, whose parents were Soapstone deacons, remembered that "we were just glad as kids to go to different churches. . . . It was kind of a thrill for us just to meet different people."

Saturday evening, folks prepared for Sunday services. Judith White remembered that "the fathers had maybe two suits and mothers had two dresses." Mrs. White recalled her mother patching together her clothes on Saturday night to prepare for Sunday, and sometimes she would look "as ragged as a can of kraut," Mrs. White admitted. Mable Clarke recalled her own preparations: "Well, you would make sure your dress was ironed, or the boys had to make sure their pants was ironed." Mable used an old metal iron, warmed in the fireplace and smeared with tallow to help the iron glide across the clothes without scorching them. The Owens children would "get everything laid out for Sunday morning," Mable observed. Over in Greenville County, Elaine Parker remembered "sitting on the porch, you know, polishing our shoes and combing our hair, and rolling up our hair on this brown paper."

"And Sunday morning you get up," Mable continued, "and you do your regular chores and kind of swiftly move along and get ready to make the walk from the home . . . up here to the church." Another woman, the daughter of deacons, recalled, "We came to church on Sunday morning [because] . . . it was your duty to come." "Daddy would bring us up here" to Soapstone, another woman recalled, "and so we had to come with him . . . whether we wanted to come or not." The church had two doors; men entered through the left-hand door and the women to the right; the congregation sat generally segregated by gender. Then Mable Clarke's nephew rang the church bell to call together the worshippers. Sunday school started at 10:00 A.M., and the service began about an hour later.

By midcentury, Mt. Nebo Church, about two miles south (see map 3), held services the second and fourth Sundays and Soapstone Church had its services on the first and third Sundays. Because few families had cars or the gasoline to fill the tanks, this meant that in order to attend weekly services, families had to cross the Oolenoy River valley either way. Jessie Owens remembered walking with his family from Liberia, his mother Lula leading the way, and "you could hear them singing. . . . Momma said, 'We're going to miss something if we don't get there early!' So we'd run maybe a quarter of a mile to get to Mt. Nebo to be on time. And those were the good ol' days. Back then, when they had church, they had *church*!" What Mr. Owens meant was that the "old folks used to fire up the service before they'd have the preaching. I mean, you had to get there to really get into the spirit."

Some congregants recalled being well behaved in church as children, partly because they loved the services and partly because their parents were deacons. One woman, for example, remembered donating all of her allowance into the Sunday school collection: "I wouldn't keep it, you know, and buy bubble gum and things." "And then Sunday school I had to sit there with my little book, you know, right there and listen," she added. On the other hand, Mable Clarke and her best friend and cousin Judith White always sat toward the back. "And we were back there talking about something and either her mother would turn around, or mine; we shut it up . . . right there," Mable Clarke admitted. "But they knew those two little hens had something going on," Judith White confessed. "And weren't paying attention to what the preacher was saying," Mable quickly added. Since at various times the parents of both girls were elders of the church, and since the congregation was very small, misbehavior stood out dramatically and would be corrected "with just a look of the eye," Mable recalled.

Local historian Luther Johnston listed some of the pastors and their deacons, and many of them are buried in either the old or new Soapstone cemeteries.[32] Unfortunately, because the church records burned in 1967, only some of the dates of residency have been recorded, and many of these are from congregants' recollections. Robert Parker, himself a minister, remembered that the old-time pastors would stay until they would "get so old, then they just resign." Others, both he and his wife noted, "would stay there until they died."

Whenever Liberia residents would pass away, the deceased would be taken to a black funeral home in the area for embalming (funeral homes and mortuaries were segregated as well). Sometimes the older residents would be taken back home to their own parlor (rather than the funeral parlor) for visitation, "and people would sit up all night with you," Angela Young recalled. Mable Clarke added that community families would bring food—"it would just be so much food . . . you would think you were at a picnic or something." Bernard Quinn, a funeral home director, felt that people at these gatherings seemed more emotional; "it looked like their only hope was gone when the person left," he remembered. While most people respected the ceremony and remained "very sanctimonious," Quinn also admitted that parties and wakes in people's homes might have offered occasional drinking.

To indicate the funeral the next morning, someone would ring Soapstone Church's bell, and then, Mable Clarke observed, "people in the community would know that somebody's died." The funeral service would have a lot of singing, Mable Clarke added, "and maybe three or four people from the community would get up and share some remarks about the person that has passed on. And then [there would] be more singing and then they would do the eulogy and go to the cemetery," right beside the church. The deacons of the church maintained the cemetery and had staked out the gravesite; men in the community dug the grave. After the ceremony, everyone would gather at the adjacent Soapstone schoolhouse "and eat again," Mable Clarke added; "so there was always a lot of eating."

Before Baptist churches built interior baptismal pools, traditional baptisms were outside, either in specially built pools (such as the one at Oolenoy Baptist Church), or actually in rivers, which could be cold, muddy, or alive with fluvial creatures. Several Owens family members recalled being baptized in the placid Oolenoy River, just upstream from the bridge below the old Keith homestead, in a pool barely deep enough for dipping. "And you would have all the church members, deacons and deaconesses all standing around on the bank," Jessie Owens recalled, "and the preacher having to march down into the creek to be baptized." All those to be baptized wore white. "And there'd be so much spirit there that you'd think you was in church," one woman remembered. As a child, she recalled crying in fright at the shouting and spirit possession of the faithful. "And they would bring you from the creek . . . back to the church," Jessie Owens continued; "it didn't stop there at the river. It came back into the church and everybody fell in and rejoiced. . . . It was a grand time!" Despite the modern comfort of an indoor baptismal pool, Mr. Owens especially appreciated the biblical symbolism of being taken to the river for a baptism. In fact, the recollection of these old-time baptisms triggered the Soapstone congregation one morning to sing, "Take me to the river, take me to the river, take me to the river, to be baptized."

Frequently, baptisms were held during revivals or homecomings.[33] "A revival meeting would start like seven o'clock," Jessie Owens recalled, "and back in the old days, there was no such thing as leaving and going home early. . . . Everybody came in and had a good time." The meetings would run from Monday through Friday, and would feature guest ministers from the other black churches in the association. Homecomings were annual affairs, the first Sunday in May at Soapstone, and marked a return to the "home" church for former members, long-separated family, and even retired ministers. "Everybody come home," Elaine Parker observed. Mable Clarke explained, "We would have two services. We'd have morning service, then we'd break and we would eat, and then we'd come back in and have an afternoon program. And then . . . sometimes they'd let the young adults, you know, participate in the afternoon program." Between three huge oak trees alongside the schoolhouse, the men would erect tables of wooden slats in a circle, and the women would cover the boards with tablecloths and as much food as the tables could hold. "And nobody wasn't scared to eat," one woman recalled. "Oh, my goodness, we would fry chicken," Mable Clarke exclaimed. She continued: "Then they would have like . . . smoked pork chops like they smother them with gravy and onions and then you would have collard greens, green beans, . . . black-eyed peas, macaroni and cheese, candied yams [sighs]. And then all the cakes: coconut cakes, red velvet cakes, carrot cakes. . . . And then they would make lemonade." "And the mothers of the church," Elaine Parker remembered—"you know, they didn't have utensils to serve. . . . They used their hands. Their hands have cake icing and— seemed like that made the cakes better." Mable Clarke recalled: "Everybody out there just eating and fellowshipping and talking and people you hadn't seen for a long time, a lot of hugging and . . . a celebration. Like everybody . . . coming home." Everyone shared this homemade feast, physically located between the cemetery and the church, symbolically linking those past and present and anchoring both the living and the dead to their home place and to their God.

Education with Segregation

From Mable Clarke's birth in 1943 until after she left the area in 1961, public schools in Pickens County (and across much of the South) continued to be segregated. For the children of the Liberia community, then, this meant attending classes in the tiny clapboard schoolhouse built in 1928 or 1929 (described in chapter 4; see figure 7). By 1949, a visitor described the schoolhouse as "a one-room white wooden structure, which needs repainting and recovering. The interior is ceiled but unpainted, the floors are unoiled and dirty, and the blackboards are poor and insufficient in number. Kerosene lamps are used for lighting the room and a wood heater is used for both heating and cooking purposes. The children sit in double seats, but the teacher has no desk. The windows had curtains but posters on the walls were almost entirely lacking. Library materials are 'nil.' Type B lunches are served with the teacher preparing the meals. The toilets are the outdoor-pit type, as water is secured from a near by residence. . . . The teacher attended Seneca Junior College for two years."[34]

Mable Clarke and her seven siblings attended Soapstone School, along with about three other neighborhood children. Mable recalled a typical day: "We had one teacher [Mable's mother's sister, Lilly McJunkin]. She would teach first grade [through] . . . sixth grade. . . . And she would teach up until eleven o'clock. At eleven o'clock class was stopped, and she would send us with the buckets to go down the hill from the back of the schoolhouse to a little spring. And we had to bring the water up so she could cook for us. So the teacher would cook our lunch, and then we would help clean up the dishes, and then, after that, we would start school back up about one o'clock. And we'd stay in school from one 'til three." When the regular teacher had car trouble or otherwise could not teach, Lula Owens (Lilly McJunkin's sister, with three grades of education) walked up the hill from her home and taught school for the day.

Managing six grades in one room created some interesting learning opportunities for the pupils. Older children had chances to review lessons they had learned the year before, and younger children had previews of what they would learn in a year or two. The daily lesson plans, Mable explained, began with the teacher starting with "the first grade, . . . and then you would have to do your homework, and then she would go ahead and start with the grade books for the second grade, and . . . you'd have an assignment to get your work done. And then, . . . after she'd gone through that whole period, she would come back and check your paperwork and make sure that . . . you [were] doing what you're supposed to do. . . . The fifth, sixth, and the seventh grade, she would give you work like a day before and you need to be working on that while she's teaching the other class. . . . And then she would also let us participate with all the grades so they could even participate in helping us. . . . We was just like a whole big group learning together."

Judith White attended Soapstone School for a few years while living in the community with relatives. She recalled bringing in stove wood to heat the building during cold winter days and helping to cook the lunches of pinto beans, turnip greens, black-eyed peas, and cornbread—what would be called "soul food" today, Mable Clarke added, but back then "we just called it food." Government surplus commodities provided supplemental monthly cheese, dried fruit, powdered milk, and concentrated juice. "We'd get the leftover," Michael Owens admitted; "a pot of milk, a pot of eggs, old beans that's been around for a long time, . . . old peanut butter, stuff like that."

Black schools also got secondhand textbooks, and the children knew it. "My Daddy would hire whites to help us work in the field," Mable Clarke recalled, "and they would see our books and say, 'What [are] you doing with this book? These books's outdated; we had those books years ago.'" "There was mold, missing pages," Michael Owens noted. "It was just another way of keeping us back," Mable Clarke believed. As discussed in chapter 4, state history texts also reminded black pupils of their "inept" and "corrupt" ancestors who had governed the state under Reconstruction, while hidden transcripts of black family memories countered the prevailing "truth."

During recess, both black and white children played similar games on their separate schoolyards. Alice Jackson recalled that she and her white classmates "played ball and we played marbles. . . . Wore out our pants legs. . . . Did you ever play hopscotch?" she then asked Mable Clarke, who assented. "Drawing on the ground and then use a piece of broken glass, or dish" to sketch out the design, Mrs. Jackson continued; "and just regular old games that you never see nor hear of anymore." Both women laughed at the recollection of playing "doodle bug." "We would get some little sticks and we would crawl up under the schoolhouse" or other undisturbed places to find the small cones of ant lions' (*Myrmeleon* sp. larvae) nests. The children would chant, "'Doodle bug, doodle bug, your house is on fire!' And that little doodle bug would come up out of the dirt, sure would," Mrs. Jackson chuckled.[35] "Wasn't a lot to do," Mable added wryly.

Mable Clarke noted proudly that her mother strongly pressured her children to learn as much as they could, despite her relative lack of a formal education. Mable remembered her family subscribing to *Reader's Digest* every month: "And I used to get that little book, and just read different stories. Because what I found . . . the more you read, the more you understand. . . . And I remember we had this little old raggedy dictionary. The words I didn't understand, I would look them up. . . . And by doing that at a young age, it made it much easier for me once I became a young adult."

Integration for South Carolina schools became an increasing likelihood in the early 1950s as *Brown v. Board of Education* moved to the Supreme Court; to postpone what seemed inevitable, South Carolina's governor James Byrnes proposed a compromise. He argued that the optimal way to avoid desegregating South Carolina's schools was to consolidate rural, one-room school districts, to add school buses to transport black pupils for the first time, and to build brand-new grade and high schools for black pupils, so that separate and unequal could become separate and equal. Should that plan fail to meet the feared Supreme Court decision that separate schools can never be equal ones, Byrnes proposed closing all South Carolina public schools entirely.[36]

Besides a genuine desire to improve both black and white educational opportunities, Byrnes (like most South Carolina whites) desired to maintain segregated schools for as long as possible. To do so, he wanted to be careful to place the new black high schools nearest to black centers of population (paralleling northern de facto segregation), to prevent black pupils from being bussed past white high schools and thus having the NAACP "insist that Negro students be allowed to attend the white school which is nearer their homes."[37] Underlying his concern about integration, Byrnes ultimately feared miscegenation. Drawing upon the familiar trope of the black male rapist myth, Byrnes accused the "leaders of the colored race" as visualizing "the young [white] girl in high school playing tennis in shorts. They visualize traveling on a bus to a football game or a basketball game, . . . coming home at late hours of the night." From these daytime leers at tennis shorts or nighttime embraces in darkened buses, miscegenation occurs. And, Byrnes concluded, "trouble comes from people who are neither one race or the other and . . . want to make others unhappy."[38]

Byrnes's "educational revolution" directly affected the Oolenoy Valley. By 1953, the rural schoolhouse at Liberia closed, as districts modernized and consolidated. Four children remained. Several had not yet finished grade school, while others were entering high school, and this presented the Pickens County School District with a problem—the legal requirement of guaranteeing a free public education to all young citizens (black and white) while at the same time maintaining school segregation. Mable Clarke finished grade school at the black school in the city of Pickens, but the nearest black high school, Clearview, was in Easley, about ten miles away. Several of her siblings had already started school there; the Owens family had to rent rooms from friends and board their high school–aged children during the week (an added expense for black families not faced as often by white ones). After a strong protest from Lula Owens (see later in this chapter), the county modified a little yellow station wagon that drove up to Liberia at 6:30 A.M., picked the school children up, dropped some off in Pickens, and transported the rest on to Easley. The children had to eat their breakfast (cold bologna sandwiches) on the bus. In adjacent Greenville County, school children "had previously walked to school regardless of weather conditions" until James Monroe McJunkin obtained the first school bus for black children living north of Greenville, as part of Byrnes's "revolution." The drivers were McJunkin's son James Edward McJunkin and his cousin Spann Cruell Jr.[39]

Once she was old enough to drive, Mable carried her brother and herself in the little station wagon bus, down to Pickens to catch the main school bus to the black high school in Easley. Along the way, Mable passed the white Pickens High School, and (just as Governor Byrnes had feared), "I would say to my parents, . . . 'Why we got to go past this school?' We get up at five o'clock in the morning and we be on that poor school bus riding from here all the way to Easley. . . . And then [on the way back] when we got to Pickens we had to get off that bus and wait for the little small bus for here. So that's another forty-five minutes just standing . . . there in the yard of the elementary school waiting for the bus to make the round dropping the city kids off to come back and get us little country kids, bring us to the mountains."

Even at an early age, Mable Clarke noted the irony of segregation: "I didn't understand that, . . . because here my parents is interacting with whites coming sitting at our table eating, but we can't go to the same school. But you could sit here and you could eat my food!" By the penultimate years before desegregation in the mid-1960s, Don Owens was the only child left in Liberia, and he had to drive only himself in a thirty-student bus to Pickens, await the black school bus to Easley, and reverse the pattern on the way home every evening. The county schools finally desegregated by 1968, residents recalled, and Liberia's youth would have gone to Pickens High, but by this time no school-aged children remained in Liberia.

Like most rural children now consolidated in the more "urban" schools of the mill, railroad, or commercial towns like Pickens or Easley, the "country" Liberia kids faced typical taunts from their more sophisticated classmates. Philip Owens lasted only two years in Clearview High School because "I was always getting into fights. Broke my leg down there, fighting. . . . It was kind of rough!" Because the Owens children had to do farm chores before leaving for school in the mornings, Mable recalled, "you [had to] run back in there [the house] and try to freshen yourself up so you [could] get rid of the cow smell."

By the late 1950s, rock-and-roll music had become firmly planted into popular culture, even penetrating Upstate South Carolina. Southern adults (both black and white) viewed these new musical traditions as lewd and suggestive, while daring black and white teens challenged parental restrictions by embracing this music.[40] In her Easley high school, out of her rural environment, Mable Clarke encountered many new ideas. As "a little girl, you get a little fast, right?" she admitted, and continued: "So they would tell me about all these little new songs and things—you know, they weren't Christian songs. . . . And they had a little radio for me to listen to and I'm hearing all these little hip hop songs and all that stuff. So I came home and I was in the room there, . . . doing my little hip hop beat. My Momma looked at me and she said, 'Young lady, I don't know where you [are] picking that up from. You better take it back and leave it where you got it!' "

White Neighbors

Throughout their lives, Liberia's black residents had known white neighbors—as coworkers on the farms, the owners of the crossroads stores, the operators in the saw and grist mills, and the merchants in the shops in downtown Pickens and Easley. Whites controlled political offices and policed the streets as well. As discussed in chapters 3 and 4, blacks in the Oolenoy Valley (like their compatriots in the state and throughout the South) recognized the fine line of deference, respect, and humility that must be offered in the presence of unfamiliar whites in unfamiliar places, coupled with the friendship and camaraderie granted to familiar whites in the local area (the "normalizing gaze" of those in power). At the same time, as the civil rights movement gained momentum throughout the nation, the old-fashioned attitudes of deference and humility were gradually being replaced with attitudes of an increasing pride and directness, especially in the younger generations. The key to survival for blacks, however, still remained in knowing the rules for the appropriate type of performance in varying social circumstances (the infrapolitics of the powerless). "The subculture is essentially a set of adjustment devices for the restricted," sociologist Hylan Lewis argued, but it is also possible to apply more theoretical perspectives to examine the complexities of power relations during this time.[41]

"Many older Negroes have cordial sentimental relations with whites with whom they grew up or for whose families they have worked," Lewis noted about Kent, South Carolina (York County, see map 1).[42] "Back growing up on the farm," Jessie Owens reminisced, "we used to pick cotton. It was black and white out there in the cotton field." The integrated fields of the Oolenoy Valley reinforced the social connections between races.[43] Chris Owens hired white farmhands to work alongside his family in the fields, the Owens children remembered, and they shared chores and vegetables. Other whites pitched in with minor tasks when they came for a visit or a meal. Despite the fact that outside of Liberia drinking fountains and bathrooms were segregated by race, Jessie Owens remembered the farm workers boldly violating that law as they refreshed themselves from the well bucket during breaks: "and you'd just dip down and take a sip, and you'd pass it on to the white folks, and they'd take a sip and pass it to the black; they would take a sip." In fact, "my father used to chew tobacco," Owens continued, "and he'd bite off a chew of tobacco and he'd pass it to his white friend and they'd pass it to the next person and they'd pass it back to my father. That's how things worked back in the old days."[44]

One common memory for all the adult Owens siblings was the fact that virtually every day, some white friend or neighbor sat at their mother's table in their humble kitchen and shared the wonderful country cooking of Lula Owens. "I mean every day," daughter Mable Clarke recalled, "they'd know about noontime she would have food, and they'd just come right in, pull up a chair and sit down just to eat her cooking. And she enjoyed it. She always made enough, she did. . . . She didn't just cook for . . . the ten of us in the house." A Burgess family daughter remembered that "everything was just ready for the next meal."

Wherever he went, Chris Owens had white friends. In fact, "he had more white friends than he had black," a grandson recalled. "And the truth I tell you," Mable Clarke recalled, "when I grew up, I kind of grew up wondering, 'Where's the black people?'" "It was always traffic" past the Owens home, Mable Clarke asserted; "somebody's going to pull in here, wanting to buy a bushel of potatoes, a gallon of buttermilk or something." Sometimes neighbors would leave vegetables as well. White and black "hunting buddies" brought in "sacks of squirrels and rabbits," Mable Clarke explained. One area white woman recalled stories about her father sleeping at Chris Owens's home after the two of them had spent a long night hunting and "tasting" moonshine up by Table Rock. Other whites sat on the Owens porch and requested Chris Owens to sing hymns, and "they would sit there for hours," daughter Mable Clarke confessed; "they would just come here just for fellowship." Chris Owens "never met a stranger," a white neighbor added; "and you'd never thought they didn't know you all their life when you went over there."

As in previous decades, the Owens family name carried weight outside of Liberia as well. William Owens grumbled about having to work in the fields while his father sat down at the Burgess Store in Pumpkintown, shared a nickel Coke with his white friends, and socialized. Another white neighbor remembered driving around with his grandfather and Chris Owens, visiting white and black neighbors throughout the Oolenoy Valley; someone had bought a pint of moonshine, and both black and white men would share the jar. Peddling brought the Owens family in touch with an even wider network of white customers who then became friends as well. For example, Elizabeth Yeats, living in a valley above the Oolenoy, remembered Chris Owens selling vegetables to her family when she was a little girl, "and he always called me his baby." When Mrs. Yeats's father died, she poignantly recalled that Chris Owens paid his respects, and that he had bought a new pair of overalls (with the tag still attached) especially for the occasion. "He didn't have to do that," she concluded somberly, but she genuinely appreciated the fact that he had.

As in previous decades, white friendships established during these moments of mutual interaction might prove extremely valuable at later times and places in life.[45] It is possible to view this network of white patrons established by less powerful blacks as another hidden transcript, or a method by which those with less power manipulated those with more. For example, after leaving Liberia and joining the service in the 1950s, Philip Owens came home on leave but needed to buy a bus ticket to return to his unit on time or risk going AWOL. While in the uniform of a U.S. soldier in Greenville, he tried in vain to get the attention of the white bus station clerks from the small "blacks only" window in the back. Increasingly desperate to buy a ticket to catch his bus, he entered the "whites only" door and "next thing I know two [white] MP's, they came in, one on both sides, jacked me up like so [under his arms]. . . . They lift me up, set me out on the sidewalk." The MPs demanded to know where he needed to go, and then one entered the station, bought his ticket for him, and said to a surprised Philip Owens: " 'Take care, sir. I'll see you later. 'Cause I remember you from [your job as a carhop at] the Varsity Restaurant.' " In other words, a short-term "good" black carhop created social relationships that in the future became valuable. The more of these relationships established, the greater the chances one of them might save a life someday.

Ironically, while whites ate at Lula Owens's table and swapped stories on Chris Owens's porch, the Owenses could not attend the same churches, send their children to the same schools, and encourage their offspring to date white neighbors. It is these "experienced indignities" of daily life, James Scott observed, that help others to sense what that power gap feels like, to embody inequality in flesh and blood and feelings (Foucault's capillary forms of inequality).[46] For example, Philip Owens had been cautioned by his father to "go the other way" when white women offered their company; otherwise, "you'll get lynched." Michael Owens remembered eating in the back room in Woolworth's in downtown Greenville and riding in the back of the bus. His sister Mable Clarke described the separate bathroom facilities in more detail:

> They didn't say black then, they said "colored." And they were around back. They weren't close. . . . The whites [would] be all up near the front. . . . And you didn't know what was back there going to knock you in the head or whatever. . . . And water fountain if you was thirsty, you had to walk all the way around the back. And you find the old water fountain, and it was so dirty and nasty when you look at it, you . . . walk away. . . . When I head to the courthouse in Pickens, they had the same thing. Here's a courthouse, that's supposed to be . . . equally fair for everybody . . . citizens that pay taxes. And you got to go around to the back if you got to go to the bathroom, or water fountain. And if you was in court for something, . . . you couldn't sit in the courthouse with the whites, then, you had to go over there in your little corner that they had sectioned off.

Doctors had separate waiting rooms, Don Owens recalled, and the Owenses and other blacks parked behind and entered downtown Pickens stores through the back entrance; "and you [were] spending your money there to buy shoes" just like the whites, Mable Clarke added ironically.

Highlighting the racial divide were individuals who represented the physical embodiment of integration—those of mixed racial ancestry. Miscegenation (while illegal at this time) nevertheless took place at both a rate of occurrence and a level of consent that were impossible to document factually. Many of the residents of Liberia knew they shared last names and sometimes genetic ties with some of their white neighbors, and their white neighbors knew this as well. For example, a county official recalled a time when Chris Owens was relaxing on his porch, "and a white man came to see him and brought him a nip" of alcohol. The white man acknowledged that they were kin, "and he told him the story of how they got to be kin," the official added. At a discussion held with the Soapstone Church congregation, an African American woman recalled that when she was young, her family attended Mt. Nebo Baptist Church across the Oolenoy River from Soapstone. "And . . . there was two white ladies that would always come and sit in the back. . . . So we got to questioning, and Momma had told us . . . that those ladies back there were close kin to us." The woman added, "Uncle Will Terrell and Aunt Minnie used to tell us when we used to come up here, 'You got people that's lighter skin kin to you.'"

Despite possible (but rarely voiced) genetic and family ties, both whites and blacks recognized the invisible but all-too-real barrier of segregation, but this barrier varied tremendously in its differential impact. To whites, the barrier remained at worst an inconvenience preventing a greater degree of intimacy when socializing with black friends. For blacks, however, that same barrier created, maintained, and justified the tremendous political, economic, and social inequalities of daily life. Not violating that barrier became a constant source of stress and vigilance for every black in Liberia (and throughout most of the country, of course). Should that barrier ever be breached, then close white friends might jokingly remind their black neighbors of the boundary that had been crossed inadvertently. On the other hand, the violation of the segregation boundary might transform heretofore indifferent or barely tolerant whites into those much less tolerant and much more belligerent. Mable Clarke described the general social situation as a "climate of fear" (or Michael Taussig's culture of terror) because one never knew when whites might "turn on you."

The most effective way to avoid racial antagonism was to avoid racists, for "withdrawal and a certain passivity with respect to whites are rationalized as virtues in this subculture," sociologist Hylan Lewis observed.[47] Liberia's residents knew the rules about how to do so. Angela Young mentioned that "back in the day I don't think too many black people went to River Falls, . . . for fear there may be some trouble." (River Falls was the former plantation where Mrs. Young's great-grandfather Joseph McJunkin had been enslaved—see chapter 2 and map 2). In fact, she remembered her father talking about witnessing a Ku Klux Klan rally at a little crossroads store in Cleveland. Visiting their grandmother Emma McJunkin at Bald Rock, the Owens boys knew that they could not be "caught out there after dark," and even during the day Lula Owens shepherded her children through the woods to her mother's home rather than along the roads, to avoid white harassment. At the Cleveland resort where Philip Owens cleaned restrooms, he knew that "you cannot be on that property after five." "They had you trained to stay in your community," Mr. Owens added. Another woman remembered her father praying on the way home from night services at Soapstone that they would not have car trouble and become stranded somewhere they were unwelcome. Mable Clarke stated that "we were taught to always be aware" of strangers in Liberia as well. Her niece added that Chris Owens would "go get his shotgun, and just give them [a stranger] a warning shot, to let them know this is not the place to stop."

Even in normal social situations of shopping or socializing, Liberia's residents faced various types of harassment (additional capillary forms of social inequality). Home on leave, and while in the uniform of the U.S. military, Philip Owens not only had trouble hitching rides, but a cousin driving him to the bus station got pulled over for having "bald tires" (a police action he interpreted as harassment) and almost making him late for his bus. When Don Owens went to the Burgess Store in Pumpkintown as a boy, the white men sitting on the bench out front would "call you the N word," even though they knew his grandfather Chris Owens.

Children learned at an early age that there should always be "a measure of reserve in any relationship [with whites], no matter how cordial or benevolent."[48] In stores, while white children handled the merchandise as children typically did, black parents warned their children never to touch anything, to prevent accusations of theft. "So you always had to go like with your hands glued to your legs or body," Mable Clarke confessed, "because, you know, you just couldn't touch nothing." "And that was true the whole time you grew up," Mable Clarke continued; "I don't care what store you go into, it was somebody following you around—unless you were like in a little community store like here at Pumpkintown, where you grew up, you know. . . . And that's very uncomfortable," she acknowledged. "But you know," Mable concluded, "that kind of stuff lives with you, even 'til today."

Liberia's black residents also faced legal threats from their white neighbors. Both white and black families told stories about a prominent local white family who owned land adjacent to African American families, and members of this family used various strategies to obtain the land of their black neighbors (see chapter 4 for a similar story). One worked as a county surveyor, and "they'd have the [property] line anywhere where they wanted it to be," one man said; "and then, once it's in the [plat] book, you can't do nothing about it." Judith White recalled that same family charging her elderly grandfather with trespassing by crossing property lines, when in actuality a lawyer discovered the opposite—they had crossed *his* property line instead. Philip Owens remembered another family that cheated his mother's brother James McJunkin out of timber sales. They promised they would pay him $500 per tree stump; "they cut down all the trees and [were] gone, and . . . he [was] still there counting stumps." At that time, Owens continued, blacks had very little recourse when faced with pervasive racism and an all-white police and legal system, and their white exploiters knew it: "you go to court, and what . . . you gonna face that white judge, all right? You go to jail, you'll face the white jailer. . . . Anything you do, you got to go through the white system."

The agricultural system also favored the white landowners. Philip Owens related a story about a local white landowner who operated a typical tenant farmer scheme against Chris Owens.[49] Owens had borrowed money in the spring of the year to buy the cotton seed and fertilizer to plant a crop on land rented from the owner, expecting to make his money back, plus a profit, at harvest. After the white family had sent a truck to pick up the harvested cotton bales, they claimed to have run into a ditch and lost most of the cotton. When Chris Owens went to the mill for payment, he received a brown paper bag full of one-dollar bills. "He got in the house and counted it and said it was only something like seventy-five dollars," Philip Owens explained. With a bale then going for much more than that, and having harvested at least ten bales, Chris Owens had anticipated much more money than he actually got. Lula Owens wailed and cried, but "it didn't do no good," Philip Owens explained. As was typical of many tenant farmers (both black and white), Owens continued, "he couldn't read or write, my father, too well. He didn't have too much education" (three grades, in fact).[50]

The closing of Soapstone School during rural consolidation and Governor Byrnes's attempt to circumvent integration presented Liberia's residents with another confrontation with perceived attempts to deny African Americans equal opportunity. With the closing of the school about 1953, Jessie Owens related, the county superintendent of schools initially made no further attempt to transport the remaining Liberia children to a segregated high school; instead (according to daughter Mable), he told a complaining Lula Owens: " 'Well, you have all those kids, why don't they just stay there and work the farm?' . . . My mother says, 'No, these kids are going off to high school; they're going to get an education, and I'm going to see to that.' And she left, never heared any more from the superintendent. . . . So mother went back to Pickens and met with the superintendent and she really scolded him. . . . And Momma says, 'Look, if I have to call Columbia [the state capital], I will.' The next week, she got word that there would be a bus to take my sister and I to school." The county bought a brand-new yellow station wagon so the children (some in high school) could attend the black grade school in Pickens.

As shown throughout Liberia's history, blacks resisted the apparent hegemonic power of whites with public transcripts (as well as hidden ones), reasserting their self-respect and their humanity but potentially endangering their property and even their lives. "It used to be that if a black man did what . . . white people thought was the wrong thing, . . . they thought they had the right to whip us!" Angela Young explained; "and some of us, we were determined that we weren't going to be whipped."

On the night of July 21, 1957, eleven members of Greenville County's Ku Klux Klan invaded the home of Claude Cruell, "a moderately prosperous fifty-eight-year-old Negro farmer and Baptist deacon," living about three miles south of Young's father's home in the Gold Mine (see map 2). Four of the Klansmen chained Cruell up and beat him while the others watched. Fannie Cruell, Claude's wife, was driven several miles away and forced to walk home. The Klansmen berated the couple for "'trying to mix with white folks.'" In actuality, the Cruells had been assisting an illiterate, impoverished white handyman, his anemic wife, and seven children by renting a place to them, babysitting their children, and sharing rides.[51]

Directly in response to this incident, Angela Young stated, her father, James McJunkin, went to the local hardware store the next day and bought a gun, announcing to the store owner that he would be prepared "if they come to my house." Just a young girl at the time, Mrs. Young remembered that night of terror: her father had a rifle, her brother a shotgun, "and we girls had—Daddy popped the top off of a Pepsi bottle. So he said, 'When they come in, you girls, you all stab them with these Pepsi bottles,' 'cause see that jagged edge, that's going to startle you." Perhaps because of the advanced warning, Mrs. Young speculated, or perhaps because they never intended to attack in the first place, "they never came to our house. [But] . . . we were ready."

Angela Young recounted another time, early in her marriage, when her husband had taken their family automobile to a repair shop in Marietta. The white mechanic had fixed it once but unsatisfactorily; Mr. Young returned for a better repair job and the mechanic threatened him, saying, "'I'll kill me a nigger!'" Angela Young's father, James McJunkin, once had a run-in with the same man, who used the same taunt. To retaliate, McJunkin got his gun and parked his truck across the street from the repair store. Had that white mechanic walked across the road, Young assured her listeners, her father would have killed him. "Daddy was fearless," Young stated proudly.

Mable Clarke, Young's first cousin, remembered her father, Chris Owens, as equally courageous in the face of harassment: "They would not attack him, because they know one thing—my Daddy would fight back. . . . You didn't mess with him, period. . . . I remember one time he took the black-jack from the police and whooped him with his own blackjack. . . . But you know they would do stuff to us children. But when they saw him the fear come in, and they would never . . . call him a 'nigger' or anything like that, because . . . if they called my Daddy that, the next thing, my Daddy was so fast with the knife, you might have your throat laying there on the floor. . . . I mean that's just the way he controlled this land, and he had to."

Even black children faced life-threatening situations. For example, one morning Mable Clarke had been asked by her teacher at Soapstone School to bring up the lunch Lula Owens had prepared for the children. She continued: "I ran back down the road and was on my way back and this white man just came out of the woods out of nowhere and tried to snatch me. And I just threw down what I had and ran back to my house, and then my mother— . . . my mother was a very tall lady and she was strong and she ran and she caught him and she said, 'You see this pick [pitch] fork?' she said. 'If I ever catch you one more time on this road,' she said, 'I'll *pick* you up with this pick fork and that'll be the last of you!' So we never saw him anymore." "There's so many stories that, if you're black American, that never get told," Mable Clarke lamented.

The Owens family related another story that could have ended tragically. Jessie Owens was driving his father's '39 Chevy truck, leading another flatbed truck loaded with black and white field hands on their way to pick crops. Driving down State Highway 288, "two pretty dogs" ran into the road. Owens had been driving a school bus for two years, and so he knew that if he braked suddenly, the men in the flatbed truck would become air-borne. Thus, he reasoned, "I had to keep going. I killed one of the dogs, which hurt me very deeply. Well, the next following Saturday, I was coming from the bean field, . . . driving Dad's old car. Pulled up to the stop sign right there, at 288 and Highway 8; there was two white guys that knew my father. I stopped; they came over and says, 'How's old Chris doing?' I say, 'He's doing fine.' The next one snuck up behind him, punched me in the nose. I was bleeding *all* the way down. . . . [I drove away, but] they had a better car than I had. They beat me to the turn and blocked the bridge where I couldn't get across. They came out [with] sticks, screaming and a-hollering and using the 'word,' if you know what I mean."

Just as Jessie Owens was preparing to fight for his life, he heard his father's old Chevy truck coming up the road. The senior Owens demanded to know what was going on, and the whites claimed they had only been "talking to" his son. Owens requested that his son be allowed to pass, and they let him through to go home. However, Jessie Owens admitted he was "pretty mad," and he grabbed a shotgun and raced from the house with another brother, back to confront his attackers. "And that's when the battle started," Owens continued; "no one got killed, but . . . they knew that we meant business." The whites countered with a mob and attacked the Owens family by shooting up their house. Eventually the sheriff stepped in and calmed matters, but he also cautioned the younger Owens brother to carry an unloaded shotgun with him on the school bus. "I drove a school bus for two years with that shotgun in here," Owens admitted, and "didn't have any more trouble."

For the entire Owens family, perhaps the most traumatic event they faced occurred during Mable Clarke's girlhood, probably in the mid-1950s.[52] "It was on a Sunday," Mrs. Clarke narrated, when her father had gone to Marietta to visit his sister Willie Mae. Mable herself was about eleven or twelve, and the Owens children had gathered on the front porch of their home while Lula Owens read the Bible and told the children stories. Suddenly, they noticed their father's mother's brother, Clarence "Clance" Glenn (Grandma Rosie's brother, by now an old man), trotting up the dirt road toward the house, shouting to the family to " 'get the guns! Get the guns!' "

A white prostitute living across the road from Uncle "Clance" had been entertaining three or four nonlocal Ku Klux Klan clients, and in drunken amusement they had decided that a white woman should not live among blacks.[53] In order to drive Mr. Glenn off his land, they came upon him milking his cow in a barn near the prostitute's home, shot a hole in his milk bucket and demanded he lick the milk off the ground. "Made him take off his shoes," Jessie Owens added. Then they seized him by the neck and (Mable recalled) said, " 'Nigger, get the hell out of here!' " and told him they were going to drive all the blacks out of the area for good. "Old guy was nervous and shaking," Philip Owens noted. Fearing for his life, Mr. Glenn raced to his grandnephew's house for protection and (Mable recited), to warn his kin: " 'You all need to get your guns 'cause . . . they said they [are] going to make their way down here to kill you all!' "

Mable Clarke's voice then slowed as she continued the story. Lula McJunkin Owens, the granddaughter of a former slave and equally powerful defender of her family and her community (Patricia Hill Collins's example of an othermother), told her children to remain calm. "We were scared to death," Mable Clarke admitted. Lula Owens ordered her daughters into the house (Mable holding her infant nephew), and commanded her sons to get the family's guns and to follow her through the woods. She led her sons silently toward the back of the prostitute's home, where the Klansmen were drinking and laughing about their racist attack. Mable remembered her mother saying grimly, "'When I raise the pick [pitch] fork, I want you all to start shooting and don't stop. You got plenty of ammunition.' . . . Said, 'We got to take them down.' Said, 'If we don't, they [are] going to run us off the land.'" Lula Owens raised the pitchfork and bullets flew everywhere. From the relative safety of the Owens home, Mable and her sisters heard "the bullets just a-ringing, just a-ringing. And even as I talk about it now [voice chokes up and slows], I still hear those shots. I still hear those shots. I remember those faces. . . . It's just always been a nightmare with me."

But the Klansmen, bloodied and outraged, remained undeterred. They drove to the Burgess Store in Pumpkintown to bandage themselves up, and (Mable Clarke recalled) demanded that Mr. Burgess help them "'get a mob up, 'cause we need to go over there and kill them niggers tonight!'" Demonstrating the critical importance of white friendships as a hidden transcript means of protection for blacks, Mr. Burgess refused their request (Mable related), saying, "'You done made a mistake. . . . You best to get back across the [state] line . . . because you done messing with the wrong families over there. You're not going to run them off the land. . . . I've known that family; they're good people.'" Instead of helping to organize a mob, Burgess called the sheriff. The sheriff told Chris Owens (who by now had returned from his sister's house) that if the marauders invaded his home that night, he should kill them, drag them outside the door, and he would pick them up.

"So that night nobody slept," Mable Clarke explained; "you know we sit up in the window." Late at night, headlights dimmed, the Klansmen's car drove by as anticipated and opened fire on the little home. "But they never came close to the house, you know, just . . . passing by shooting," Mable Clarke noted. Meanwhile, Chris Owens had positioned his sons in the ditch in front of the house, and as the Klansmen's car passed a second time, Jessie Owens recited, "Daddy says, 'Boys, let's let 'em have it!'" And the Owens boys did exactly that. "We blew out one of the tires," Mable Clarke announced. The Klansmen fled for their lives and never returned, but the Owens siblings remembered the incident vividly. Mable Clarke, the youngest child, still suffers: "As children, you know, we lived in fear. . . . Every night you'd hear a little noise, you'd figure they were coming, you know. So my Dad had all the boys sleep with guns beside the bed at night" (voice chokes up).[54]

Leaving Liberia

Given the overwhelming racial tension during this time, coupled with the economic challenges promulgated by racism and social inequality, many African Americans in the South in general, in South Carolina, and in Pickens County severed their deeply emotional ties with the land of their ancestors and left the area entirely—flight being another form of resistance.[55] Despite the beauty of the landscape, many departed because, as Mable Clarke admitted, "when I was growing up . . . I kept seeing all the hard work in the field, you know, picking the cotton. . . . I never saw the mountains. . . . And that same mountain was still right there; it was on the same land, but I never saw it. . . . I saw it in the sense of a name, but not really what it represented. Because . . . you grow up here, you [are] so busy with the farm work and . . . the [racial] struggle, . . . so your mind is overwhelmed with all of that, so you don't take time to sit back and say, 'Wow!' "

As with those described in previous chapters who had left, the lives of some of the Owens siblings reflected the common trends of southern blacks in general. For example, after struggling in the segregated black schools for several years around 1950, Philip Owens was drafted into the Army during the Korean War. He left his father his '39 Buick that he had used to get to work in Greenville and departed for induction. He recalled traveling from Fort Jackson, South Carolina, to Fort Benning, Georgia, on a troop train, and being cautioned to pull the shades down on the windows because "the white folk would shoot you and kill you" because of racial antagonism directed against an African American in the uniform of the U.S. military.

After mustering out in Boston, Philip Owens had already married and had a baby on the way. While still serving in the Reserves, Owens "thought I'd want to try to find myself," he acknowledged. He worked in factories, learned to be an electrician, bought some real estate, and prospered. "I just started making money up there," Owens noted; "I never could make no money down here." When visiting his family back in Liberia, Owens conceded, "I come down looking good—you know, with a new car, new shoes, dressed up!" He bought his mother a new electric pump for her well and impressed his other siblings, including his older brother Michael, who had been struggling to find meaningful work in the segregated Upstate in the late 1950s.

Michael Owens left a series of low-paying jobs in the Upstate (see preceding section) and eventually joined his younger brother in Boston. An early job for Michael Owens was "working at a university hospital; stayed there 'til I got burnt—I got my hip burnt." He left. By now also married, Michael Owens "worked a regular job and then do a little part time work" to make more money than he had ever made down in South Carolina. After a period of about five years, with failing health and a homesick wife, Owens decided to return home—plus "we had to fight all that snow and everything."

By 1961, Mable Owens Clarke had graduated from high school and also had struggled to find meaningful employment. "I looked for jobs from Travelers Rest to Greenville—everywhere," Mable recalled. Her parents already had enrolled another brother in South Carolina State College (the principal state-supported black university), "so there was no money for me to go," she acknowledged. Increasingly frustrated by her underemployment, Mable Clarke faced a very emotional decision—to leave the land of her ancestors, that she had helped nurture, or to debase herself by taking low-wage, meaningless jobs. "There was a curtain that dropped in front of me," she admitted, "and I had to figure out, OK—I have to push this curtain back, and walk through it, and go—if I want to—be able to find myself." She called her brother in Boston and went to live with him.

As a country girl from South Carolina now living in the urban North, Mable had a few adjustments to make. She remembered smiling and waving at all her neighbors, calling across yards and just being very outgoing and friendly—"you know, the little Southern girl," she admitted. And her neighbors would just eye her oddly and not respond. On her first experience with the New Jersey Turnpike, driving her brother Philip's Buick and displaying her father's penchant for speed, "she put it through the test!" Philip Owens confessed. Pursued by a state trooper, the quiet country mouse suggested to her shocked brother that she try to outrun the patrol car, but cooler heads prevailed and they only received a speeding ticket.

During her time in Boston, Mable Clarke labored in several factories, learned bookkeeping, eventually worked for her brother's electrical firm, and even opened a clothing boutique. "And it was great," Clarke recalled, and elaborated: "I had such opportunities to meet so many great people that . . . took time to set the pace for me, being in the big city. And I learned so much. . . . And I really feel bad for the people that never had the opportunity or chance to get out of here . . . to get that opportunity to learn 'cause they missed a lot that life has to offer."

Especially liberating to Mable Clarke was living without the overwhelming and constricting gaze of white racial power. "I could walk in stores" in Boston, Mable Clarke admitted, and realize that "nobody's watching me, nobody is looking at me," expecting her to steal. She even wondered, "Is this a different America?" "I mean, you know, I was like eighteen when I went there," Mable explained, "and to see this experience I said, 'Gosh, this is really nice!'" She did not want to return to the restricted life of the segregated South. Later in life she did return, but reflecting on her flight, Mable observed, "if I hadn't a-gotten out of here . . . I know I would not have developed into the person that I am because it's just like a stifle, and you don't know how to grow and how to get out of this boundary that you're in."

Pamela McJunkin, daughter-in-law of James Monroe McJunkin, also escaped the social and physical boundaries of the area by following kin ties drawing her northward, as she left with her husband for better educational opportunities in Ohio. "He had an aunt there," she explained, "and I had an aunt there." Although both had strong ties in South Carolina, "he [her husband] couldn't find a job," McJunkin continued. Even though her husband had been offered a scholarship to South Carolina State College, Pamela McJunkin continued, "we would've wanted to stay," but "it was the segregation that drove us away. We . . . couldn't put up with that, so he just wanted to go on."

Coming Home to Liberia

Despite the tremendous forces of racial antagonism and economic desperation propelling Liberia's residents to leave their communities, two equally strong forces pulled them back: aging relatives and a longing for the land their ancestors had fought so hard to obtain and retain. These forces are intertwined, for land and people connect through memory and story in Upstate culture, for both black and white (see chapter 8).[56] Land becomes symbolically important because ancestors owned it; because descendants still own it, live on it, and tell stories about it; and because kin may have been (and continue to be) physically embedded in it (through burial). Aging relatives maintained a dwindling hold on land, and so many times (as already seen in previous chapters), children returned to care for aging relatives and to safeguard their family's heritage.

Liberia's residents proudly held onto their lands (and some of their land titles) for several critical reasons: they had struggled against racist pressures to deprive and/or cheat them of ownership, they had worked so many decades (even centuries) to earn the money to own that land, and they had established spiritual and emotional ties to that land. Many Sundays, James Monroe McJunkin came to Liberia to visit with his sister Lula

McJunkin Owens (and her husband, Chris), and the pair would spend hours poring over plat maps outlining McJunkin family property up at Bald Rock. Mable Owens Clarke remembered that "he had everything marked off and it was just like reading the Bible. And him and my mother would sit there at the kitchen table and go over it—over and over, year after year, Sunday after Sunday after Sunday." In fact, Angela Young (McJunkin's daughter) listed by memory every land purchase made by her lineal relatives, beginning with the freed slave Joseph McJunkin in 1869 (see chapters 2 and 3). "Owning land was just a priority for him," Mrs. Young added; "and Daddy went so far as to, when he drew up his will, to put in there that the land that he left us, his children, was never to be sold." "That's [the] same thing my Mom and Dad said, too," Mable added; "they instilled that in us for some reason." Even though Chris Owens had worked in Greenville around 1930 (see chapter 4), he returned to the land of his ancestors to care for his aging grandmother, Aunt Katie. By the time of Mable's childhood, nothing could have pried him from his land.

Even for those who had to leave for reasons discussed above, memory of place offered a powerful gravitational pull, reinforced with each subsequent visit home. As a child, Robert Parker loved "going up to Uncle Chris's. . . . I loved to go up to Soapstone, 'cause—something about it, you know. Daddy'd tell me about the school and all he went to up there." Whenever the family would visit, Elaine Parker's father-in-law "would get in the car with us and . . . go up to Soapstone. So see that gave him a chance to go up to his old stomping ground where he was raised and born, and where his Daddy was born and raised. . . . When I think back, it's just good memories. Good memories, 'cause we had some good times up there. To this day, I remember those good times that we had, you know, visiting family." After living in Boston for several years, Michael Owens returned home because he "missed seeing people what I know."

A white woman, born and raised in the Oolenoy Valley and now a county employee, recalled fond memories of sitting on the front porch of the Owens home with Chris and listening to his stories of the area: "I loved his story about how . . . it came to be Liberia. . . . He'd tell you about how proud he was of the land. . . . And he wanted to keep the land and had kept it in the family. And he'd point to the houses over here and the houses over here and how most of the family'd stayed there. Some had moved off and some had come back. But he was still proud of the fact that he was there on that land grant and he'd been done right, so to speak. . . . And he'd just point and be so proud of it."

In her recollection, the narrator indicated the way that memory and story become the threads tying people to place through time, and how the continued occupancy of that place makes this linkage culturally real. In fact, as a local herself, she understood better than outsiders what Chris Owens meant as he paused, silently pointing to his fields across the little country road. Standing on the porch of his family home (one that still stands), Chris Owens visually surveyed his present property and his children's homes, but through his stories, ancestors like Katie Owens and Joseph McJunkin reanimated that same landscape, thus layering it with a depth of centuries of human lives.

Conclusion

Despite the powerful hold of land and memory, by the early 1960s very few residents remained in Liberia. Those who remained, however, witnessed some dramatic changes that escalated through the next decade. Because of the nation's civil rights movement, Jim Crow segregation gradually faded, as blacks entered a diversifying workforce and a nationalizing region. From the end of World War II to the early 1960s, the Oolenoy Valley's residents had transitioned from a primarily agricultural area of self-sufficient farms to a rural workforce for city occupations. Paved roads and electricity made this rural-urban connection stronger, and various forms of mass media brought national and international news into every home. Chris and Lula Owens still bantered politely with their white neighbors, but more frequently now topics might have included thoughts on "the race problem." Perhaps stemming directly from the unspoken tension between the diminishing (perceived) loss of control by whites and the increasing (relatively) equality of blacks, Liberia soon faced the darkest episode in its history—an episode that then became its brightest moment.

6 Because Hatred Is All It Was

Death and Resurrection

· ·

A scan through the headlines of the *Greenville News* (published in the largest regional city) from April 1967 reveals the general concerns of the nation at this time. Israel was fighting with Syria in the Near East. In Southeast Asia, the Vietnam War raged on, with hundreds of American soldiers killed or wounded each month. Communist casualties (those of North Vietnamese and the Viet Cong [Vietnamese troops]) ranged into the thousands, according to official reports. President Lyndon Johnson argued with Congress over the president's Southeast Asia policy, while former vice president Richard Nixon gained in popularity among Republicans. Antiwar protesters marched in American streets. Richard Speck was on trial in Peoria for the mass murder of eight female student nurses in Chicago the summer before. Less than three years earlier, Congress had passed, and Johnson had signed into law, the 1964 Civil Rights Act and the 1965 Voting Rights Act, which drew upon the Reconstruction-era Fourteenth and Fifteenth Amendments to guarantee federal protection for African American civil and voting rights. By spring 1967, the Ku Klux Klan was marching and protesting against the growing civil rights movement across the nation, as "Negroes" across the South registered to vote in ever-increasing numbers.

On Friday, April 14, 1967, the *Greenville News* published (p. 4) an unsigned editorial calling upon the area's "Negro" population to repudiate "another self-appointed civil rights leader corrupted by power": Dr. Martin Luther King Jr., "holder of a doctorate of divinity of uncertain origin" and the winner of a Nobel Peace Prize "which robbed the award of what lustre [*sic*] it had." Accused of being a subversive and promoting a Communist agenda, King (the editorial noted) was "beginning to tie the rope around his own neck" as he alienated more and more people. His gospel of civil disobedience played into the hands of world Communism, the editorial warned, and eventually would lead to the Communist takeover of Southeast Asia. The editorial reported that "whispers are current" that local Negro leaders might want to bring King to Greenville to speak; the consequences of that visit would destroy the "growing cooperative spirit" between local leaders, and instead, "racial bitterness . . . would rise like a killing tide." The editorial concluded by declaring that local Negro ministers should reject such false prophets. Regional readers, both black and white, would have noticed the editorial's cautionary references to the "killing tide" of antagonism potentially created by King's visit and the more obvious lynching reference, triggering black recollections of past injustices. Of course, black readers (by now with an increasing distaste for traditional southern white paternalism) also would have noticed the editorial's condescending reference to King's graduate diploma and the dismissive attitude toward King's international recognition by the Nobel Peace Prize Committee.

But there is an even more subtle "truth" revealed by this editorial. Anthropologist Michael Taussig (chapter 1) described the culture of terror directed by colonial occupiers against indigenous peoples, which becomes inverted by the colonizers into indigenous violence allegedly perpetrated against colonials, thus justifying the "legitimate" and often horrific retaliation by colonial powers against indigenous peoples. As in the past with apocryphal stories of black male rapists triggering the white culture of terror toward black males, in this editorial, the historic white-led "killing tide" of racial antagonism is inverted to become a warning about a potential increase of "racial bitterness" engendered among blacks and directed against whites because of King's visit. Even more dramatic is the inversion in the lynching reference: it is King himself, not a white lynch mob, who is "beginning to tie the rope around his own neck." In this way, both white and black readers are reminded that any attempts at black self-assertiveness will lead to a lynch mob; according to the editorial, it is the black community itself that brings on the inevitable retaliation. Such reminders of hegemonic power and racialized violence reinforced the sense of inequality recognized by all of the paper's readers.

While all of these national issues affected people in the Oolenoy Valley, perhaps the greatest concern for local folks came from a mysterious rash of brush fires breaking out in the area in the late spring. On April 12, the weekly *Easley Progress* (p. 3) reported that County Forest Ranger Charlie Gravely warned that dry weather conditions had transformed wooded areas into " 'a keg of powder waiting for some fool to pull the trigger.' " At least one local fire was due to the careless burning of trash, but some of these fires, especially "about two miles north and east of Pumpkintown" (in the Liberia area, behind the church, on Gowens Creek), appear to have been set deliberately by " 'incendiaries.' " There was a report of a person seen tossing " 'a can of flaming substance into roadside bushes' " in another place along a county road. The next day, the weekly *Pickens Sentinel* (p. 2) ran approximately the same story.

By April 1967, few black residents remained in Liberia, but the old Ansel McKinney house (now abandoned) sat in the woods about 400 yards to the east of the church, the Owens family lived at the foot of the hill to the north of the church, and in front of them lived a married Owens son and his family. Soapstone Baptist Church, by 1967 about sixty years old, most likely had become a tinderbox. Described in detail in chapter 4 (see figure 6), the wood frame church sat on a knoll near exposed soapstone rocks, as it had for generations of Liberia's residents. About thirty feet southwest from the church, across a dirt parking area, sat the old one-room schoolhouse (built about 1929; see figure 7); just beyond the schoolhouse was the new Soapstone Church cemetery, with about a dozen graves by this time. Behind the church a small stream drained to Gowens Creek.

On Saturday, April 22, 1967, Lula McJunkin Owens celebrated her seventy-first birthday.[1] Undoubtedly she and her immediate family prepared for honoring her important event at Sunday services at the Soapstone Baptist Church the next day. That evening the sun had set about 7:00 P.M., and the almost-full moon was slowly rising over the hills. Well outside of the lights of any city or town, Liberia had only sporadic county sheriff protection with no rural volunteer fire department coverage at this time. The peaceful little enclave was utterly vulnerable to attack.

Don Owens, living in the brick house in front of his grandparents, remembered that he had come home from work that Saturday evening and about 7:00 P.M. had just settled down to his mother's dinner at home. He continued: "And somebody come knocking on the door, and they was knocking real fast. So I got up and opened the door, and the lady said, 'Your church is burning down up there!' And I couldn't—you know, it hits you at once. And I said, 'You sure it's our church?' And she said, 'Look!' and I looked, and I see this flame there, and I hollered at Momma, and they come out and look and so we all took off up to the church. We got up there, it was gone; I mean, it was going down. But there was a lot of people there already, I mean white friends . . . I guess they'd seen it, or heared it. A lot of people there."

And then, Mr. Owens continued, "about—I guess less than a few minutes, Furman's house [the old Ansel McKinney home], you know, right out that dirt road, it went up, it went 'Boom!' Just like that. So there was two—church was burning, and our half brother's [Furman's] house was burning down. Same time." As Soapstone Baptist Church burned furiously, and as the Mc-

Kinney home, about 400 yards away, exploded into a second conflagration, someone in the crowd discovered a chilling message. Mable Clarke had heard that someone had noticed words scrawled into the dirt parking lot: "The Klansmen paid you a visit."

With no rural volunteer fire departments, the shocked and horrified members of the crowd relied on their only viable alternative—they called the nearest South Carolina Forestry Commission ranger, who lived about ten miles up the Oolenoy River valley in the neighboring crossroads community of Holly Springs. Edgar Smith, the ranger who responded, could not remember the date of the burning, but he directly related the event to the period of time "during some of this between the blacks and whites." Smith continued: "And they called me one Saturday night and said come to Soapstone Church. And I got up there and it was burned to the ground. It was completely burned down. And I felt bad, but again I was scared, 'cause I was standing there by myself; everybody's gone. And I was standing there by myself. I didn't know who was going to be coming by. I didn't know what to expect." In that same interview, Smith verified, "I was the only one there that night" after the fire, and in a later interview elaborated: "When I drove up and seen what had happened, I was afraid." Smith's first thought was that the fires had been set deliberately by arsonists; thus, his fear that the perpetrators remained in the area and might attack the first responders. Smith's second thought, though, was anger. He recalled that he "stood there and cried to see something so uncalled for. Because hatred is all I could [think of]. That's all it was. Had to be."

While recalling events from over forty years ago, residents offered varied opinions as to the cause of the twin burnings. Philip Owens, in a discussion with his sister and brother, remembered that his mother (Lula) had told him that "they were having trouble with white folks going out there [behind Soapstone Church], . . . and they were taking girls out there with the play house, and I think they didn't want to be doing that out there on the church grounds. I think that might've set it off. I'm not sure—I'm just speculating." Mable thought that they were parking behind the church on a little dirt road and would "hide back in the back of the church." Philip Owens added that he had heard that these young adults were "breaking in the church there for a while." Another woman, in a discussion group at Soapstone Church after services one Sunday, acknowledged that "we never found quite out what happened to the first church. We don't know whether it was arson or what, but it never was proven that it was an electrical fire or anything so we just think it was arson." Most local whites never even had heard of the event, or had completely forgotten about it. Colleen Zimmerman, for example, lived about five miles away and admitted: "I didn't know about the church burning until Mable mentioned that the other day. . . . I guess I just wasn't aware of it." Only one known eyewitness to the event remains in the Liberia community today.

Although she was living in Boston at the time, Mable Clarke had been told that the county sheriff back then knew that certain locals had burned down the church; even Edgar Smith, an experienced firefighter first on the scene, agreed with the assumption of arson. In fact, standing at the scene the night of the event, Smith felt an eerie sense of danger, suggesting to him that there had been a criminal act. Given the fact that "incendiary" fires had been reported in precisely the same area for the past several weeks, given the fact that two buildings went up in flames almost simultaneously, and given the fact of the reported inscription in the parking lot, evidence strongly suggested arson.

It is also interesting to note the association between the rising tide of the civil rights movement across the United States, the anti-King editorial in the *Greenville News* from about two weeks earlier, the mysterious "incendiary" brush fires in the immediate area, and the celebration of Lula McJunkin Owens's birthday that very night. With the family undoubtedly gathered at the Owens family home below the church, with the community's attention thus directed away from the church on the hill, and with the arsonist already having gained some experience in setting fires, perhaps the suspected arson at Soapstone Church and the old McKinney home was intended as another in a long series of warnings to the Owens family to abandon the Liberia area. The Owens family and the Liberia community certainly took it that way—but the hypothesized intention backfired.

On Monday, April 24, 1967, the *Greenville News* (p. 6) broke the story, reporting from Pumpkintown that "two fires believed set by an arsonist destroyed an old church and an unoccupied home near here late Saturday night." According to the news article, the fire was called in about 8:30 P.M. (supporting eyewitness accounts). A deputy sheriff told the reporter that "about 30 minutes after the 62-year-old church flared up, a frame house about 400 yards behind the building burst into flame. Both structures were leveled" (again supporting eyewitness recollections of two fires, set at slightly different times). Furthermore, the paper observed, a detective with the South Carolina State Law Enforcement Division (SLED) was investigating the fires as arson.[2] On Wednesday, April 26, the weekly *Easley Progress* (p. 6) reported that county deputies and a SLED arson investigator continued the probe of the fires, "but no definite clues have been found so far, the officers said." The story did not appear in the weekly *Pickens Sentinel*, perhaps because nothing more newsworthy had happened over a twenty-four-hour period.

Perhaps part of the rising tide of racial bitterness predicted (or even triggered) by the *Greenville News* editorial two weeks earlier, the destruction of a small black rural church and the intimidating use of arson sparked an immediate positive response by both blacks and whites. "A lot of people gave donations right then," Don Owens recalled, " 'cause they felt bad for us." In fact, one of the first to donate was Edgar Smith, the white firefighter who had stood, forlorn and frightened, at the sight of the smoldering jumble of charred timbers and crumpled tin roofing. Smith felt so awful about the hatred that (in his opinion) had burned Soapstone Church and about his helplessness to save the building that he had decided to do something positive to help the Liberia community as soon as possible afterward. At that time, Smith explained, he was teaching "a little Sunday school class over here" at Holly Springs Baptist Church. Mr. Smith encouraged his pupils to save their "pennies and nickels, dimes, and putting [the money] in a pot to donate to the Soapstone Church. And believe it or not, we come up with about sixty-nine or seventy dollars." Later, in another interview, he exclaimed: "That was money then! And that's where I really learned to love and where they give a lot of love, Chris and Miss Lula. And from then on, Chris Owens was my buddy. We were good friends."

Additional help soon followed. While the daughter of the minister at that time recalled her father receiving donations from the ministers and deacons of other black churches in the surrounding counties, everyone agreed that Lula McJunkin Owens, by this time in her early seventies, became the principal instrument by which money was collected for the reconstruction effort. Lula Owens's emotional ties to this church ran deep. Not only was it her family's current church, but it also had been founded by her formerly enslaved grandfather, Joseph McJunkin, right after the Civil War (see chapter 3). Lula's daughter Mable Owens Clarke proudly recounted the story of her mother's crusade to restore the church:

> She took her little book—bought her a little notebook, and she went from house to house asking for donations to help build the church back. 'Cause she said, "There will be a church!" . . . And my Mom and Dad used to peddle [farm produce] on . . . Saturdays. They would go peddling like down through Marietta, Travelers Rest, and

ended up [in] some parts of Greenville with their vegetables and milk and butter and the eggs. And on her peddling route she would take her book and she would collect money to—"Help my church out; my church [has] been burned." And everybody would give money. In the grocery store where she'd shop to buy her groceries, she would ask the man [who] owned the store, "My church [has] been burned; can you help me?" And that's the way she got the money to buy the [cement] blocks and build the church back.

A current Soapstone Church congregant remembered that "Sister Owens . . . would come up and almost every Sunday she would bring . . . some money that was given to her from someone. . . . She would always bring it here and give it to the church." Don Owens, her grandson, estimated that 90 percent of the donations came from white folks.

With the money, both white and black neighbors and friends pitched in to help rebuild the church. Judith White listed Raymond Owens, Eugene Whiteside, Justin Williams, and Andrew McGowens as members who "spent a whole vacation up here, getting the foundation and building this church." Everyone helped whenever they could, doing whatever task they could. No one charged for their time. Mable Clarke remembered that Reverend William, the pastor, "was very handy and knew a lot about carpentry." Mable's father, Chris Owens, "knew a lot about carpentry, too, and they pretty much built the church back with that and some volunteers from the community." Materials were also donated by friends with connections to the construction companies. Bankers gave discounts on loans, and "a lot of the companies give lumber," Don Owens recalled. Other neighbors donated pews. William Owens (Mable's brother) remembered a white man in a Greenville-area construction company who "told my Daddy, said, 'Chris, I'll tell you what. I'm going to get you as many [concrete] block that you want to build this church back. And . . . it ain't going to cost the church nothing.' He said, 'I feel like the Lord blessed me to do that.'" During the rebuilding, neighboring churches (both white and black) opened their doors to host Soapstone's services. On September 25, 1967, the cornerstone was placed and the church reopened.[3]

Much work still needed to be done, and volunteers again pitched in to help. Even after the church was finished, Mable Clarke noted, Edgar Smith enlarged the pulpit and "pulled the church further back to put the baptistery in." No longer desiring baptism in the Oolenoy River as in previous generations, the congregation of Soapstone Church had Smith install a modern baptismal pool in the back of the church. This facility allowed for full immersion, in full view of the congregation, without having to worry about the long trek to the river, the variable temperature of the water, and the mysterious creatures in the stream.

As the building rose and expanded (see figure 1), American society changed. Pickens County (and the rest of the nation) desegregated, and the social world of racism that had fueled the hatred that had burned Soapstone Church retreated but did not disappear. The congregation aged and diminished in numbers through time. Clarence Glenn, the initial victim of the racial violence in chapter 5, died in 1974 and was buried near his ancestral land in Soapstone's new cemetery, in view of the rebuilt church. Owens and McJunkin children still visited their parents in Liberia, Marietta, and Bald Rock, but life on the farm seemed more anachronistic and almost unfathomable to visiting grandchildren more used to urban noise, indoor plumbing, and accessible stores. Of course, home-cooked meals of salt-cured ham, free-range eggs, handmade biscuits, and handpicked vegetables compensated fairly well for the rustic shortcomings. The welcoming hugs of country cousins and aunties, filled with never-ending tales of ancestors who walked the same hills visible to the guests, transformed every visit into a living family history lesson and further rooted distant kin back to their homeland.

Other social changes shook the foundation of long-established traditions. Colleen Zimmerman, a Yankee from Connecticut, married and moved onto Chris and Lula Owens's peddling route in the late 1950s; by 1973 she and another outsider had started the Table Rock Extension Homemakers Club, a group of upper–Pickens County women. "And we met once a month and the county agent would come and talk about canning, or vegetable gardening, or some new thing in sewing, or just general health and domestic issues," Zimmerman recalled. Wanting to be neighborly, and in keeping with her religious background, Mrs. Zimmerman invited Lula McJunkin Owens, granddaughter of slaves, to join the all-white group of women; she did. In Mable's presence, Zimmerman stated that "my friend and I used to pick your mother up and take her to the meetings. . . . And she always enjoyed those, and we enjoyed having her." According to Mable, group members always requested her mother's specialty—homemade coconut cake with real grated coconut icing.

Although introduced in earlier chapters, Lula McJunkin Owens is worth a closer look. She epitomized what sociologist Patricia Hill Collins termed an othermother—a black woman who, in the process of raising her own children in a social structure of gendered, racial, and class inequalities, also struggled to improve the lives of others around her, and in so doing, improved her community as well. "These women often remain nameless in scholarly texts," Collins asserted, "yet everyone in their neighborhoods knows their names."[4]

In chapter 5, Lula McJunkin Owens worked full time on her family's farm, raised her eight children, and supported her husband's truck-farming operations on weekends. Although with only three grades of formal education, "Miss Lula" encouraged Liberia's children to attend their only school, even teaching the children herself in emergencies. She successfully fought the county for a school bus to continue that education when rural schools consolidated, she protected her daughter (and her community) from a sexual predator, and she led her sons in a retaliatory strike against armed assailants. Drawing on her good name, family ties, and wide supportive network of friends and allies (both white and black), she worked tirelessly and selflessly to rebuild her community's church, destroyed (most likely) by a criminal act. By means of all these activities, she exemplified Collins's "socially responsible individualism."[5] By helping her own children survive and thrive, Lula McJunkin Owens, granddaughter of enslaved human beings, helped Liberia to survive and thrive as well. In addition to preserving her community and church as her legacies, Lula Owens left one other legacy as well: as Collins noted, othermothers typically "raise daughters who are self-reliant and assertive."[6] Lula McJunkin Owens raised her youngest daughter, Mable, to carry Liberia on into the twenty-first century.

Conclusion

The resurrection of Soapstone Baptist Church in 1967 symbolized the resurrection of the Liberia community. Despite the fact that Owens family members were now scattered between Boston and Pumpkintown and Marietta and Cleveland, Ohio, more importantly, the Owens family still owned land in Liberia. That land continued to be a magnet, drawing grandchildren back for nostalgic visits and warm hugs, and children back for the reinvigorating smells and exhilarating views of their family's ancestral lands. Despite the inevitability of generations aging or leaving, African Americans still owned the same lands once owned and/or occupied by ancestors like Katie Owens and Joseph McJunkin. Equally important, descendants still possessed stories and memories of these people. As members of the Soapstone congregation left their newly rebuilt church on a Sunday afternoon in fall 1967 and stood atop that familiar soapstone boulder, they felt tremendous pride in knowing that their ancestors had suffered so much for that same land, and yet they had persevered through injustices and emerged steadfast and strong. The struggles of Soapstone Baptist Church and the African Americans of the Liberia area were not over yet, but Liberia's residents could now face whatever might come with the knowledge that they had a wider network of allies and a strengthened hope for a better future.

7 This Is My Home

Into the Twenty-First Century

. . . .

The Oolenoy Valley that Mable Owens Clarke had left in 1961 for better economic opportunities and less racism up north had transformed completely by the time she returned in 1983 to care for her aging parents, like so many of her friends and relatives had done in past decades. The horror, shame, and fear felt by Edgar Smith the night he stood helplessly amid the ruins of the old Soapstone Baptist Church had retreated (but not completely disappeared), now metamorphosed into a mutual effort by many whites and blacks to rebuild the church and simultaneously construct an entirely new set of social relations. Faded (but not gone) was the visceral culture of terror in blacks who had been raised to fear lynching by white mobs or the humiliating subservience to whites while maintaining a culturally appropriate social and physical distance between races. On the other hand, still present were all the positive interracial social interactions of the past—the heaping plates of food on Lula Owens's kitchen table and the reciprocal work in the Owens fields that might yield a fresh watermelon or a bushel of corn. By the early 1980s, the social interactions between blacks and most whites on a local level had not changed that much, but the rules governing those interactions, as well as the cultural context explaining and justifying them, had transformed completely. The informal racial integration that always had been a part of Liberia's story now was formally legal and socially more acceptable to most of the region's residents.

But more importantly, during Mable Clarke's absence, social ties between Liberia and neighboring communities had expanded significantly. As white residents such as Edgar Smith learned about the community, more and more friendships developed. These friendships helped integrate Liberia's residents into a wider social network beyond the upper sections of Pickens and Greenville Counties. As the tides of the civil rights movement flooded over the nation (supported by the constitutional amendments from nineteenth-century Reconstruction governments), and as the mass media of newspapers, magazines, and television further linked local residents with national and international information, the blacks of Liberia integrated more completely into the general social life of the country. In fact, by the 1980s, these Oolenoy-area *black* residents had become Oolenoy-area *rural* residents, seen by most people as not much different from their white neighbors. While the resurrection of Soapstone Baptist Church symbolized the resurrection of the Liberia community, the survival of that institution equally symbolizes the survival of the Liberia community today.

The Liberia Community in the Twenty-First Century

The Pumpkintown General Store (the old Burgess Store) still sits at the four-way stop, across the intersection from the expansive (former) Sutherland home (see map 3). While the building is still owned by the Burgess family, the business is not; the store now sells a narrower range of merchandise than in decades past.[1] The grill and a few small tables allow travelers to enjoy the three meals advertised on the building's side: breakfast, dinner, and supper, utilizing typical southern terms. After a meal, a driver might follow State Highway 288 out of Pumpkintown toward Marietta, keeping the Oolenoy River on the right. About a mile and half down the road, a left turn onto Liberia Road leads past the legendary site of Cornelius Keith's first cabin in the valley (see chapter 2), and then the newer campus of Miracle Hill Children's Home (an evangelical Christian orphanage). The road curves around several modest houses, with a few mysterious side roads leading into the woods, and then heads up a longer hill to the crest. One might stop there and take in the scene (described in chapter 1). Now this sight may provide the viewer with added significance, because the soapstone rocks, the church, the schoolhouse, and the names of those residing in the cemeteries now bear deeper levels of cultural meaning.

Ironically, many of the structures currently visible in this scene were built by Edgar Smith, the same man who stood and watched helplessly the night Soapstone Church burned. Smith helped to rebuild the church, and his construction company also built several homes and the church's Fellowship Hall as well. In fact, Mable Clarke told him during a mutual interview, "You built the whole community out there." They both counted the homes—Smith's company built houses for two of Chris and Lula Owens's daughters, another for a son, and a fourth for a grandson. Smith modestly admitted this was more of a coincidence than a feeling of guilt over his inability to save the church in 1967, but the Owens family had met him that fateful night and had not forgotten him. Thus, when seeking a respected local construction company, the Owens family turned to Smith as someone they already knew and trusted.

This pattern of household clusters is typical of settlement patterns in southwestern North Carolina as well, folklorist Michael Ann Williams observed. Despite the fact that many people move away, Williams continued, "it is not uncommon for young adults, including some young professionals, to build a house and raise a family on land carved out of their parents' or grandparents' tract. Even those who have moved away are sometimes given a parcel of land in case they wish someday to return. In keeping with tradition, new ranch houses and mobile homes encircle the bungalows and other dwellings built by the parents' generation in mid-century."[2] As will be argued in chapter 8, this clustering of multiple generations in rural areas typifies much of the southern Appalachian region and reflects a deeper connection to both the "homeplace" (Williams's focus) and ancestral land more generally.

Because of the symbolic power of the homeplace and family lands, generational ownership of family land in the region is critically important.[3] Typically, Williams found, family land is inherited equally between male and female children. As a consequence, "the continual dividing of land made it difficult for families to keep large tracts of land intact and impeded the development of a stable rural elite."[4] Thus in Liberia today, the Owens farmland has been divided between the surviving children, with some ranch-style houses located near the homeplace and others located on their own parcels of land, protruding through the trees on elevated hills.

Because of its symbolic importance to a family, inheritance of the homeplace raises a great deal of social tension and legal entanglements.[5] For example, Mable's oldest brother continued to live in his parents' home, across Liberia Road from his youngest sister, Mable (and her family) and in their direct long-term care until he passed away in 2014. According to Mable, her brother's estranged son, never a resident of Liberia, then challenged his Aunt Mable in court over ownership of his father's home—the Owens homeplace. During a contentious court battle, Mable provided documents proving her social and medical care for her brother, and (based on that evidence) she successfully retained legal control of the Owens homeplace, now occupied by another Owens relative.

Of course, Edgar Smith did not build most of these neat brick bungalows in the midst of expansive vegetable garden patches because most of the area's farms had disappeared by that time. In a newspaper interview in 1983,

Lula Owens observed that almost all of the former homes had "rotted or been torn down."[6] Nevertheless, the area around Liberia still remained lightly populated and undeveloped. Mable Clarke remembers bringing her fiancé down from Boston to visit her family in Liberia for the first time. An international hairdresser and world-traveled sophisticate, Mable's fiancé enjoyed his first sights of Greenville but grew increasingly uncomfortable as they drove into smaller towns, turned onto a rural highway, and entered what to the visitor seemed to be wilderness. By the time they had reached the Owens family home, the fiancé wondered aloud what people did for a living out here, and what he would do specifically if they were to move back to Liberia. After a week's visit, Mable had shown him that there were indeed stores and urbanity in Pickens, Easley, and Greenville, and he felt a little more comfortable.

As historian Gilbert Fite noted for the South in general, by the 1980s, "the agriculture of hoe, mule, and cotton was gone forever." The same was true in upper Pickens County. Despite the general decline in the number of family farms in the area, Chris Owens continued farming into the 1980s.[7] Interviewed by two local historians in 1979, Owens was described as "a grand farmer" with seventy-two acres; Lula Owens gardened, milked cows for fresh buttermilk, churned butter, and raised chickens. She also maintained "a porch full of flowers."[8]

As in decades past, the multiple livelihood strategies of "the Kentucky way" enabled rural folks to maintain ties to the homeplace while participating to an extent in the capitalistic market system.[9] Established in earlier decades by Liberia's residents to maintain and protect political and economic independence, the Kentucky way enabled Chris Owens and his neighbors to maintain sufficient extended family income and relative independence almost to the twenty-first century. Today, Halperin's description of the "shallow rural" of Kentucky and that of many southern areas also characterizes Liberia. In between the isolation of "deep rural" and urban environments, Liberia's residents (like their rural white neighbors) operate in both worlds, seeking to maintain self-sufficiency and to resist "dependency upon capitalism."[10] As in other Appalachian regions, Liberia's residents today combine wage labor jobs with household gardens and informal markets (such as flea markets, garage sales, or home-based self-serve produce stands). Moreover, residents are linked by extended family ties, where kin exchange labor, cash, tools, and food, especially for family celebrations or crises.[11] Churches in the area exchange congregants, food, and fellowship. While in the past these strategies allowed Liberia's residents to maintain their relative independence from white hegemonic control, today this same pattern functions to support the entire region's emphasis on "individualism," a fundamental southern value.[12]

During his lifetime, Chris Owens's agricultural lifestyle provided his grandchildren and urban relatives with a never-ending source of humorous stories and exotic experiences. For example, concerned about his daughter's urbanized husband's lack of "practical" knowledge, Chris Owens did his best to help educate him properly. The most challenging chore was to shovel manure out of the chicken house, load it onto a truck, drive the truck to the garden, and spread the manure on the garden; " 'The smell was killing me,' " Mable remembered her husband saying. After spreading the manure and before heading into the house for Lula's noontime dinner, the men passed the corn crib, and Chris Owens invited his son-in-law inside for a special treat. Hidden in an old churn was a bucket of homemade wine, and the urbane city dweller watched in horror as Chris's hand, fresh from the chicken manure, dipped into the bucket for a cup full of wine. " 'Here, take you a good swig,' " Chris had said. At that moment, "I think he was ready to move back to Boston," Mable admitted to a group of friends.

Mable Clarke recognizes that her city-dwelling friends face "difficult" challenges when visiting her in Liberia even today. They do not tolerate the ubiquitous insects, including those infesting garden vegetables when visitors have been asked to pick some fresh greens. Bears and snakes are perceived as more dangerous than anything faced in an urban environment. Most troubling to these visitors to the mountains is the darkness. Thus, Mable acknowledges, most of her urbanized friends leave before darkness falls lest they be stranded "in the mountains," for them a place akin to a foreign land.

Relatives visiting from Boston discovered another world in the rural landscape of upstate South Carolina. Owens relatives from the North thrilled at the freedom of the farm but stifled under the isolation. "We'd come down here to get some fresh air," a visitor remarked; in Boston, "you don't have land to really just be free." Philip Owens tried to encourage his Boston-born daughter and her family to visit more often, but they came only once. "They [are] born and raised in the city, you know," Owens admitted, "where people [are] stacked on top of each other. . . . Everything [is] convenient. . . . Not like here. You got to go miles and miles, you know, to get something" from a store. Another visitor admitted: "I loved coming down to see my grandparents, but it was so boring, 'cause there was nothing to do. There was nothing here. It was just, you know, trees and cornfields, and . . . cows and stuff. . . . So all we did, me and my siblings, was fight all the time 'cause we had nothing else to do. But, as I got older, I learned to appreciate coming home."

Now mothers themselves, the Owenses' urbanized granddaughters enjoy bringing their own children to the countryside because, as one woman admitted, "I could turn them loose and didn't have to watch them for hours." Of course, she quickly added: "Not that I'm not a good parent, but it was safe! . . . They could just run and play all day." "I don't have to worry about my kids when I'm here," another Owens granddaughter acknowledged; "at night time, they stay out 'til nine, ten o'clock sometimes playing 'Hide and Seek,' that we couldn't do . . . in Boston, you know what I mean?" One of the women's daughters shyly mentioned to a gathering of her extended family that during her summer visits she enjoys riding her bike along the empty rural roads, playing in the little creek below the soapstone boulders, and helping to pick garden vegetables from her grandparents' garden. And as everyone in that room silently recognized, this young Owens girl walked the same fields, waded in the same creek, and climbed on the same boulders traversed by her formerly enslaved great-great-great-grandmother Katie.

Soapstone Baptist Church in the Liberia Community

The social activities hosted by the church founded by Joseph McJunkin over a century and a half ago generally remain the same today, but they are attended by fewer people. As historians Thad Sitton and James Conrad discovered in their Texan freedom colonies, "the demise of church congregations often signaled the real death of a community, or at least the beginning of that death."[13] Soapstone's remaining congregation recognizes this demographic process all too well. A generation ago, Mable Clarke acknowledged, the church had almost fifty members; now the number at services averages about ten. Church activities have declined only gradually, however. The first McJunkin Family Reunion, for example, held Sunday services at the church in August 1986. Other church members remember old-time revivals continuing into the 1980s as well, with the ladies of the church preparing a different meal for several nights. "And that was just something different that they don't do anymore," a woman lamented. During the 1990s, Colleen Zimmerman noted that her church, Pleasant Grove Baptist (a white congregation about a mile from Soapstone; see map 3), allowed the congregation to hold various events such as Chris Owens's centennial birthday celebration in 1996 and fish-fry events in order to help them raise the money to build the church hall.

A recent Soapstone Annual Homecoming, the first Sunday in May, offered a smaller celebration than in years past (see chapter 5). Sunday school (an informal discussion of Bible verses led by a deacon) began about 10:30 that morning, and the formal service started about an hour later. At the opening of the service, there were perhaps ten people in the congregation. Several women (especially older ones) wore white dresses or skirts, and one Owens brother wore a white suit. After a formal communion service, the congregation (by this time perhaps about thirty people) sang a closing hymn, and everyone drifted into the Fellowship Hall for dinner.

Using the same food trays and station as the monthly fish fry, several employees dispensed homemade food (a slightly less diverse offering than at the fish fry). These laborers then freed Mable Clarke and the other usual fish-fry volunteers to circulate and socialize more effectively. The minister blessed the meal, and then families gathered around the circular tables while the church musician entertained the audience on an electronic piano. The white minister from Pleasant Grove Baptist Church and the black minister from Soapstone Baptist Church sat by themselves and shared a meal, symbolizing the ecclesiastical cooperation in the area today. A few families traded photo albums and reminisced over their meals. Couples and families began to leave by early afternoon, and by about 3:00 P.M. the room had emptied. Unlike in years past, there was no evening service.

As reflected by the ministerial camaraderie at the recent homecoming, the rural Baptist churches in the area "nurture each other" today, Mable Clarke observed. At Pleasant Grove, Mable and the white female congregants "meet there at the first Tuesday in the month. We have a little women's organization; we take a little potluck there. And we sit there and we do Bible study," Mable elaborated. Occasionally the churches hold services jointly, and Mable acknowledged, "I've got friends up there; we just hug and laugh and talk and share food and different recipes," especially at the potluck suppers. At these events, "it may be two tables [with] just desserts," Mable observed. Most importantly, Mable continued, she knows that "the church is a community. . . . When something [may be] going down with the one family or something, we kind of make sure that somebody get[s] to the hospital to visit somebody there, send flowers, cards. . . . And it all just comes together. . . . You know, it's just like a big community with your arms stretched wide open and everybody reach out and just hug each other."

Soapstone's Fellowship Hall has become the focal point of Liberia's community socializing. Called upon for the construction job (beginning about 2004) was Edgar Smith, by then well known in the Liberia community specifically and in the surrounding area more generally. Mable Clarke recalled that Smith worked some of the time for free on the hall, donating his time and building supplies for the cause. Smith also loaned the use of his construction license to permit the work. Volunteer laborers came from area churches such as Pleasant Grove and surrounding areas. "If you fooled with Chris Owens," Smith quipped, "you was going to work for free!" (Readers may recall the "Hard Times" appellation Owens had earned throughout his life, by getting the best deal possible because of his charm and persuasive ability; see chapter 5). Depending on the availability of funds, "we pieced it [together] little bit by little bit," Mable noted, and the hall was completed by November 2006. On the day the building was finally dedicated (June 24, 2007), Smith stated, "there was as many whites there as there was blacks." "More whites," Mable Clarke corrected. "Yeah, I guess there was," Smith admitted. In fact, Dr. William McClain, the black minister from Washington, D.C. invited to speak that day, was quite surprised to discover that "'we got more white [people in attendance] than we have black,'" Smith noted.[14] He then remembered Mable commenting, "'We don't know the difference here.'"

Today, one of the most important activities held in the Fellowship Hall, with the same degree of interracial harmony as exhibited in other community activities, is the monthly fish fries held the third Saturday of every month (except December) in order to raise funds to pay the mortgage for the church and hall. Several days before each appointed Saturday, Mable Clarke begins preparing trays of fried fish, fried and baked chicken, barbecued ribs, pulled pork barbecue, and vegetables including several types of beans and peas, candied yams, squash, corn, and several casseroles, and always including macaroni and cheese. Diners get a "meat and three" vegetables plus a choice of corn bread or roll and a side of coleslaw. Desserts (which vary each month) may include pound cake and fresh strawberries, carrot cake, or pies (popular in the fall). Sweet and unsweet tea along with lemonade and coffee accompany the delicious food. On the scheduled day, a small team of employees (with volunteers such as cousin Judith White and Soapstone's minister) collect the admission charge, serve food (from a cafeteria-style steam table), and bus tables, while Mable navigates between supervising the food service, greeting guests, and circulating among the tables for hugs and laughs. Hundreds attend, and serving continues from noon until 7 P.M.

In many ways, this interracial repast models the kitchen table in Lula Owens's home that Mable Clarke remembers from her girlhood. As described in chapter 5, the Owens home continually hosted white visitors for a variety of reasons: vegetable purchasers, buttermilk samplers, and visitors who wished merely to hear a song or story from Chris Owens. Like her mother before her, Mable especially enjoys when her guests have their meal and then sit as they gaze out the expansive windows of the hall across the soapstone boulders to the views of Table Rock and Caesar's Head in the Blue Ridge about four miles away. "Some of them stay two or three hours," Mable stated; "they just sit in there, just socializing, fellowshipping, and just talking." Sometimes her guests admit to Mable that "it's something about [I] feel like I'm glued to the seats here" because they do not want to leave. "So we try to make everybody feel so welcome," Mable added, "and want you to feel relaxed."

One of the most newsworthy community activities linking Liberia's remaining population with their ever-widening network of white supporters has been the resurrection of the older slave cemetery near Soapstone Baptist Church. As described in chapters 3 and 4, this cemetery holds the remains of many former Liberia residents, including James Kemp and his grandmother Chaney, a former slave (and perhaps Hattie [James's wife] and Emerson Kemp [his father] as well). A few of the stones have legible inscriptions (see appendix 1); most of the other marked graves have merely a fieldstone. Depressions in the soil undoubtedly indicate additional graves.

For some reason, individuals began to be interred nearer to the church by the late nineteenth century (or the graves were relocated; for example, Willie Owens died in 1879, W. R. Edens in 1903; see appendix 1), but the old cemetery remained in use at least through the 1930s (for example, James Kemp died in 1938). However, sometime after that, the old cemetery gradually fell into disuse, and decades later it had become overlooked and almost forgotten. Dirt roads leading off to several newer homes outlined the ill-defined boundaries, and a power line cut through one side. By March 1983, Lula Owens described the old cemetery as "overgrown" and "littered."[15] Leaves, brush, and shrubs obscured many of the stones and the depressions, concealing the cemetery completely.

While surveying a property line in 2007, workers rediscovered the cemetery and notified the community's local historian, Mable Clarke. After being contacted, Mable described herself as unable to rest until she could provide some dignity and respect to those buried in what her family had always called the slave cemetery (some, but not all buried there, had been born a slave; see appendix 1). Using her extensive network of friends and relatives, Mable Clarke made calls and rallied an army of about thirty-five volunteers to clean the cemetery in late April 2007. One state employee arrived about 7:30 A.M. "and I felt like I was an hour and a half late. Everybody was out there." Representatives came from "eleven different churches," Mable recalled, as well as local Boy Scouts and volunteer fire personnel. People donated their time as well as their equipment: chainsaws, brush hogs, bulldozers, and trucks.

Several years later (February 2011), after some vandalism to the isolated site, Mable Clarke solicited more volunteers, this time from Clemson University's Anthropology Club, to rake off the cemetery, draw in the coordinates for every gravestone, and record and photograph the inscriptions on the legible stones, to prevent further destruction and to provide increased publicity (therefore protection) for the place. Utilizing grant money from the Accommodations Tax Fund from Pickens County (obtained from the county council), Mable and another group of volunteers then initiated a third project two months later: the addition of more attractive landscaping, an expanded parking lot, and the construction of a split-rail locust fence around the site for further protection. A kiosk now offers visitors a brief historical summary of the cemetery and its place in the Liberia community, and an explanatory brochure is now available as well (laid out by more volunteers from a Clemson University writing class). At the slave cemetery's rededication ceremony in May 2013, Mable Clarke solemnly and proudly declared that she had finally restored respect and dignity to some of Liberia's oldest inhabitants.

Contemporary Social Interaction

The daughter of othermother Lula McJunkin Owens, Mable Owens Clarke continues her mother's legacy. Mable faced the culture of terror as a young girl, helping to protect her nephew and her sisters from murderous gunfire in her own home. Knowing education was critical to her success, she struggled to learn in a poorly heated one-room schoolhouse, and later drove herself and her siblings and neighbors dozens of miles along country roads to continue her education. After a significant portion of her adult life, she returned to her home community to care for her aging parents and oldest brother. Her resolve to maintain her church and to protect the burial site of her elders, along with her political activism to secure funds for these projects, again exemplify sociologist Patricia Hill Collins's othermother, a woman whose self-sacrifice improves her own family's life and then simultaneously that of her community. "When you look for it," Collins concluded, "people who are actively engaged in changing the terms of their everyday relationships with one another surface in surprising places"—including upper Pickens County, South Carolina.[16]

Neither passively tolerating contemporary challenges nor patiently depending on white largesse, Liberia's blacks, under Mable's informal leadership, continue to claim, defend, maintain, and expand their own social status and physical place on the landscape—just as their ancestors had done for over a century. Much easier today than in decades past, Liberia's path forward has not always been effortless even after Mable's return.

Negative Interactions with Whites

The continuing irritation over protecting the slave cemetery from vandalism illustrates an unfortunate part of the legacy of Liberia, traced throughout all previous chapters—the interaction between whites and blacks in the Oolenoy Valley has not always been peaceful and harmonious, as portrayed in local histories.[17] The relatively small number of racial incidents faced by Liberia's African Americans in the past several decades demonstrates several social facts. They reflect the continued harassment and negative experiences today faced by blacks specifically and by many minorities of color generally. However, these experiences are no longer the product of institutionalized racial inequality (at least not to the scale of Jim Crow segregation laws and the culture of terror from the Klan) but instead occur due to the lingering effects of personal misunderstandings by certain individuals, generally speaking. Nevertheless, regardless of the cause, the episodes still hurt. The other social fact reflected by these stories is the reminder to those of primarily European heritage that racism and inequality still persist in this country and in this state, and that African Americans continue to face embarrassing or painful experiences that whites as a group of people generally do not face. "You know, we're not being hung in trees and shot at and all that" anymore, one African American observed, but this person recognized that racism continues in a more subtle sense, and reported instances still occur.

As in earlier decades, some of these negative experiences could be ignored or dismissed by blacks. For example, one Liberia resident, in line to vote in the 2008 presidential election, was vehemently and publicly told by a white resident not to vote for Barack Obama because he was a "terrorist." Mable Clarke related a tale of her shopping for a blouse in a regional mall store. The blouse fell to the floor and Mable bent to pick it up; almost immediately the clerk came to see what had happened and (in Mable's mind) to prevent her from shoplifting, reminding Mable about the way that merchants had mistrusted all black customers in her childhood. Another episode reminded Mable of another painful childhood experience. In line to renew her Greenville YMCA membership, Mable had been questioning a clerk about a detail when, in the midst of helping her, he shifted his attention to a white couple who had just entered, thereby ignoring Mable. "I guess I just became *invisible*," she concluded. Then Mable added: "I went through this as a child growing up, and I'm still . . . experiencing this same kind of thing but in a different form." Here, as in eras past, a reader may comprehend Foucault's capillary form of inequality, implanted in individual human bodies and still viscerally felt even decades after the dominating power structure has been removed. As similar episodes have happened to them, other blacks reported that they have learned to try as best as possible to ignore these slights.

Blacks have also felt the familiar sting of segregation relatively recently as well. An African American married couple had decided to open up a business on Main Street in downtown Greenville in the early 1980s, and they successfully had placed a contract and a deposit on a prime location. Three days before closing, the real estate agent returned their check with an apology: " 'I'm not really supposed to tell you,' he said [as a woman reported], 'but I'm a Christian man.' And he said, 'I hate to really say this to you but [pause] we'll have to return your check; he [the owner] won't let me make the sale.' " The reason, spoken but unwritten, was that a city official did not want another black-owned business on Main Street in Greenville. Eventually the couple found another location several blocks farther away.

The old rules for segregated businesses still linger as well. As a member of a regional bank's board, an African American woman reported that she and a friend had been invited to attend a business reception at an expensive restaurant in downtown Greenville several years ago. There were "probably only three blacks in the whole place" among perhaps hundreds of people, she observed. While sitting at a table conversing and enjoying their hors d'oeuvres, the two black women were approached by a white woman who demanded, "How do you all get in here? Do you just walk in off the street?" One African American woman quickly replied, "We got invited here! Did *you* walk [in] off the street?"

As in previous decades, Liberia's residents have had to defend their property against encroachment. Besides having to protect the older slave Soapstone cemetery, the Owens family in earlier decades confronted trespassing timber cutters. When challenged by Chris Owens for crossing property lines, some white neighbors took him to court, a newspaper story related. " 'I had my piece of paper (title and deed), and they had to go by the oldest survey on record, and I had it,' " Chris Owens recounted.[18] The McJunkins in the Bald Rock area faced a similar circumstance. As noted in chapter 5, the grandchildren of former slave Joseph McJunkin, including Lula McJunkin Owens and her brother James, had memorized every marker and every line on their family's property. Over the years, however, a real estate company had occupied hundreds of acres of McJunkin land and had even built the Mountain Lake Colony (wealthy estates) on some of that land, under the nose of Caesar's Head and adjacent to Bald Rock (see map 2). Knowing in his heart and on his deed that the land was his, James McJunkin went to court in 1992, and under cross examination by the judge, he produced deeds and plats as well as cited from memory every tree and rock marking his property. McJunkin's daughter-in-law proudly concluded: "And I think that the final thing that convinced the judge was one of the lawyers from Mountain Lake Colony asked him. And he said, 'Mr. McJunkin, you think you *own* that land, don't you?' So Dad answered, 'No, I don't *think* I own the land, I *know* I own the land.' " The jury unanimously decided in McJunkin's favor.

At the same time, Liberia's blacks have faced more subtle attempts to erase them from the landscape. When the highway department reorganized all the county's roads for the EMS system several decades ago, the Miracle Hill Children's Home asked that Liberia Road be renamed after the home. Outraged, Lula McJunkin Owens (Liberia's othermother) soon appeared at the County Highway Department and demanded that the road upon which her family had been raised be restored to its original name. She succeeded. Liberia Road leads through the community to this day.

Sometimes it is difficult to distinguish between wrongdoings committed against Liberia's residents because of their race from those committed because of their rural, isolated residence—in other words, problems frequently faced by country dwellers in general. For example, Mable Clarke described a time when her elderly and trusting parents admitted a stranger to their home, ostensibly to inspect for termites. The "workers" went throughout the house, including the attic's storage space. The next day, Mable had heard, the same culprits hid in the woods until Chris and Lula Owens went to their fields for the day, and then they broke in and stole her father's (and father's father's) antique hunting guns. The robbers took about a dozen guns in all, some over a hundred years old. Old farm equipment suspended on the walls of Owens farm outbuildings has also disappeared over the years.

Having spent their childhoods and perhaps even their youth at times fearing for their lives should they utter an "inappropriate" comment or commit an "inappropriate" act (having lived under Foucault's normalizing gaze of generalized observation and Taussig's culture of terror), Liberia's blacks no longer feel they face the same gauntlet of carefully negotiated social interaction they had faced in earlier times. Nevertheless, certain events might seem for whites to be coincidental, peculiar, or perhaps threatening; for blacks, on the other hand, these same activities are perceived through the additional weighty baggage of their earlier experiences (the embedded and embodied inequality) and thus take on added connotations. For example, Mable Clarke related a recent incident that she faced while driving home late at night from Greenville. Alone on a rural road, in the dark, she noticed that she was being followed by a car that flashed its lights at her, speeding up as she did and slowing down as she did. The car continued following her onto Liberia Road, and, knowing her husband was not home, Mable instead pulled into her brother's driveway and promptly honked her car horn. At that moment, she noticed the mysterious car had turned around and gone back the way it had come.

While reflecting on the challenges she had faced as a child in the Oolenoy Valley and continues to face as an African American woman in American society today, Mable Clarke summarized her survival strategy: "As you live . . . you try to get stronger to surpass that [the past experiences] and to look back at it and say, 'It's nothing wrong with us; it was the other way.' So once you try to arrive at that you're able to try to put your own life together and make some steps forward instead of just standing in this one spot dwelling on what's wrong with them. So at some point you have to come to peace with it. But it's a road to get to that peace. It doesn't happen overnight."

Legacy of Interracial Relationships

Despite centuries of legal and social segregation, whites and blacks have maintained sexual relationships under a variety of conditions (from coerced to consensual). In the past secretive and rarely shared with those beyond immediate family members, stories of these relationships persist in the hidden transcripts of the Liberia community today, reflecting (in fact sometimes literally embodying) the tremendous variety of interracial social interaction that always has characterized the Oolenoy Valley.

For example, on his trips back home before he had permanently returned, Jessie Owens remembered that "two white ladies would come over in the afternoon around three o'clock, and they'd come sit on the front porch with Momma and Dad. They'd sit there and they'd talk and they had their little conversation." Eventually he got up the nerve to ask his mother who those women were. "And she kind of downed her head, and she looked at me with a smile on her face and said, 'Those are your cousins.' It best goes to show you," Mr. Owens concluded, that "you may be out here fighting [interracially, but] . . . you may be fighting with your cousin over here, all right? You got to be very careful out here—very, very careful."

Probably the most curious interracial interaction concerns the story of Esley Owens. Esley Owens first appeared in chapter 4, as Rosa Glenn Owens's second son, younger brother of Chris Owens (see appendices 1 and 2). According to family stories, at least one, perhaps three, of these children had been fathered by an unnamed white man through an indeterminate type of relationship. Family legend also told that Esley Owens fled the Oolenoy Valley sometime in the early twentieth century, escaping the Ku Klux Klan, "because a young white girl was liking him and he didn't know whether he was black or whether he was white," as a nephew had stated. He had disappeared somewhere up north.

Always curious about the family legend, Jessie Owens decided to track down his long-lost uncle sometime around 1967 or 1968 (he could not recall the exact year, but he said he was about forty at the time). He contacted the American Red Cross, and they identified a man by the name of Es Owens living then in Trenton, New Jersey. Owens called the stranger, "and we started to talk. And he says, 'Well, who[se] boy are you?' I says, 'I'm Chris and Lula's son,' and he says, [pause] 'Well, how's ol' Bubba doing?'" Eventually Owens and another of his brothers arranged to fly themselves and Chris and Lula Owens up to New Jersey to reconnect with this long-lost relative. They took a cab to the residence, and the family hesitated for a moment outside until Jessie finally went up and knocked on the door. "Here this big tall guy come on out," Mr. Owens stated; "look[ed] just like any white man with long curly hair." "Are you Esley Owens?" Jessie inquired, and the man responded affirmatively, and then asked who Jessie was. Jessie continued: "I said, 'I'm [name] Owens,' and he says, 'Where's your Daddy at?' And them two old guys got together; . . . they just had a very good time. We stayed there all day long and almost [chuckles] missed the flight back to Boston because they was having such a good time. But that just goes to show you how things were back in the old days. . . . So I was thrilled to have that opportunity to get to meet my uncle—a man I had never seen. . . . And what a feeling that was—what a feeling."

Positive Interactions with Whites

Despite the occasional negative experience, every interview with every African American always equally if not overwhelmingly has emphasized the positive experiences blacks have with their white neighbors today. As with the negative experiences, these may range from relatively mundane to profound and life-changing interactions.

"We have a lot of good white folks in this community," Jessie Owens asserted, and they continue to help support the church through the monthly fish fries. During one such gathering, Mr. Owens remembered being out in the parking lot and a white woman came up to him and said, " 'I just want to stop and give a donation.' So she gave Mable a nice check there, which I thought was very, very, very, very nice." Another time, Mable needed emergency assistance because the handicapped van used to transport her older brother (crippled by polio) had broken. None of her other relatives were around, so she called a white neighbor and said that her disabled brother needed help. The woman raced out to the field to get her husband, having promised Mable that he would be there as soon as possible. "So I mean that's the kind of community" that exists here, Mable observed, "that you know that you can just pick up the phone and get some help."

Even today, the name Chris Owens carries much weight. "Very respected family," proud daughter Mable Clarke noted; "the Owens was a name that goes a long way. You can ask anybody." In another interview, Mable offered evidence of this. Several years ago, the park manager at Table Rock State Park invited community members, including Clarke and her nephew, to come collect storm-downed timber for firewood. As they arrived, older white men clustered around her and asked if she was Chris Owens's daughter; when she replied affirmatively, everyone started sharing stories about Chris, and they all helped Mable and her nephew load the truck. "And that's what this community's about," Mable concluded; "reaching out, touching and helping, and you don't find that every place you live."

Carl French first ventured into Liberia while campaigning for sheriff in the late 1970s. There he met Chris and Lula Owens and became their lifelong friend. On another visit he recalled being invited to eat at Lula's table and being served poke sallet (a wild leafy green) just like his own mother (also from Pickens County) used to make. He stayed over an hour listening to Lula Owens tell of her trip to the Holy Land in the early 1980s.

According to family history, daughter Mable and son Philip accompanied their eighty-something-year-old mother, who had always wanted to "see where my Jesus walked," Mable remembered. Lula Owens became an othermother on the trip, as the tourists increasingly turned to her for biblical information and ignored the less-informed official guide. Because Lula Owens had always wanted to float in the Dead Sea, she asked Mable to buy her very first bathing suit; "not like the girls wear today," Lula had cautioned her daughter, but something more appropriate for an older woman. Lula first forced her daughter Mable to float in the water, just in case something went wrong, but Lula eventually floated herself.

Another time, while on a visit to downtown Pickens, Chris Owens stopped to visit the sheriff at the county jail, and the white lawman showed the old black farmer the facilities. " 'Well, I've never had the occasion of coming— being brought here,' " the sheriff remembered Owens had quipped. "And to my knowledge, he never had," the sheriff added somberly. Although unable to attend Chris Owens's funeral, the county sheriff did attend that of Lula Owens.

Lula Owens nearly killed Edgar Smith once, and Smith and Mable chuckled over that particular story during a joint interview. Shortly after Smith completed Mable's sister's home (situated above the old Owens homestead), he and Mable were showing it to a couple who had expressed an interest in having a home built in a similar fashion. Night was falling, and Lula Owens in her home downslope heard strange voices coming from a house she thought was empty. Recalling all the struggles she and her family had faced throughout her life, including the burning of her church and the shooting at her home, this granddaughter of slaves imagined the worst. She stood on her porch and demanded, in a loud, threatening voice, that she would begin firing her double-barrel shotgun at the intruders. "Mike [addressed to the author], she meant business!" Smith assured his audience. Panic stricken, Smith pleaded that Mable alert her mother immediately, and so without hesitation Mable raced downhill toward her mother, shouting " 'Momma, it's me; don't shoot! It's me,' " Smith recalled. After Mable had calmed her mother, she realized that she had run downhill toward the barrel of a loaded shotgun while Smith stayed behind in the safety of the house. "I'd rather be a live coward than a dead hero anytime!" Smith quipped, and both he and Mable chuckled. "I told Mable that would have made good headlines in the paper the next day: 'Black Woman Kills White Man and Daughter for Being in the House!'" The room erupted in laughter.

It was during the building of another of those Owens homes that Smith learned a valuable lesson in an embarrassing way. Smith had been asked to build a home for Chris and Lula's grandson Don, directly in front of their own home. However, "every time I'd see him, he's sitting in that [front porch] swing at Chris's," Smith confessed. He sarcastically stated to himself, "Fella, to build a house, you gonna have to get out of that swing and go to work." To appease him, Smith sent him to Pickens Savings and Loan, expecting him to be turned down for his home loan. The loan officer called Smith back, he remembered, and said, "'Get your "A" up yonder and start that house. That boy makes more money than me and you put together!'" The grandson drove a truck for a major retailer, and Smith always had caught him lounging at his grandparents' home on his days off, waiting for his grandmother Lula's home-cooked meals.

The relationship between Edgar Smith and the Owens family, including Mable Clarke, epitomizes the typical interracial relationships in the area today. From the lone first responder the fateful night of the church burning in 1967, Smith had evolved to be a literal builder of the community, raising funds for and assisting in the reconstruction and expansion of Soapstone Church as well as building several of the Owens family homes (see chapter 6). In fact, Jessie Owens did the electrical wiring for Smith's construction company, and he trusted no one else with the work. "Between me and Chris," Smith observed, "we never looked at races. . . . And Chris, oh, I just loved him. I loved him." "But if you want to feel at home, just go over there and sit down on the porch" of the Owens home, Smith observed; "you felt just as at home as you did right here." Edgar Smith "is like my father," Mable acknowledged during their joint interview; "me and him carry on all the time."

In an earlier interview without Mable being present, Smith related a poignant story that he felt illustrated his personal feelings toward the Owens family. Raised in exactly the same era of institutionalized racial inequality and assumed white superiority as virtually every other white Pickens County resident, Smith had acquired a different outlook on life during his decades working in Liberia (of course, not unique to him or his family, either). As he was building Jessie Owens's home, Smith remembered that Mr. Owens "took a liking" to Smith's grandson. For Christmas that winter, Owens brought the boy some toys from Boston, which the child cherished. Years later, Smith's grandson returned one winter from college and was asked about the toys that he had kept all those years. When reminded that the toys had been given to him by a local black man, the grandson (Smith proudly noted) then replied, "'I remember him as a good man; I don't remember him as being black.' And he still don't to this day. And—that'd be good if the whole world could see through a good eye like that," Smith concluded. As a final sign of friendship, both Mable Owens Clarke and her brother Jessie Owens attended Edgar Smith's funeral service at Holly Springs Baptist Church in May 2010.

Returning to Liberia

According to historian Gilbert Fite, after the Great Depression, World War II, and the modernization of southern agriculture in the 1950s, "a sentimental attachment to the soil could no longer have practical meaning to the great majority of southerners, who had been separated from the land by technology, public policy, and economic change" for the past several decades.[19] While many southerners indeed lost this critical connection and moved away, many others, especially in the mountains, did not.[20]

As in previous decades, distant kin always have maintained their connections to relatives in Liberia (the cultural implications of those ties are explored in chapter 8). These kin connections tie people to place despite great distances. Although some elderly residents such as Elaine Parker lamented, "We don't have the time to visit family like we used to, 'cause everybody [is] . . . so busy doing other things," others have always tried to maintain their ties to their home-based kin. For example, even while living in Boston, Mable Clarke returned home "three or four times a year," especially "for holiday times" such as Christmas, Thanksgiving, and the Fourth of July. In fact, returning to Boston after being home with her parents created in Mable "like an emptiness inside." Eventually she knew, "I gotta go" back home—and she did.[21]

Mable's niece, a self-described "big city girl" visiting Grandma Lula's farm decades ago, now brings her own children back to Liberia. She then elaborated: "I love coming back here; my kids enjoy coming here now, you know. It's just nice to see everybody. It's just a community. I told people—the Kennedys have a compound; the Owens[es] have a compound [all laugh]. . . . My parents are here, my aunts and them are here, and you know we're just a very close knit family. And this is what my grandparents built for us, so it's home. You know, this is my home."

Of course, as with all kin relations, social ties bring social obligations. In a group interview one time, Mable Clarke related the dilemma of living in an idyllic paradise, at least when compared with the crowded streets of Boston. She vividly remembered hosting sixteen of her northern nephews and nieces at her modest home in Liberia for two weeks one summer. Despite the fact that they were all cousins, small squabbles broke out and people maintained a variety of daily regimens. "It was a bit much," Mable sighed. For any future trips, Mable and her husband had both decided, the cousins would visit in shifts.

The unspoken consequence of these regular visits by kin is that some relatives connect so strongly with the place that they eventually return. As in previous decades, one of the strongest pulls drawing people back to Liberia has been to help aging relatives. Like adult children elsewhere, Liberia's adults always have demonstrated a strong sense of filial piety, and places of residence often have fluctuated because of kin obligations. Angela McJunkin Young, the youngest daughter of James McJunkin, initially moved in with her parents when she first married (as young couples sometimes do) but then built her new home adjacent to her father's, on his land in the Gold Mine area north of Marietta (see map 2). She and her husband eventually left for Florida to seek better economic opportunities, but after four years they moved back to be near her father again. "Daddy was getting of age," Mrs. Young explained, "and I felt that I needed to be near Daddy, so we come on back, and I've been here ever since." Young's first cousin, Mable Clarke (the youngest daughter of Chris Owens), returned from Boston in 1983 for exactly the same reason. "And in my heart, in my heart," Mable explained, "I felt the need, the responsibility, and the love to come back and spend some quality time with them [her parents] while they were still up moving." Even though she knew she was still Chris and Lula's child, Mable recognized that her relationship with her parents had changed. "You know, you talk to them in a different way," she observed; "we talk about different things. We can laugh, we can joke, and you know . . . just sit and have a good time. . . . And that was really important to me, to come back and be able to do that."

Reflective of these close personal ties between elderly parents and their adult children is the retention of the homeplace as a symbol of these connections. As in other Appalachian regions, both Mable Clarke and her cousin Angela Young built their ranch homes very close to those of their parents; those houses stood as long as possible (Mable's childhood home still stands).[22] As Williams argued, though, at some point "the symbolic significance of an old dwelling decreases, rather than increases, with age," and it might be torn down, as Young's father's house was.[23] Both Mable and her cousin are also the youngest children (and youngest daughters) in their respective families, and so, according to Appalachian values, were most likely to take on the task of caring for their parents as they aged.[24]

One activity that Mable specifically enjoyed with her parents was the simple pleasure they all got when they would "just sit out there on that porch and just look out into the mountains." In fact, Mable's front porch today faces the tableau described in chapter 1—the Blue Ridge Mountains about four miles away, framed by Table Rock and Caesar's Head (see map 2). As folklorist Henry Glassie observed, front porches link together the private home interior with the public exterior, and thus Mable's front porch symbolically connects her directly to the mountains (see chapter 8).[25] The panoramic view from her porch is one Mable never tires of, for it changes constantly: "And at night, . . . when the sun is starting to set, sometime[s] it sets on a certain area of the mountain, . . . and you can just sit there, and just see how the light just shift[s]—and come back to that same window, within an hour, it's a whole 'nother picture there. . . . I can go home now, and sit and I have a cup of tea, and I sit and just look out that window and meditate." Judith White, while living away from Liberia during part of her life, mentioned missing this exact same view, only from a slightly higher elevation—sitting on the soapstone boulders above and behind Mable's home. "'Will I ever be able to see the big rock again?'" Mrs. White had wondered; "and then when I did come back and I was able to go and all I could say was, 'Thank you, Jesus!'"

Indeed, the very beauty of the valley was a powerful magnet to keep some relatives in place and to pull others back home. During an interview one autumn, when asked why people would continue to live in the area, Mable responded incredulously, "Driving through the beautiful foliage, why wouldn't you want to live here? I mean, all this beauty that you can just look out at, that's why they choose to stay here [as] opposed to being in the city where you [are] looking right out to another house." After she and her sister-in-law had taken a ride deeper into the mountains to view the fall colors, Mable heard her companion describe the trees as "God's paintings," and Mable was struck by that description: "Those *are* God's paintings," she realized; "those trees in all different colors, all different shapes, all different sizes—all this He gave for our beauty. It's a gift, Mike. It's not a gift that man created."

Even visitors like Bernard Quinn, with only friendship and business ties to the Liberia community, described himself as being enraptured by the beauty of the place, "especially when the sun is there about almost down. You can kind of look like you're going to get close to something." When asked what he felt he was getting closer to, Quinn elaborated, "Well, the Good Master, I guess. It look[s] like you can see some of His workings. We don't know nobody else who could do all that!"

The beauty of the place further inspired in Quinn and in many others an almost indescribable sense of place that some residents had a difficult time articulating when trying to explicate their specific feelings about the area. A few people, like a younger woman in the Soapstone congregation, related her spiritual ties to the church to a greater spiritual sense of place: "The only thing I can summarize up is that at Soapstone it is a special place. . . . It's just something about when you come back here—it just feels a different atmosphere than the bigger church or whatever. There's just something special about this church. . . . It's just like you just want to come back sometime and it just gives you a—filling you up with a . . . different feeling that you just get from coming here. . . . I don't get to come as much as I'd like to but when I do come it's just something there that just kind of builds me up and that's what I can say."

Mable Clarke and her cousin Judith White expanded upon the feelings that visitors to the fish fry got from their experience, as well as the feelings she and her cousin sensed around Soapstone Church and the Liberia community. Mable remarked, "When people enter that grounds, they feel that sense of peace there. You know, there's no discord; there's that peace that's been planted there for years. Years. You know, they [are] walking on grounds where people—." Here Mrs. White interjected: "Kind of feel like sacred ground." Then Mable continued: "Yeah. For over a hundred years, you know?" While mentally wrestling with attempts to describe that feeling, Mrs. White stated: "You can feel it and you sense it and you're talking about like, what is it? . . . I feel that there is something there and I guess that's why I said 'sacred' a few minutes ago. But you just feel it."

Conclusion

Trying to capture the essence of the feeling Liberia's residents have while standing atop the soapstone boulders, gazing at Table Rock across the little Liberia Valley, has become one theme of this book. Despite overwhelming odds, enclaves of African Americans have held steadfastly to ancestral lands in northern Pickens and Greenville Counties for over fifteen decades. Their story reflects the greater struggles of many similar groups—blacks in the South and minorities in general, rural landowners in a globalizing economy, and perhaps even indigenous groups in Southeast Asia and throughout the world. While Liberia is, of course, unique, it is also typical of many types of communities, and typical of many types of social, economic, and cultural struggles by myriad groups fighting to maintain their land and culture (the other theme of this book). Thus, the story of Liberia transcends the little valley in which it is located and becomes a case study illustrating larger theoretical concepts and deeper cultural insights. By parsing out the cultural logic of the meaning of "land" to Liberia's residents, readers may discover the essence of the "feeling" Mable Clarke and Judith White found so difficult to describe, and by doing so, unravel a larger cultural meaning about land that may be applicable to a much wider range of regional and cultural groups.

One afternoon, while sitting in the Fellowship Hall of Soapstone Baptist Church, Mable Clarke explained her feelings about Liberia, and in doing so, she transformed her physical sense of place into a metaphysical sense of peace—about that place. Her voice slowed as she thought carefully about her precise words: "So it's a sense of peace. Peace. You can feel it. . . . There's something about once I hit to make that turn right here at Liberia Road, it's just the serenity and the peace. It's just overpowering. You can't explain it; you have to feel it. And it's there and it's real. It's very real. And when you break around this corner, that little curve right there, I take a moment and just apply my brakes. *That whole area just opens up its arms and just hugs me* [emphasis added]. You can't get past that spot right there without feeling it."

In this quote, Mable Clarke anthropomorphizes the actual landscape she occupies. What is the cultural logic by which this metamorphosis occurs? How do the natural essences of soil and rock become infused with both a supernatural sense of peace and a humanlike quality to embrace? In other words, how does this landscape become animated and anointed? This process occurs through an interlocked series of cultural concepts, outlined in this chapter, which both illuminate the special quality of Liberia and explain the ties to land felt by many residents of the Appalachian region in general. While this latter topic is postponed for a later work, this chapter outlines the cultural process that happens within the Liberia community by which ordinary landscapes become vitalized with symbolic power and simultaneously become another member of an extended, and vitally important, network of kin.

Many scholars have examined critically the power of culture (human perception) to transform ordinary physical landforms into extraordinary cultural places. For example, Miles Richardson described place as both "something you can walk on and something you can speak, a curious and uneasy product of experience and symbol." Edward Casey distinguished between "space," a "neutral, pregiven medium, a *tabula rasa* onto which the particularities of culture and history come to be inscribed, with place as the presumed result." Fritz Steele then further "distinguished between a 'sense of place' (the feelings of individuals in that place), and the 'spirit of place,' which is the combination of characteristics that give a place a special feel or personality." "To get into the spirit of a place," Casey elaborated, "is to enter into what makes that place such a special spot, into what is concentrated there like a fully saturated color." Steele also noted the critical importance of "past memories" to expand perceptions "beyond a single point."[1]

In the seminal work by anthropologists Steven Feld and Keith Basso, the authors sought to understand the processes by which "places are metonymically and metaphorically tied to identities."[2] Edward Casey philosophically connected people to land by concluding "that as places gather bodies in their midst in deeply enculturated ways, so cultures conjoin bodies in concrete circumstances of emplacement." Basso used the Western Apache as an example to illustrate "the ways in which citizens of the earth constitute their landscapes and take themselves to be connected to them." Basso further argued that shared experiences of place produce this connection, "a social and moral force [that] may reach sacramental proportions, especially when fused with prominent elements of personal and ethnic identity."[3]

One could add "regional identity" to Basso's list as well, for social scientists also have examined the sense of place in the South in general, South Carolina's Low Country, and in Appalachia.[4] For example, Ronald Eller tied land to "a set of relationships—human relationships that define personal identity, establish a shared history, and define patterns of expectations and behavior." "Mountain people," Eller continued, "tend to be tied not only to a specific plot of land (the 'home' place), a specific . . . locality but to people (kin) and to memories (shared experiences)."[5] In her book *Homeplace*, folklorist Michael Ann Williams described the specific symbolic connection between a physical structure and a family whose ancestors had inhabited that structure, linked through oral narrative. Homeplaces may even become "a site for family reunions," a stage upon which to demonstrate family ties. Because of these connections, the homeplace symbolizes all the memories of family experiences, preserved in narratives. "Through these stories, people may still travel home," Williams concluded.[6]

"The mountain family is rooted in the land," Patricia Beaver noted; "land is symbolically associated with family and has often been in a family for several generations." In fact, Barbara Allen described this connection between families and land as a "genealogical landscape." Allen Batteau also recognized the close tie between land and kin, but argued for land's importance as stemming more from a class-based struggle over a commodity.[7] While this perspective is certainly valuable, there is also a symbolic meaning to land that is equally intriguing. But, Gary Cox observed, mountain people "have great difficulty in verbalizing" this association between land, people, and memory."[8] Melinda Wagner's cultural analysis uncovered two explanatory metaphors (from her southwest Virginia consultants) that help clarify this association: land becomes a family member, and land takes on a spiritual essence. Cox elaborated: "It [land] is the locus of his [mountain resident's] memories, the place he reared his children, the final resting place of generations of his ancestors, and the place where he will be returned to the earth." "In Appalachia, mountains and home are synonymous," Davis concluded.[9]

As has been shown throughout the story, Liberia's residents reflect these very same Appalachian values. But the cultural analysis needs to go further. Readers still need to understand the symbolic process by which people and land become intertwined, both in Appalachia in general (it is assumed) and in Liberia in particular. To comprehend this process, the emic cultural logic will be unraveled by means of a "thick description" of local cultural perceptions in a six-step analysis.[10]

Step One: Ownership of Land

Because their ancestors had labored so long and had fought so hard to retain their land, Liberia's residents believe that the continued ownership of that land is critical for those remaining on it. When asked about the importance of her family's land in the Bald Rock area (see map 2), Angela Young (daughter of James McJunkin) explained: "Well, now, I can speak for Daddy. Owning land was just a priority for him. . . . And Daddy went so far as to, when he drew up his will, to put in there that the land that he left us, his children, was to never be sold. He said, 'I don't want it ever sold. Not ever, ever, ever!'" Pamela Williams noted that Mr. McJunkin "made sure we knew every corner, every rock, every tree, every stump, . . . to make sure that land stayed, because it was given to them, and then they purchased a lot of it."

Mable Clarke, in a newspaper interview in March 1983, "recalls her father telling his children: 'I've worked hard all my life and all I have to give you is land and it's yours.'"[11] A granddaughter of Chris and Lula Owens really appreciates "the work they had to do because we know they had to fight every day for this land. So it really means a lot to us." So important is family land that Mable equates the potential loss of her family's land with a loss of the importance of that land: "I like the community over there [in Liberia] the way it is. I would not want to see a subdivision or anything like that come in there. . . . Our parents left the land for the land not to be sold off. . . . Some new people that just moved in that don't have the same love of the land as we do . . . have came and talked to us about, you know, . . . getting city water through there and making a resort. So, you know, people are looking to come into the Liberia area. . . . But you can lose the value of the land and it would not be the same. It would not hold the same meaning." "Our roots was up there" at Soapstone, Elaine Parker stated.

Step Two: Occupancy of Land

Not only do Liberia residents own ancestral land, but they continue to occupy it, physically connecting their bodies to their ancestors in that critical space. As Chris and Lula Owens aged, they watched with pleasure as Edgar Smith constructed homes for their children on the family's ancestral land. "That was their joy," Mable recalled; "they saw the children was going to be coming back." In fact, Mable continued, Chris Owens was quite adamant: "And Daddy, he would say to us, he'd say, 'Now, before my eyes are closed, I want to see . . . some wood and sticks start going up, or some modern bricks.' He would get on us all the time, every summer we'd come home [for a visit]. . . . He just kept pushing us. You know, like you got to build a house!"

Over in Bald Rock, on Joseph McJunkin's ancestral land, great-granddaughter Angela Young tries to get up there "about every two weeks," she estimated, because she had promised her father that she would always keep an eye on the property in order to protect his hard-won real estate. Sister-in-law Pamela Williams has decided to build a home on the property because "Gramps [James McJunkin] wanted this land to stay in McJunkin [ownership], so y'all have to figure out how we [are] going to keep it in McJunkin land. That's why I decided to go ahead and put a . . . house there." Despite irritants such as bears, rattlesnakes, and social isolation, Mrs. Williams's daughter continues to live on that McJunkin ancestral land on the eastern slope of the Blue Ridge Mountains, at the end of an unpaved road culminating in wilderness. Even after losing her water pressure and facing a washed-out driveway after a thunderstorm, she told her concerned mother: " 'I love it; I wouldn't go anywhere else.' "

Step Three: Family Memories Infuse Family Land

In addition to the historical ownership and contemporary occupancy of ancestral lands, these places draw additional symbolic power from their current owners' memories of the collective pasts of generations of ancestors
who occupied that same land. The association of land with these layers of
meanings energizes the landscape and connects people to place through
time. For example, as an elderly member of the McJunkin family (by marriage), Pamela Williams has reminded her younger relatives that "'we're sitting on something that has so much history.' [We] wouldn't dare think of
selling it. But [we need to] try to come together and put something there so
that our great-grandchildren will keep that legacy alive." Even though she
dwells in Boston, a granddaughter of Chris and Lula Owens considers Liberia to be "home" because "we have a lot of history here as well. . . . It's a nice
legacy that my grandparents left for us to carry on." Judith White directly
linked land and family as she explained the importance of Soapstone Church:
"This is a family. Everybody that was there in that area [Liberia], even
though I was born and raised in Slater, but that's still part of my home too
because that was my Momma and Daddy's home and that's where we went
to church. So that's my home; that's family. It's family ground, home ground."
Every time Judith White stands on the soapstone boulders outside the
church, she thinks "about Aunt Lula, Uncle Chris, [and] my grandmother
and grandfather. I wish that they could be standing there with me."

As places become enlivened by family memories, they generate their own
power as interpreted by the occupiers. For example, one time Judith White
and Mable Clarke had been discussing the old time Soapstone Church homecomings formerly held outside under the huge oak trees, and how as girls
they had to scramble to safeguard the food in case it rained. Just then,
Mrs. White observed from the shelter of the Fellowship Hall that it had
started to rain. "It was amazing how I just said that," she reflected. Sometimes Mable travels to the church or fellowship hall but forgets why she
went. Unabashedly she admits, "It's like [a] magnet. It just draw[s] you, you
know? You go there."

Family stories are the history of the places, directly interweaving people
into place through time. Sitting in her childhood kitchen, surrounded by
members of her extended family, Mable Clarke recalled memories of her
mother in that same kitchen, pointing to the exact place where she had kept
the pies, cobblers, and sweets Mable so loved as a child; her nephew then
indicated the storage cabinet with the bins for flour and sugar, noting that

the piece was "older than I am" (at least five decades). Through her family memories, Judith White also linked place to kin and embodied both: "And until today I can still taste Aunt Lula's corn that she cooked and it's just like it's still in my nostrils. I can smell it cooking and that taste! I still can . . . just walk in the house and you get that good old country smell of food. . . . And sometimes, in a way, I wish I could go back. . . . It'd be great but we know we can't. But we hold those memories, hold them very, very dear and it means a lot."

Step Four: Embedded and Embodied Memories

Ownership and occupancy of ancestral land, together with memories of past relatives in those same spaces, become even more meaningful by embedding those people literally into the landscape through burials. Recently, Pamela Williams reported, her son told her: " 'Before I go back to Philadelphia, I got to go to the mountains [to McJunkin land].' . . . And he said, 'I just want to sit out . . . by the graveyard . . . with my folding chair and my Bible. I just want to sit there quietly.' " In fact, Mrs. Williams observed, whenever members of the family pace out the property lines of McJunkin land, they all recognize that "you're also communing with the people who were there way before you even knew anything about the land. . . . This is where they were; this is where your grandparents, where your great-grandparents, those people who saved it when they were enslaved. They saved the land. So you're communing with them. . . . You have a presence when you go to the cemetery. . . . It's like it's sacred ground. . . . Those lands have special meaning for me personally because my husband was buried there. . . . You have that feeling that everything's at peace, and you're at peace."

When she walks on the grounds of Soapstone Church, Mable Clarke thinks of "the struggle and the hardship that the ones that's gone on that put into that church just to hold on to that church, just to keep that church alive." Her cousin Judith White added: "Every one of them that's out there [in the new cemetery] that we knew as we grew up played a big part in our lives. . . . That's another good feeling like when she [Mable] has that, comes over you when you're there. You're close by."

Step Five: Merging Land, People, and Memory

As generations of family members own, occupy, discuss, and ultimately enter (through burials) their landscape, an intriguing transformation occurs—land and people merge. Pamela Williams described a weekend she spent recently by herself in the wilderness of ancestral McJunkin land, "listening to the birds and listening to the ripple of the water. To me that's—you can't buy that, you know; you can't give that away. You just—*that's in your bones*" (emphasis added). In either Soapstone Cemetery, Mable Clarke does not have a "little creepy feeling." Instead, she explains, she feels that her ancestors are "just right there just watching over you." "Everybody that's buried out there in that cemetery," Mable explained, "it's like somewhere along the line they gave [me] some kind of guidance," that (along with her own life experiences) "the two come together and make you a better person." In fact, Mable can "just walk through the graveyard and I hear the people. . . . It's not a cemetery like okay this is just dead people. The people that's lying there is people that connected my life, that form and shape my life and other peoples' lives. You know, they're not just bones and stuff's just laying there."

Step Six: The Anthropomorphic Landscape

As land and people merge, it is as if the land itself then becomes animated—another person in the extended family kin network. On the day she buried her husband in ancestral McJunkin family land, Pamela Williams remembered how the pink dogwoods were in bloom and "everything just seemed to say, 'Welcome home!'" Mable Clarke on multiple occasions (including earlier in this chapter and in the book) has described the sensation she feels when she reaches the crest of the knoll with the church on her right: "it's like the mountains just reach out and just hugs you and say, 'Welcome home.'" Then, while sipping tea before her expansive picture window overlooking Liberia Valley and the Blue Ridge beyond, Mable anthropomorphizes her landscape further: "The beautiful rocks and the trees . . . peep out at you. . . . And every time you look at them you see something different. They have a different message for you every day. . . . Sometime you can look at the mountains; they pull the shade down. They actually close you right off. Like 'Today I'm not going to let you look in.' And then the next day the curtains open back. They open the shades up. . . . Then some days they just give you a little small peep."

Perhaps because the landscape comes alive, losing this significant land, embedded with memories and with kin, held by families through the tribulations of centuries, would be unimaginable. For example, when asked what might happen if the Liberia Valley were ever to be sold to developers,

Mable Clarke stated: "I think it's too painful for me to think about right now . . . because it's just—when you talk about it, it's like something's piercing my heart."

This multilayered cultural process by which ordinary dirt and rock ultimately become another member of an extended family network linked through generations explains the magnetic pull of the land to draw long-absent kin home, the justification of the life-endangering struggles to retain ownership, and the pain felt by those who, for whatever reasons, must surrender their family land to various types of injustice, development, or abandonment. While this process specifically explains the strength of family ties to land in the Liberia area, this same process also explains the equally strong ties to land felt by other mountain residents, regardless of race, in Appalachia.[12]

Epilogue

The story of the Liberia community opened with the tragedy of the church burning and challenges to the "truth" of the Liberia story, and this book has presented evidence that the community persists despite that event and other equally pernicious ones. Today, large portions of ancestral McJunkin and Owens family land remain in family ownership and will continue so into the near future. Owens and McJunkin descendants still occupy that same land, family members still tell stories about their ancestors, and new generations continue to be buried (embedded) in that family land. Through this process, these lands become for the residents of Liberia not only sacred but animated—another member of their extended families. This metamorphosis of rock and soil into an old and familiar relative provides the centripetal force drawing long-distant kin back to visit all of their ancestors, including the very ground upon which other ancestors had once trod.

As one stands on the soapstone boulders beside the little church on top of the knoll and gazes across the terraced fields of Chris Owens's old farm to the pedestal of Table Rock, a viewer sees the same general panorama that Katie did as a ten-year-old enslaved black girl in 1850. At that time, she had no last name and virtually no human rights. Perhaps at some point, pausing in her enforced and unrewarded labor, the young slave girl may have gazed upon that same mountain across that same field, and wondered if she (or her grandchildren) might ever be free. Young Katie never could have imagined the tremendous social forces that eventually would wash over that bucolic scene, or the turmoil and trouble her descendants would face but ultimately transcend.

Over a century and a half later, Mable Owens Clarke, the great-granddaughter of that same enslaved little girl, now owns that land upon which her ancestor had worked, now has human and civil rights, and now has a last name. Soapstone Church "is still sitting here" on the same rock overlooking the same valley it did over a century and a half ago, Katie Owens's great-grandson stated proudly; "and I'm so happy today" to see that. A woman in the Soapstone congregation directly connected the church to both past and future generations, using the institution as a fulcrum to balance time periods: "Soapstone will always function. It will always be here. . . . I mean, even with the grandkids, like even now, they don't know it, but hey, we'll instill it in them. . . . But it's just like we have learned so much from our forefathers. . . . We're still taking that torch and we're still carrying it on, carrying it on. We can't let it go out. Just can't let it go out."

This "great commission"—to carry on the legacy of Katie Owens, Joseph McJunkin, and the others by means of Soapstone Baptist Church and the Liberia community that it anchors—has been expressed most poignantly by Mable Owens Clarke, the direct descendant of both of these former slaves, as she recalled her mother's final wish:

Nothing could ever change . . . what you feel when you walk . . . on the grounds of that church. You know you think of the struggle and the hardship that the ones that's gone on that put into that church to just to hold on to that church, just to keep that church alive. That ground. And I recall when my mother had her stroke, . . . she'd lie there in that bed and she grasped my hand and she said to me, "I want you to make me a promise." And she looked [at] me—I remember her eyes never blinked. She said, "You make sure as long as you live and the breath of God is in you, that you keep the doors of that church open." And she held my hand so tight, she said, "Will you make me that promise? Whatever it takes, whatever you have to do to keep that church doors open. Don't let that doors close." [pause] And that's why I do what I do.

And that is the reason for this book—to document and honor the hard-won legacy of Katie Owens and her relatives, her friends, her neighbors, and her descendants, and to add back to the history of the state and nation just a fragment of the myriad histories of human beings who lived, loved, labored, and died alongside their majority neighbors and yet who remained largely invisible to them and to recorded history. The Liberia story is the story, the countermemory, of all of these heroic people—men and women, young and old, black and mixed race (and white), wealthy and poor, and from all levels of education. Ultimately the Liberia story is also the story of the strength of the human spirit.

Appendix 1

Soapstone Baptist Church Cemetery Grave Names

Kin relationship to Mable Owens Clarke [MOC], unless otherwise indicated. Names are generally alphabetical, but relatives are grouped together.

GRACIE LOUISE BLAKELY, born January 15, 1943; died March 8, 2016
MOC father's mother's daughter's daughter (daughter of Rosa Glenn and Tom McGowens)

MAURICE BLAKELY JR., born June 28, 1940
Husband of Gracie Blakely

D. M. "DOCK" CHASTAIN, born June 4, 1886; died June 13, 1952
MOC father's mother's daughter's husband's father

LOUISE MCJUNKIN CHASTAIN, born October 25, 1891; died October 1, 1929
MOC mother's father's sister (?) and wife of Dock Chastain

EDDIE ARVEL COOPER, born August 13, 1947; died February 17, 1995
MOC husband's brother

COLUMBUS FERGUSON, born June 25, 1886; died May 25, 1960
Husband of Queen Anthony

QUEEN ANTHONY FERGUSON, born September 12, 1886; died ___
Daughter of King and Lucy Anthony

CLARENCE WILLIAM GLENN, born October 15, 1888; died August 5, 1974
MOC father's mother's (Rosa) half brother (?)

ARTHUR C. HAGOOD, born December 4, 1903; died April 13, 1955
MOC father's sister's husband

WILLIE MAE OWENS HAGOOD, born February 19, 1904; died May 12, 1981
(tin marker)
MOC father's sister

MARY HILL, born 1877; died November 3, 1910
Wife of W. M. Hill

WILLIAM M. HILL SR., born June 15, 1871; died September 4, 1938
Husband of Mary Hill

ANDREW MCGOWAN, born August 18, 1912; died February 18, 1968
MOC father's mother's (Rosa) son

O'DELL MCGOWANS, born ___; died November 1, 1979 (cannot locate grave)
MOC father's mother's (Rosa) son

W. MCJUNKIN (stone covered by bush)
MOC mother's brother

A. B. SALOM BENUM [ABSALOM] MCJUNKINS, born March 6, 1896;
died February 3, 1976
MOC mother's brother

REV. HENRY MCJUNKIN, born May 31, 1904; died October 7, 1984
MOC mother's brother

VERA PORTER MCJUNKIN, born March 7, 1910; died July 21, 1991
MOC mother's brother's wife

W. R. EDENS, born 1834; died August 27, 1903
Kin relationship unknown

SOPHIA ELLA AMANDA EDENS MILES (no birth or death dates)
Wife of Henry Miles (blank tombstone next)

CHRIS OWENS, born November 3, 1893; died February 21, 2000
MOC father

LULA MAE OWENS, born April 22, 1896; died March 25, 1999
MOC mother

ALBERT CHRISTOPHER "A C" OWENS, born September 26, 1924;
died May 20, 2014
MOC brother

GROVER E. OWENS, born March 10, 1930; died October 29, 2015
MOC Brother

ELFORD OWENS SR., born September 4, 1934; died August 15, 1993
MOC brother

MINNIE OWENS BOWENS, born December 9, 1935; died May 10, 2012
MOC brother's wife

ALMA BENNETT, born July 2, 1928; died March 22, 2008
MOC sister

GEORGE W. BENNETT, born April 13, 1915; died November 13, 1969
MOC sister's husband

WILLIE OWENS, born 1854; died 1879
MOC father's father

EBBIE EUGENE WHITESIDE, born November 29, 1929; died July 15, 2002
MOC father's sister's (Willie Mae Owens) son

FRANCES ZEOLAR WHITESIDE, born October 17, 1929; died February 9, 2015
Wife of Ebbie E. Whiteside

TINNY BELL WHITESIDE, born January 28, 1914; died October 8, 1943
MOC father's mother's (Rosa) daughter (wife of E. E. Whiteside)

ROOSEVELT E. WHITESIDE, born September 18, 1933;
died November 16, 1952
Son of E. E. and T. B. Whiteside

BILLIE JOE WHITESIDE, born July 17, 1935; died October 7, 2001
Son of E. E. and T. B. Whiteside

GENEVA WILLIAMS ANDREWS, born ___; died September 14, 1983
Sister of Chester Williams Sr.

ALEXANDER D. WILLIAMS, born ___; died December 23, 1979
Brother of Chester Williams Sr.

BESSIE LEE WILLIAMS, born October 4, 1916; died October 15, 1998
MOC father's mother's (Rosa) daughter

CHESTER WILLIAMS, born May 23, 1912; died May 17, 1970
Husband of Bessie Lee (Gowens) Williams

CHESTER WILLIAMS JR., born March 21, 1948; died October 23, 2002
Son of Chester and Bessie Williams

FLOYD WILLIAMS SR., born February 24, 1938; died August 1, 1998
Son of Chester and Bessie Williams

DANNY L. BARTON, born November 21, 1951; died December 14, 2000
Husband of Rodessa Williams, daughter of Chester and Bessie Williams

Soapstone Baptist Church (Slave) Cemetery Grave Names

Chapter references and U.S. Census records included
Pumpkintown District unless otherwise indicated

QUEEN, dau of C. H. and E. A. Anderson, born December 28, 1896;
died February 25, 1903
[carved epitaph:] "Asleep in Jesus"

RHODA GOWANS, died May 17, 1882; aged 45 years [born 1837]
(First wife of A. R. Gowens. Mentioned in 1880 Census; see also note 67 to
chapter 3) [carved epitaph:] "Farewell my husband / Dear keep Christ the /
Lord in your heart / In heaven we all / Should meet we will / shout around /
the Saviours feet"

ADLINE GOWAN, died October 4, 1890; aged 36 years [born 1854]
(Second wife of A. R. Gowens. See also note 67 to chapter 3) [carved epitaph:]
"Farewell my husband / child dear keep / Christ the Lord in / Your [curved symbol]
If in Heaven / We all should meet / We will shout around / The savior's feet"

REV. A. R. GOWENS, 1845–1928 / His dau Charlota / Wife of A. P. McKinney,
1884–1925
(footstones marked A.R.G. and A.P.M.)
(A. R. Gowens, mentioned in 1920, 1910, 1900, 1880 Census; discussed in chapter 4)
(dau. Charlotte, mentioned in 1920, 1910, 1900 Census; discussed in chapter 4)
Ansel "Anse" McKinney, mentioned in 1940, 1930, 1920 Census, Pickens District
165; 1880 Census, Eastatoe District; discussed in chapters 3, 4 and 5)

JAMES KEMP, died July 19, 1938 [S. C. Franks and Son Funeral Home marker]
(Born about 1868, mentioned in 1930 Census; 1920 Census [Pickens District 164];
1880 Census; 1870 Census, Dacusville District; discussed in chapter 4)

CHANIE KIMP, died Aug. 6, 1884, age 60 years [born 1824]
(Mother of Emerson Kemp; discussed in chapter 2)

Appendix 2

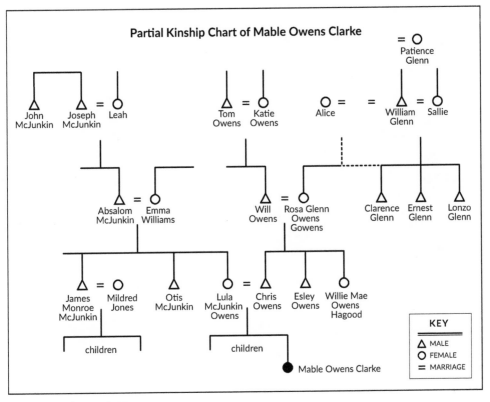

Partial Kinship Chart of Mable Owens Clarke

Chart by Sarah Moore.

Appendix 3

Names of Contemporary Informants

Pseudonym	Relationship
CARL FRENCH	Owens family friend
ALLEN HILL	Friend of Don Owens
ALICE JACKSON	Owens family friend
DON OWENS	Mable's brother's son
JESSIE OWENS	Mable's brother
MICHAEL OWENS	Mable's brother
PHILIP OWENS	Mable's brother
WILLIAM OWENS	Mable's brother
ELAINE PARKER	Owens family relative
ROBERT PARKER	Owens family relative
BERNARD QUINN	Owens family friend
EDGAR SMITH (real name)	Owens family friend
JUDITH WHITE	Mable's cousin
PAMELA WILLIAMS	Owens family relative
BETH YEATS	Owens family friend
ANGELA MCJUNKIN YOUNG	Mable's first cousin
STEPHEN YOUNG	Angela Young's husband
COLLEEN ZIMMERMAN	Owens family friend

Notes

Chapter 1

1. Megginson, *African-American Life*, 4. Hereafter abbreviated *AAL*.

2. See Halperin, *Livelihood of Kin*.

3. For the geology of the area, see Murphy, *Carolina Rocks!*, 20–21 and 30–31.

4. Foner, *Nothing but Freedom*, 44; Foner, *Reconstruction*, xxiv; and Foner, with Brown, *Forever Free*. For the classic "Reconstruction as failure" white perspective, see Robertson, *Red Hills and Cotton*, 259–63.

5. See Foner, *Reconstruction*. The argument is summarized from 158–70, 177–216, 304–64, 353–72, and 389–459, and also Foner, *Nothing but Freedom*, 60–71.

6. Foner, with Brown, *Forever Free*, xxvii.

7. Foner, *Reconstruction*, 602–11; and Foner, *Nothing but Freedom*, 71–73.

8. Foner, *Reconstruction*, 610.

9. Baker, *What Reconstruction Meant*; countermemory description, 70; countermemory persistence, 112–33. See also Foner, with Brown, *Forever Free*, xxv–xxvii.

10. Baker, *What Reconstruction Meant*, 113. See also Foner, with Brown, *Forever Free*, xxvii.

11. Ringer, "Intellectual Field," 270. Ringer cites Bourdieu, "Intellectual Field."

12. Zerubavel, *Recovered Roots*, 11.

13. Clifford, "Introduction"; consecutive sentences' quotes from 2, 7, and 13.

14. Marcus and Fischer, *Anthropology as Cultural Critique*, 26.

15. hooks, *Yearning*, 125–28; quote from 133.

16. Harrison and Harrison, "Introduction," 1.

17. Tyler, "Post-modern Ethnography," 131.

18. Collins, *Black Feminist Thought*, 286.

19. Coates, *Between the World and Me*, 44.

20. Foucault, "Power and Strategies," 142.

21. Foucault, "Prison Talk," 39.

22. R. Lynch, "Foucault's Theory of Power," 26.

23. Hoffman, "Disciplinary Power," 32.

24. Feder, "Power/Knowledge," 59. Feder refers to Foucault's *History of Sexuality* 1: 96. The concluding comment is from Feder, "Power/Knowledge," 60.

25. See a discussion from Coates, *Between the World and Me*, 145.

26. Scott, *Domination*, x–xiii; quotes from xiii.

27. Scott, *Art of Not Being Governed*.

28. Ibid., 329; see also Halperin, *Livelihood of Kin*, 4.

29. Scott, *Art of Not Being Governed*, 237.

30. Scott, *Domination*, 62n31 on slavery; see also 82 on hidden transcripts.

31. Ibid., xi.

32. Sitton and Conrad, *Freedom Colonies*, 3.

33. Schweninger, *Black Property Owners*, 165.

34. Sitton and Conrad, *Freedom Colonies*, quote on defensive black communities from 4; other quotes from 18–19.

35. Montell, *Saga of Coe Ridge*, 3.

36. Sitton and Conrad, *Freedom Colonies*, 179.

37. Schweninger, *Black Property Owners*.

38. Tolnay, *Bottom Rung*; and Fite, *Cotton Fields No More*.

39. Chafe, Gavins, and Korstad, *Remembering Jim Crow*; quotes from xxiii–xxiv and xxvii.

40. Holt, *Making Freedom Pay*.

41. Schultz, *Rural Face of White Supremacy*, 14 and 170.

42. Reid, "Researching African American Land," micro-level studies, 315, and oral interviewing, 311. See also Baker, "'Recourse that Could Be Depended Upon,'" 22.

43. The community is "Promised Land" on maps, but Bethel's book title differs. See Reid, "Researching African American Land," 311; Schweninger, *Black Property Owners*, 165; Bethel, *Promiseland*; and Wideman, *Fatheralong*. Lewis, *Blackways of Kent*; Stack, *Call to Home*; Falk, *Rooted in Place*; and Dyer and Bailey, "Place to Call Home."

44. Coates, *Between the World and Me*, 103.

45. Foner, *Nothing but Freedom*, 40–43 on the Haiti revolt; Collins, *Black Feminist Thought*, 147. See also Schultz, *Rural Face of White Supremacy*, 136, and Gilmore, *Gender and Jim Crow*. Schultz speculated that the myth might have been a response to white male frustration at women's rights issues, while Gilmore connected it to a Social Darwinist fear of racial impurity.

46. See Tolnay and Beck, *Festival of Violence*; terrorism quote from 50. See also Gilmore, *Gender and Jim Crow*, 92.

47. "Billie Holiday—Strange Fruit Lyrics," songlyrics.com, accessed June 22, 2017, http://www.songlyrics.com/billie-holiday/strange-fruit-lyrics. One can also access Holiday's performance online, and see her nuanced facial and tonal comments on the lyrics.

48. DuBois, "We Are a Nation of Murderers," public amusement quote from 123, and 125–26.

49. Taussig, "Culture of Terror." Specific quotes in consecutive sentences are from 492, 469, 495 (twice), and 468.

50. Turner and Cabbell, "Preface," xiv. This is a somewhat curious statement, given Lynwood Montell's (1970) oral history of Coe Ridge, Kentucky, *Saga of Coe Ridge*; and folklorist Richard Blaustein's reference to "Free Hill," Tennessee, in his Review of "Free Hill." Both communities, however, lie in the central (not southeastern) Appalachians.

51. L. Williams, "Vanishing Appalachian," 204; Culpepper, "Black Charlestonians," 362; B. Smith, "De-gradations of Whiteness," 43; Nash, *Reconstruction's Ragged Edge*, 2; Barnes, "Archaeology of Community Life," 699–700; Hayden, "In Search of Justice," 124; and Turner, "Demography of Black Appalachia," 260.

52. Inscoe, "Introduction," 2 and 6 (for the Beech Creek reference); and J. L. Smith, "Negotiating the Terms of Freedom," 220. For more information on the three North Carolina communities, see Ostwalt and Pollitt, "Salem School and Orphanage"; Butcher, "Religion, Race, Gender, and Education"; and Keefe and Manross, "Race, Religion, and Community"; the "accommodation" quote is from the last article, 258. See Culpepper, "Black Charlestonians" (see 371 for the "Happy Land" reference). For more information on "Happy Land," see Bryan and Bryan, "Kingdom of Happy Land." See Megginson, *AAL*, 331–32, for information about Maxwell and Liberia.

53. Jackson, "Shattering Slave Life Portrayals."

54. Megginson, *AAL*; and Dunaway, *Slavery*, 12.

55. Megginson, *AAL*, 171.

56. Chafe, Gavins, and Korstad, *Remembering Jim Crow*, xxviii; Jackson, "Shattering Slave Life Portrayals," 458; and Inscoe, *Race, War, and Remembrance*, 60.

57. Inscoe, "Introduction," on agency, 10; center stage, 11; women, 12; obscure individuals, 11; wide open, 11.

58. hooks, *Talking Back*, 15 and 18.

59. Collins, *Black Feminist Thought*, 3 and 229.

60. Collins, "Shifting the Center." See also hooks, *Feminist Theory*, 15, and hooks, *Talking Back*, 21. The intersectionality quote came from a talk by Patricia Hill Collins at Clemson University on March 2, 2016; motherwork quote is from Collins, "Shifting the Center," 47.

61. Collins, "Shifting the Center," 49–59. See also Collins, *Black Feminist Thought*, 174–94. For an additional perspective on black grandmothers, see Jimenez, "History of Grandmothers," 525. See also Megginson, *AAL*, 171–73, on interracial sex and exploitation.

62. Collins, *Black Feminist Thought*, 269. See also Chafe, Gavins, and Korstad, *Remembering Jim Crow*, 91.

63. For those tracing genealogy, Ancestry.com presents interesting challenges. The site reprints actual handwritten copies of the census forms, with a searchable typed index below. Since most of the locals in Upstate South Carolina were poorly educated, and the census takers may have been as well, the names on the forms are often phonetically rendered, as they would sound to an Upstate southern speaker. For example, "Terrell" may be spelled "Turl" or "Camp" as "Kemp." Compounding the difficulty, the volunteers for Ancestry.com may have misread the handwritten forms or repeated the original, incorrect spelling in the searchable index. Thus, genealogists doing a name search may be unsuccessful. Caution and patience are advised.

64. Historian Theda Perdue noted that the term "mulatto" entered the U.S. Census by 1850, as whites "began to see 'Mixed Blood' as a specific category with

its own inherent characteristics distinct from either parent." Perdue argued that the term originally designated children of Native American and European parentage, but later included children of European and African ancestry as well. By 1850, Perdue concluded, the category had gained social significance and thus had become relevant enough to record in the census. The term disappeared from census use early in the twentieth century. For the discussion, see Perdue, *"Mixed Blood" Indians*, 86.

65. J. L. Smith, "Negotiating the Terms of Freedom," 231; Schultz, *Rural Face of White Supremacy*, 201; and Megginson, *AAL*, 355.

66. B. Reece, *History of Pumpkintown—Oolenoy* (hereafter cited as *HPO*), 7; Lynch and Ellison, *Echoes*, 13; and J. Reece, *Rambling from the Mountain*, 6–7.

67. Chafe, Gavins, and Korstad, *Remembering Jim Crow*, 58.

68. As will be seen in chapter 2, McJunkin's grandfather recalled quite specific details that, when compared to U.S. Census data, validate his memory through over a century and a half of oral tradition. James McJunkin had been interviewed twice about his collection; see Cornelison, Fant, Hembree, and Robertson, *Journey Home*, 19; and Clark, Foster, Lewis, and Sorenson, "Memories," 38.

69. Holder, "Notes," 3.

70. See Megginson, *AAL*, 330, who described Liberia as functioning "harmoniously with local whites most of the time. Post–World War books and newspaper articles by whites have stressed this harmony."

71. Sitton and Conrad, *Freedom Colonies*, 4 (see also 30 for the mention of county records). See also Allen and Montell, *From Memory to History*, and Schultz, *Rural Face of White Supremacy*, 228–33.

72. Allen and Montell, *From Memory to History*, 21; see also Scott, *Art of Not Being Governed*, 237.

73. Montell, *Saga of Coe Ridge*, viii.

74. Baker, " 'Recourse That Could Be Depended Upon,' " 22.

75. Jackson, "Shattering Slave Life Portrayals," 457 and 458.

76. The author first cleared the project through the university review process and then contacted possible contributors, asking to speak with them in a place and time of their choice and with whomever else they wanted to be present. Most interviews were conducted at residents' homes, but a few were held at places of business. About seventeen African Americans and about ten Euro-Americans were interviewed specifically about Liberia, for a total of about twenty-seven hours of conversation. Interviews ranged from thirty minutes to several hours, and participants may have been asked for follow-up interviews as well. Transcripts of every interview were done by paid undergraduates, double checked against the original interview tapes by the author, and then returned to every participant by mail. All contributors had been promised anonymity during the interview sessions, in keeping with the best practices of anthropological research. On the other hand, if individuals approved the use of their names with their quoted information, then their actual names were used. If published accounts (such as local histories) provided real names, then those real names were included here. In all other instances with living

individuals, pseudonyms were used. For issues involving deep background or for especially sensitive topics, the level of anonymity was raised to "a resident" or "an older woman." Every word quoted was actually said, but sometimes those speakers remain anonymous or pseudonymous. Rather than correcting the grammar of recorded speech, the book uses verbatim quotes. It is recognized that grammatical errors may occur in actual human speech, and these errors are not corrected in the text, in order to avoid distractions and to preserve authenticity. On the other hand, for unusual constructions in recorded speech, [*sic*] is used.

77. Collins, "Shifting the Center," 48–49.

78. Collins, *Black Feminist Thought*, 72; hooks, *Yearning*, 153.

79. hooks, *Talking Back*, 43–46.

80. Chafe, Gavins, and Korstad, *Remembering Jim Crow*, xxxv.

Chapter 2

1. See Klein, *Unification of a Slave State*; see also the map on 111. Dunaway, *First American Frontier*, 16–18; Perdue, *"Mixed Blood" Indians*, 3; and Groover, "Evidence for Folkways," 58.

2. Edgar, *South Carolina*, 208, for the date of 1763 quote; the date of 1776 quote is on 229.

3. Dennis, "American Revolutionaries," 215–16. See also Edgar, *South Carolina*, 229.

4. Seaborn, *Hawkins's Journeys*, 1–2.

5. Ibid., 2. On map 2, this line would begin at the North Carolina–South Carolina state line approximately under the *R* in "North Carolina," on a straight line clipping the top of the *S* in "South Carolina."

6. Dennis, "American Revolutionaries," 264.

7. Seaborn, *Hawkins's Journeys*, 2. Megginson, *AAL*, 21–23, described the frontier closing.

8. See, for example, D. Williams, "Georgia's Forgotten Miners."

9. Edgar, *South Carolina*, 270–75.

10. Wright, *South Carolina*, 163–66.

11. Ibid., 167–71; and Edgar, *South Carolina*, 287.

12. The Keith migration story may be found in Overman, "Keith Family in South Carolina," 2.

13. The April 1795 date comes from John M. Keith, "To the Tenth Generation," 13. The denial of any earlier date is from 12. See also Edgar, *South Carolina*, 229; Holder, "Notes," 11 and 16; and Holder (ibid., 11) also offers the criticism about the pony legend.

14. See Dunaway, "Speculators and Settler Capitalists," 62.

15. Reece, *HPO*, 11–12; map for Keith's home, 61. The Reid story comes from Helen Reid Roberts, "Sir Thomas Reid of Inverness-Shire and His Descendants of Pickens County, South Carolina," a private manuscript made available by the Sutherland

family during the third annual "100 Year Reunion of Upstate Families," Southern Wesleyan University, June 23, 2012, 4.

16. The Pumpkintown description comes from the "Keith Family" Overman manuscript, 2. The naming story comes from Neuffer, *Names in South Carolina*, 159.

17. Moragne's description may be found in Craven, *Neglected Thread*, 180, and Richard's description comes from "Table Rock," 1. At this time, local sources mention corn as the principal crop in the region; these observations are supported by the U.S. Agricultural Census, available at USDA Census of Agriculture Historical Archive, Albert R. Mann Library, Cornell University, http://agcensus.mannlib.cornell.edu/AgCensus/censusParts.do?year=1850 (accessed December 3, 2016).

18. Overman, "Keith Family," 3, suggests the earlier "nobility" of the Oolenoy Valley names. The local domination of families is described by Inscoe, *Mountain Masters*, 115, and Dunaway, *Slavery*, 29.

19. The correlation between status and settlement comes from Inscoe, *Mountain Masters*, 116. Dunaway, "Speculators and Settler Capitalists," 68, noted the polarization; see Nash, *Reconstruction's Ragged Edge*, 11, for the comparative percentage. Overman described the local power of her ancestors in "Keith Family," 2.

20. These family history stories come from Rhyne, *McJunkin*. The pony story and the land purchase may be found in Banks, Crapps, Nix, Richards, and Stinnett, "Cleveland," 66. The story of Joshua Burgess came from an interview with his descendant Mark Burgess published in the *Greenville News*, May 25, 2016, 6A.

21. Holder, "Notes," 11, for a list of criticisms. See Swanton, *Indians of the Southeastern United States*, 349.

22. The institution of slavery in the Appalachian Mountains has been well documented by Inscoe, *Mountain Masters*; Nash, *Reconstruction's Ragged Edge*, 17–18; Dunaway, *Slavery*; and Dunaway, *African-American Family*, map from 9. For more specific details about Upstate South Carolina, see Megginson, *AAL*.

23. Inscoe's conclusion is from "Race and Racism," 122–23, with the quiltlike quote from 123. For the geographical distances, see Inscoe, *Mountain Masters*, 159.

24. The statements on Appalachian local elites may be found in Dunaway, *Slavery*, 29, 37, and 241; the local merchants quote is from Dunaway, "Put in Master's Pocket," 130. For the economic health of mountain slavery in North Carolina, see Inscoe, *Mountain Masters*, 81. See also Drake, "Slavery and Antislavery," 16–17.

25. U.S. Census information has been acquired from the website Ancestry.com; various dates. The 1860 U.S. Census recorded no free blacks living in the Pumpkintown Post Office census district and only three free black families (sixteen people) in the adjacent Dacusville Post Office tract. See also Poole, *Never Surrender*, 11. See also Inscoe, *Mountain Masters*, 62, for an estimate of the enslaved population.

26. Dunaway's estimate is from *Slavery*, 25. See also Megginson, *AAL*, 124.

27. J. Reece, *Rambling*, 6; and Reece, *HPO*, 41. J. Reece (*Rambling*, 6) adds the other names.

28. Estimates of slave ownership are supported by Megginson, *AAL*, 27. Overman's quote is from "Keiths," 23. The second quote is from Reece, *HPO*, 40. Historian Bruce Baker (personal communication) believes that Keith's estimate of the number of her family's slaves may be too high.

29. Overman, "Keith Family," 7.

30. Dunaway, *Slavery*, 61. James Hester's story is from a private manuscript owned by the Sutherland family and accessed by the author during the fourth annual "100 Year Reunion of Upstate Families," Southern Wesleyan University, May 6, 2013. In the 1870 Census, Kemp's name is spelled "Camp"; in later years it is spelled "Kemp" (perhaps a local mispronunciation).

31. See Overman, "Keith Family," 8 (first 2 sentences) and 18.

32. Reece, *HPO*, 41; Lynch and Ellison, *Echoes*, 21 (1836 date) and 44 (1845 date).

33. Doyle, *Etiquette of Race Relations*, 16; and Inscoe, *Mountain Masters*, 96.

34. Inscoe, *Mountain Masters*, 104–5.

35. Historians documenting Upstate slave life include Hahn, *Nation under Our Feet*; Inscoe, *Mountain Masters*; Megginson, *AAL*, 157–70; Edgar, *South Carolina*, 315–18; and Saville, "Measure of Freedom." The leading sociologist would be Dunaway, *African-American Family* and Dunaway, *Slavery*.

36. Megginson, *AAL*, 163; housing descriptions come from ibid., 160–63; Edgar, *South Carolina*, 316; and Dunaway, *African-American Family*, 89; sanitation problems from ibid., 93.

37. Saville ("Measure of Freedom," 6–7) and Edgar (*South Carolina*, 315) describe gardens and foods, respectively, with the specific quote from Edgar, *South Carolina*, 315; see also Dunaway, *African-American Family*, 106–7 and 179 (malnourished quote). See Megginson, *AAL*, 163–65 for additional information.

38. McJunkin's story may be found in Clark, Foster, Lewis, and Sorenson, "Memories," 42.

39. McJunkin's quote is ibid., 42. Dunaway, *African-American Family*, 85, and the journal entry is from Dunaway, *Slavery*, 55.

40. Women's work is elaborated in Dunaway, *African-American Family*, first quote from 164 and second quote from 168. See also Blassingame, *Slave Community*, 250–54; Anglin, "Lives on the Margin," 187–98; and Megginson, *AAL*, 113–20.

41. Dunaway, *African-American Family*, 152–53. See also Reece, *HPO*, 41. See Megginson, *AAL*, 165–66, on herbal cures. See also Jimenez, "History of Grandmothers," 528, for the important work of grandmothers as community healers and midwives.

42. Dunaway, *Slavery*, 250. See also Blassingame, *Slave Community*, 105; and Megginson, *AAL*, 123 on slave subculture.

43. Jimenez, "History of Grandmothers," 527.

44. Dunaway, *African-American Family*, 278; and Dunaway, *Slavery*, 255. See also Megginson, *AAL*, 123; and Blassingame, *Slave Community*, 147.

45. Discussion of slave marriages may be found in Edgar, *South Carolina*, 317; Blassingame, *Slave Community*, 151–53; and Dunaway, *African-American Family*, quote from 67. See also Megginson, *AAL*, 140–56, on slave families.

46. Edgar, *South Carolina*, 317. See also Blassingame, *Slave Community*, 172.

47. Megginson, *AAL*, 118; and Hunter, *Nickel and a Prayer*, 160.

48. The McGowens story is from Gracie Blakely, ed., "The McGowens Chronicle" (n.p., 1994), a private manuscript owned by Mable Owens Clarke, accessed on May 5, 2013. Dunaway, *African-American Family*, both quotes from 53, supports these memories.

49. McJunkin's story comes from Clark, Foster, Lewis, and Sorenson, "Memories," 43–44. Dunaway, *African-American Family*, 65. Angela Young provided the author with a photo of her father, James McJunkin, plowing a field with his mule Tobe and a handheld plow sometime in 1968.

50. Luke Terrell's story may be found in Reece, *HPO*, 42. The quote from the will of Alfred Hester was accessed at the seventh annual Reunion of Upcountry Families, March 12, 2016. Although the (copied) will spells her name "Chancy," her tombstone reads "Chanie," as does a later census form. It is easy to see how an *E* could be misread as a *C* from an old text. Lynch and Ellison, *Echoes*, 86, briefly mention Kemp, also eulogized in the *Pickens Sentinel* on December 29, 1927, 1. Dunaway, *Slavery*, 61. James Hester's corn crib story is from the private Sutherland family manuscript accessed May 6, 2013 (see note 30 to this chapter). Megginson's observation is from *AAL*, 48.

51. Sam "Goob" Keith's childhood story appears in Reece, *HPO*, 42; and in Lynch and Ellison, *Echoes*, 76.

52. The 1860 Slave Census may be found through Ancestry.com.

53. Dunaway, *Slavery*, 205; see also Barnes, "Archaeology of Community Life," 691.

54. The Joseph McJunkin story is from Clark, Foster, Lewis, and Sorenson, "Memories," 43 and 41. See also Inscoe, *Mountain Masters*, 102–5, for background; and Blassingame, *Slave Community*, 120, for information about patrollers. The war quote comes from Ruth McJunkin Adams's "Joseph McJunkin story" in Johnson, Hightower, Ladd, Jameson, and Cruell, "Oolenoy River Baptist Missionary and Educational Association: 2nd History Edition" (n.p., 2013), private manuscript loaned by Rev. Chester Trower, Soapstone Baptist Church.

55. The McJunkin detail of the drowning comes from an interview between James Monroe McJunkin and Jimmy Cornelison, "James McJunkin, Chronicler of his people," *Greenville News*, May 25, 1983, 1B. Additional details of the story may be found in Clark, Foster, Lewis, and Sorenson, "Memories," 38–39. It is recognized that "zip" is an anachronism in this story, for the verb in this sense did not come into use in English until the early twentieth century, according to the *Oxford English Dictionary*.

56. Dunaway's generalization is found in *Slavery*, 246. The comment on disguising sales is from Dunaway, "Put in Master's Pocket," 122. Clark, Foster, Lewis,

and Sorenson, "Memories," 41, support her story. See also Megginson, *AAL*, 81–87, for a discussion about escape and resistance by slaves. Scott, *Domination*, xiii.

57. See also Clark, Foster, Lewis, and Sorenson, "Memories," 41. It is interesting to note that the gender of Joseph's owner has come down through fifteen decades of oral history as having been female, lending credence to the possibility that his owner was indeed Sarah McJunkin, and that Daniel McJunkin owned Joseph's half brother John.

58. Scott, *Domination*, 67.

59. Collins, *Black Feminist Thought*, 72; and Scott, *Domination*, 3. See also Collins, *Black Feminist Thought*, 97–98.

60. Megginson's comment is from *AAL*, 124; the social interaction statements are from 174–75. Doyle, *Etiquette of Race Relations*, 4.

61. Tindall, *South Carolina Negroes*, 296; Collins, *Black Feminist Thought*, 162; the purity comment is from 145–46, and black female resistance quote is from 162; and Tindall, *South Carolina Negroes*, 296. See also Edgar, *South Carolina*, 307.

62. See Blassingame, *Slave Community*, 154–56.

63. Dunaway, *African-American Family*, 120–21.

64. Pat Todd, "Rooted in the Past; Reaching for the Future: The 2002 Talley Family Reunion," n.p., n.d., private manuscript. Accessed March 12, 2016, at the seventh annual Reunion of Upcountry Families.

65. McJunkin's interview is from Cornelison, "James McJunkin," *Greenville News*, May 25, 1983, 1B, 4B. The survival strategies are discussed in Blassingame, *Slave Community*, 284–322. See also Edgar, *South Carolina*, 317–18. Hunter, *Nickel and a Prayer*, both quotes from 37.

66. Clark, Foster, Lewis, and Sorenson, "Memories," 41. Starks Adams's interview may be found in Duncan, Thompson, and Young, "Place called Adamsville," quote from 61.

67. Doyle, *Etiquette of Race Relations*, 80; Dunaway, *Slavery*, 171–97; and Scott, *Domination*, 87.

68. The Suddeth story is from Clark, Foster, Lewis, and Sorenson, "Memories," 44. For other discussions of resistance, see Blassingame, *Slave Community*, 192–222.

69. Dunaway, *Slavery*, 244 and 249–50; quote from 244.

70. Reece, *HPO*, 43. See also the Sutherland family's Reid manuscript, 4n28. (See note 15 to this chapter).

71. Reece, *HPO*, 12.

72. De Forest, *Union Officer*, 92.

Chapter 3

1. See Foner, *Reconstruction*, for a detailed explanation.

2. Hahn, *Nation under Our Feet*, 127–28, quote from 128; Schweninger, *Black Property Owners*, 143–44; and Fite, *Cotton Fields No More*, 1–6.

3. Andrews, *South since the War*, 195; last sentence from 197.

4. Foner, *Reconstruction*, millennial quote from 104; and Andrews, *South since the War*, 197.

5. For confiscation concerns, see Saville, "Measure of Freedom," 22–24; Hahn, *Nation under Our Feet*, 129; and Abbott, *Freedmen's Bureau*, Saxon reference from 6–8. By September 1865, President Johnson had returned almost all confiscated land to the original owners (ibid., 12). See also Foner, *Reconstruction*, 68–71; Megginson, *AAL*, 205; and Bleser, *Promised Land*, 11.

6. For the general history of Reconstruction, see Foner, with Brown, *Forever Free*, 79–81; and Foner, *Reconstruction*, 128–42, 177–216, 228–80, 304–72. For additional details, see Foner, *Nothing but Freedom*, 49–53. Additional sources include Bass and Poole, *Palmetto State*, 53–56; and Tindall, *South Carolina Negroes*, 7–8.

7. Nash, *Reconstruction's Ragged Edge*, power struggle discussion on 4 and white support commentary on 56.

8. Bass and Poole, *Palmetto State*, 53–55.

9. Foner, *Reconstruction*, 389–459 and 511–63. For additional sources, see Poole, *Never Surrender*, 99; Bass and Poole, *Palmetto State*, 56–62; Edgar, *South Carolina*, 399–406; Tindall, *South Carolina Negroes*, 19–22; and Nash, *Reconstruction's Ragged Edge*, North Carolina reference on 120 and the rise of the Klan discussion on 146. For an alternate view of the period, see Baker, *What Reconstruction Meant*.

10. Robertson, *Red Hills and Cotton*, 262–63; and Lynch and Ellison, *Echoes*, 78.

11. Foner, *Reconstruction*, 570–82; Megginson, *AAL*, 374. For a modern analysis of the 1876 gubernatorial election, see King, "Counting the Votes."

12. For an overview, see Foner, *Reconstruction*, 587–601; and Foner, *Nothing but Freedom*, 60–71. See Hemmingway, "Beneath the Yoke of Bondage," 52, for shifting northern interest. See Abbott, *Freedmen's Bureau*, sharecropping quote on 64.

13. Tindall, *South Carolina Negroes*, 44–73; and Edgar, *South Carolina*, 411–16.

14. Gilmore, *Gender and Jim Crow*, popular culture commentary on 61–62, black male rapist discussion on 67–70, and political party affiliation discussion on 70–72. See Tindall, *South Carolina Negroes*, segregation commentary on 291–95.

15. Tindall, *South Carolina Negroes*, 74–89 and 291–95; see also Hemmingway, "Beneath the Yoke of Bondage," 45; Doyle, *Etiquette of Race Relations*, 136–42; Poole, *Never Surrender*, 170; Edgar, *South Carolina*, 430–48; Megginson, *AAL*, 378–90; Baker, *What Reconstruction Meant*, 13–27; and Woodward, *Origins of the New South*, 212.

16. Poole, *Never Surrender*, 175; and Hemmingway, "Beneath the Yoke of Bondage," 54.

17. Hemmingway, "Beneath the Yoke of Bondage," 54–61.

18. Tindall, *South Carolina Negroes*, 302.

19. Woodward, *Origins of the New South*, 212; and Petty, "Jim Crow Section," 31.

20. Gilmore, *Gender and Jim Crow*, 117 and 131.

21. Devlin, "South Carolina and Black Migration," 25 and 67.

22. See Foner, *Reconstruction*, xxii–xxiii, on active agency; and Foner, "Prologue," xxi, on black heroism.

23. Tindall, *South Carolina Negroes*, 305; see also 305–6; Saville, "Measure of Freedom," 145–46 on literacy. New employment opportunities come from Tindall, *South Carolina Negroes*, 305–6; see also Saville, "Measure of Freedom," 188–207.

24. See Holt, *Making Freedom Pay*; and Gilmore, *Gender and Jim Crow*, 119–20, for additional sources of power.

25. Edgar, *South Carolina*, 379; and Megginson, *AAL*, 202.

26. Dunaway, *African-American Family*, 217–18; see also Hahn, *Nation under Our Feet*, 128; and Overman, "Keiths," 23.

27. Megginson, *AAL*, 205.

28. Clemson's observation may be found in McGee and Lander, *Rebel Came Home*, 92.

29. Foner, *Reconstruction*, 128–42. See also Megginson, *AAL*, 209–12; Nash, *Reconstruction's Ragged Edge*, 37–42; and Abbott, *Freedmen's Bureau*, 68, on labor contracts.

30. Nash, *Reconstruction's Ragged Edge*, social inferiors idea defined on 53; and Fleming, *Documents*, 20.

31. Megginson, *AAL*, 205.

32. The contract, along with several other documents relating to Jameson's life, may be found in the Pickens County Museum storage room (there is no file name), accessed January 22, 2015. In an 1863 will, Jameson disposed of his property, including the slaves Moses and Faith (they were freed before the will took effect). There is also a printed contract for them, dated January 1, 1866, and extending for a year, with some conditions written in by hand. The fact that the latter contract had been printed demonstrates that there was a much greater need for such contracts after 1865. See Abbott, *Freedmen's Bureau*, app. D, 141–42, for a typical labor contract. Abbott's example contains most of the phrases that appear in the Jameson document, but not the added phrase. See also Holt, *Making Freedom Pay*, on the importance of black household income.

33. McGee and Lander, *Rebel Came Home*, 93.

34. Devlin, "South Carolina and Black Migration," 32; second quote from Webster, *Operation of the Freedmen's Bureau*, 29 (citing *The Nation* 1, 393 [Sept. 28, 1865]).

35. Foner, *Nothing but Freedom*, 44; see personal freedom discussed on 45; Abbott, *Freedmen's Bureau*, 52; Schweninger, *Black Property Owners*, 145; and Foner, *Reconstruction*, 104.

36. The quote is from Saville, "Measure of Freedom," 171. See also Abbott, *Freedmen's Bureau*, 57; and Baker and Kelly, "Introduction," 1–3.

37. Edgar, *South Carolina*, 396.

38. Ibid., 379; Nash, *Reconstruction's Ragged Edge*, 3.

39. Dunaway, *African-American Family*, 225; Edgar, *South Carolina*, quotes from 381. See also Hahn, *Nation under Our Feet*, 166–67, quote from 459; and Schweninger, *Black Property Owners*, 162.

40. Nash, *Reconstruction's Ragged Edge*, 28; and Edgar, *South Carolina*, 381. See also Bleser, *Promised Land*, 11–28; and Tindall, *South Carolina Negroes*, 93.

41. Megginson, *AAL*, 330.

42. Reece, *HPO*, 42–43; cf. another local historian, McFall, *It Happened in Pickens County*, 87. See also Holt, *Making Freedom Pay*, 55.

43. J. Reece, *Rambling from the Mountain*, 6. See a parallel story in Sitton and Conrad, *Freedom Colonies* (25) from Texas.

44. Megginson, *AAL*, 236. See also Schultz, *Rural Face of White Supremacy*, 51–52; and Sitton and Conrad, *Freedom Colonies*, 37.

45. Megginson, *AAL*, 136.

46. See Fulmer, "Analytical Study," 10, for a 1939 map of the county's major roads, with the main highway extending from Pickens to Pumpkintown (currently SC Highway 8), then turning northeast and following the Oolenoy River valley toward Marietta.

47. Quote from Schweninger, *Black Property Owners*, 162; see also Sitton and Conrad, *Freedom Colonies*, 3; and Megginson, *AAL*, 331.

48. Reece, *HPO*, 43. See Jackson, "Shattering Slave Life Portrayals," 453, for South Carolina's Low Country. See also Sitton and Conrad, *Freedom Colonies*, 20, for similar outcomes in Texas.

49. Megginson, *AAL*, 128; and Holt, *Making Freedom Pay*, 64. See also Bleser, *Promised Land*, 17; and Montell, *Saga of Coe Ridge*, 63, in Kentucky.

50. Megginson, *AAL*, 330–31; and Sitton and Conrad, *Freedom Colonies*, 30.

51. Avery, *Dixie after the War*, 213–14. See also Bleser, *Promised Land*, 12; and Fleming, *Documents*, 45.

52. See Scott's *Domination*, 114–24, and *Art of Not Being Governed*; and Sitton and Conrad, *Freedom Colonies*, 4.

53. Devlin, "South Carolina and Black Migration," 65 (symbolic gesture); and Foner, *Reconstruction*, 79 (symbolic authority). See also Sitton and Conrad, *Freedom Colonies*, 1; and J. L. Smith, "Negotiating the Terms of Freedom," 225.

54. Reid, "Introduction," 6. For another example of a free black settlement in northern Georgia, see J. L. Smith, "Negotiating the Terms of Freedom," 220.

55. The sense of blackness quote is from Barnes, "Archaeology of Community Life," 673. Scott, *Domination*, 123 (defended), Scott, *Art of Not Being Governed*, 265 (define and defend), and Scott, *Domination*, 124 (strongest evidence).

56. Lynch and Ellison, *Echoes*, 166.

57. See Devlin, "South Carolina and Black Migration," 84, for Liberia as a potential destination, and 86 for the departures, citing the *Charleston Daily News*, February 27, 1867.

58. For information on the emigration movement, see Devlin, "South Carolina and Black Migration," 88–100; and Tindall, *South Carolina Negroes*, 154–57. The specific quote from Tindall may be found on 154; see 155 and then the summary on 169–73.

59. Megginson, *AAL*, 362. For information on the well-documented community of "Promised Land," see Bethel, *Promiseland* and Wideman, *Fatheralong* (note that the community's name is two words but Bethel's book title is one word); also men-

tioned in Edgar, *South Carolina*, 396. For information on "Happy Land," see Bryan and Bryan, "Kingdom of Happy Land." Liberia (Warren County) North Carolina, about fifty miles northeast of Raleigh, was founded by freed slaves after the Civil War and "most likely" named "in honor of the West African colony of Liberia" (Nancy Van Dolsen, "National Register of Historic Places—Nomination and Inventory." North Carolina State Historic Preservation Office, 2005, 4; PDF document located on the Web). I also have found the name "Little Africa" in Spartanburg County (South Carolina), but have not visited the place.

60. Lula Owens's quote is from Jimmy Cornelison, "Little Liberia: A Grand Legacy to Inherit," *Greenville News*, March 23, 1983, 1B. The McJunkin information is from Cornelison, "James McJunkin," *Greenville News*, May 25, 1983, 4B.

61. De Forest, *Union Officer*, 36–37.

62. Saville, "Measure of Freedom," 177–79; Megginson, *AAL*, 140 and 240; and Dunaway, *African-American Family*, 259–60; quote from 260. See also Megginson, *AAL*, 235, for reuniting families.

63. Megginson, *AAL*, 238.

64. Rich and Holder, "Oconee and Pickens Counties," date information given on iv, number data from xxiii, and the list of names from 39–41. Black voters' names include Charles Anthony, Adam Blythe, James and Henry Chastain, William Edens, Andrew, Edmund, Henry, Mack, Reubin [*sic*], Robert, and Roy Gowan, George Hendrix, Burr Hill, Andy, Ben, Samuel, and Thomas Keith, Emmerson [*sic*] Kemp, Joseph McJunkin, Jacob, Prestley, and Samuel Southerland, Curul [*sic*] and Milan Talley, and Benjamin, Edward, Henry, Lewis, Lewis, and Thomas Terrell. Reece, *HPO*, 44. Names from Reece are Charles Anthony, Jim Blythe, Miles Burgess, Riley Chapman, Dock Chastain, Will Glenn, Andy Gowan and wife Emily, Bailus Gowan, Emerson Gowan [Kemp?], wife Mariah, Thomas Gowan, Will Hagood, Burr, Jim, Sam, Thomas, and Will Hill, Goob Keith, Jim Kemp, George Kirkland, Ansel McKinney, Henry Miles, Dock Owen, James Owen, Tom Owens and wife Katie, Rufus Ponder, Luke Terrill, Martin (Mart) Terrill and wife Nancy, George Ruff, Bayless Sizemore, and Curl Talley.

65. Megginson, *AAL*, 180.

66. Blakely, "McGowens Chronicle," (see note 48 to chapter 2) incorrectly names Chris Owens's mother.

67. In the McGowens family history is a copy of the "License to Preach the Gospel" at Mt. Nebo Baptist Church, issued to Andy Gowens on November 22, 1874. Another document indicated that "Brother Andrew Gowens was ordained to the work of the Gospel Ministry by prayer and the laying on of hands of the Eldership" on January 10, 1885. Ordaining council members included Joseph McJunkin, Robert Gowens, and "Enderson" [Emerson] Kemp. Sources: Blakely, "McGowens Chronicle" (see note 48 to chapter 2); and Johnson, Hightower, Ladd, Jameson, and Cruell, "Oolenoy River" (see note 54 to chapter 2). In the older slave Soapstone Baptist Church Cemetery (see appendix 1) there is a hand-carved soapstone marker that reads: "Rhoda Gowans Died May 17, 1882 Aged 45 years." Most likely, this is the

first wife of Andrew Gowens and a woman born into slavery. In the minutes of the Oolenoy River Association meeting in October 1891, there is a report of deceased ministers, deacons, and wives, specifically mentioning "Sister Adeline Gowan, wife of Rev. A. R. Gowans [*sic*] [who] died a few days before our last Association, one who was mild, one who was kind and loveable, one dear little girl, and her husband to mourn her loss. She was a member of Mt. Nebo Church." Source: "Minutes of the Seventh Annual Meeting of the Oolenoy River Baptist Association," 11, South Carolina Baptist Historical Collection. In another of the few marked graves in the older slave Soapstone Church cemetery, there is a more elaborate tombstone inscribed "Rev. A. R. Gowens (1845–1928) / his dau Charlota / Wife of A. P. McKinney (1884–1925)." Nearby is another hand-lettered soapstone marker inscribed "Adline Gowan / Died Oct. 4, 1890 / Aged 36 years." See appendix 1.

68. Dunaway, *African-American Family*, 259; see also Jimenez, "History of Grandmothers," 526.

69. Sitton and Conrad, *Freedom Colonies*, 30.

70. Barnes, "Archaeology of Community Life," 691.

71. L. Smith, "Grandpa's Olden Days," 36–37.

72. Megginson, *AAL*, 243.

73. Coggeshall, *Carolina Piedmont Country* (hereafter cited as *CPC*), 181–88. See also Holt, *Making Freedom Pay*.

74. For corn in Pickens County, see the 1880 Agricultural Census, USDA Census of Agriculture Historical Archive, Albert R. Mann Library, Cornell University, http://agcensus.mannlib.cornell.edu/AgCensus/censusParts.do?year=1880. Accessed December 3, 2016. For cotton as the major crop, see Fite, *Cotton Fields No More*, 9. For black tenants and landowners, see Holt, *Making Freedom Pay*, 87, discussion of role models on 83–84.

75. Sitton and Conrad, *Freedom Colonies*, 2; and Barnes, "Archaeology of Community Life," definition on 692–93, heterogeneous discussion on 674–75, and final quote on 697.

76. See also Montell, *Saga of Coe Ridge*, 67–70, for descriptions of late-nineteenth-century homes.

77. Barnes, "Archaeology of Community Life," 686. See also Holt, *Making Freedom Pay*.

78. Barnes, "Archaeology of Community Life," discussions of laundress, midwife, and situation on 689, 692, and 694, respectively. See also Sitton and Conrad, *Freedom Colonies*, 62, on this last point.

79. Dunaway, *African-American Family*, 274. See also Fite, *Cotton Fields No More*, 28; and Coggeshall, *CPC*, 181–88.

80. Pickens, *Bursting Bonds*, 4. See also Holt, *Making Freedom Pay*; and Sitton and Conrad, *Freedom Colonies*, 80–171.

81. Hunter, *Nickel and a Prayer*, 32; also cited in Tindall, *South Carolina Negroes*, 94–95. See Montell and Morse, *Kentucky Folk Architecture*, 16 and 42, who note

that weatherboarding and framing replaced logs for cabins after the Civil War. See Dunaway, *African-American Family*, 264, for domestic work.

82. Hunter, *Nickel and a Prayer*, 33 and 46. See also Schweninger, *Black Property Owners*, 210, on black farm owners.

83. Holt, *Making Freedom Pay*, 1–3.

84. "Minutes of the Tenth Anniversary of the Oolenoy River Baptist Association," 8, South Carolina Baptist Historical Collection.

85. Holt, *Making Freedom Pay*, double farming explained on 84 , and strategies defined on 88–94. See also the *Greenville News* (October 21, 2016, 11A) for a story about wealthy black landowner Anthony Crawford, lynched in Abbeville County in 1916 because "he was too successful," according to his great-great-granddaughter.

86. Fite, *Cotton Fields No More*, 20; Holt, *Making Freedom Pay*, 133; Megginson, *AAL*, 330–31; and Schweninger, *Black Property Owners*, role models discussed on 232. See also Baker, " 'Recourse That Could Be Depended Upon,' " 35, for additional economic strategies.

87. Reece, *HPO*, 41–42. Burr Hill is mentioned in the 1868 voter's registration list and among the "original founders of Liberia." See note 64 to this chapter.

88. See Burkette, " 'Stamped Indian,' " 324–25 for the Native American discussion.

89. Luke Terrell is mentioned in the 1868 voter's registration list and among the "original founders of Liberia." See note 64 to this chapter. For information about James Bland and the lyrics to the minstrel song, see *BlackPast.org*, "Online Reference Guide to African American History," http://www.blackpast.org/aah /bland-james-1854-1911 and http://www.loc.gov/jukebox/recordings/detail/id /756/. Accessed November 7, 2016. These songs may be found in *Folk Songs of North Carolina*, ed. H. Belden and A. P. Hudson, vol. 3 of the *Frank C. Brown Collection*, ed. White. Specifically, "Black-Eyed Susan" is item no. 311, 366–67, recorded in 1915; "Cripple Creek" is item no. 299, 354–55, recorded in 1922; "Turkey in de Straw" is item no. 94, 130–31, recorded in 1923. "Shortnin' Bread" and "Git Along Home, (Lu)Cindy" are both identified as "Blackface Minstrel, Negro Songs" by the editors. The former is item no. 461, 535–38, recorded between 1921 and 1923, said to be a "favorite song, especially of the blacks, throughout the South" (535). The latter song may be found as item no. 404, 482–85, recorded in 1915.

90. The entire quote about Terrell is from Reece, *HPO*, 42. While witchcraft belief is well established in Euro-American folklore, for the African American beliefs in witches, see Puckett, *Folk Beliefs of the Southern Negro*, 79–166; for divination by coffee grounds, see 355. For the Euro-American tradition of coffee ground divination, see *Popular Beliefs and Superstitions*, ed. Wayland Hand, vols. 6 and 7 of the *Frank C. Brown Collection*, vol. 6, 645 and vol. 7, 172 (a "very old person" has this power). The Brown collection also cites Puckett, but it is beyond the scope of this book to determine whether these beliefs originated in Euro-American tradition and were adopted by African Americans, whether they originated in African (or

African American) tradition and were adopted by Euro-Americans, or whether the belief developed independently.

91. Pickens, *Bursting Bonds*, 8.

92. See Lynch and Ellison, *Echoes*, 21 and 44 for the Oolenoy Church information; Reece, *HPO*, 20 and 43. Williamson, *After Slavery*, quote from 180; denominational discussion 180–208.

93. Lynch and Ellison, *Echoes*, 44. See also Holt, *Making Freedom Pay*, 104.

94. Megginson, *AAL*, 112; and Tindall, *South Carolina Negroes*, 206.

95. Tindall, *South Carolina Negroes*, 208; Hahn, *Nation under Our Feet*, 232–34; Devlin, "South Carolina and Black Migration," 49; Dunaway, *African-American Family*, 250; Barnes, "Archaeology of Community Life," 691 and 694; Holt, *Making Freedom Pay*, 124 and 129; and Sitton and Conrad, *Freedom Colonies*, 83.

96. Holt, *Making Freedom Pay*, household income defined on 99. Foner, with Brown, *Forever Free*, centers quote on 87. J. L. Smith, "Negotiating the Terms of Freedom," 225. See also Barnes, "Archaeology of Community Life," 694.

97. Holt, *Making Freedom Pay*, 102.

98. Williamson, *After Slavery*, 194.

99. Reece, *HPO*, 43. See also Sitton and Conrad, *Freedom Colonies*, 30–31, on black congregations dividing; Schultz, *Rural Face of White Supremacy*, 105, for land donations; and Megginson, *AAL*, 294, for the church founding. Megginson (ibid.) cited a *Pickens Sentinel* article from October 28, 1880, that Soapstone Baptist Church was founded in the late 1870s (495n40), but this could have been the permanent structure. See Edens, Elrod, and Gilcrease, *History of Oolenoy Baptist Church*, 251, for the Owens interview. See also Holt, *Making Freedom Pay*, 124, for black church descriptions.

100. Hunter, *Nickel and a Prayer*, 55n5.

101. Clarke's recollection may be found in "History of the Soapstone Baptist Church," private document, loaned by Mable Clarke, n.d.

102. McFall, *It Happened in Pickens County*, 87; L. Johnson, "Oolenoy River Baptist Association," 17; and Reece, *HPO*, 43. The 1873 quote is from L. Johnson, "Oolenoy River Baptist Association," 17.

103. Williamson, *After Slavery*, 194.

104. Megginson, *AAL*, 293; Tindall, *South Carolina Negroes*, 282 (monotony).

105. For example, from the minutes of the Seventh Annual Session (1891), a statistical table indicated Soapstone with thirty-three members and Mt. Nebo with sixty-six. The next year, in 1892, Soapstone's membership was thirty-eight, Mt. Nebo's fifty-eight. Mt. Nebo Church sent W. R. Edens and R. P. Gowens; Soapstone sent no representatives. For the Seventh Annual Session (1891), the same two individuals represent Mt. Nebo, and Willis Glenn (father of Rosa, Clarence, Lonzo, and Ernest) attended from Soapstone. Sources: "Minutes of the Third Annual Session of the Oolenoy River Baptist Association," 3; "Seventh Annual Session," 3, the table from 15; "Eighth Annual Session," 13. "Minutes of the Tenth Annual Session," 13. SC Baptist Historical Collection.

106. Holt, *Making Freedom Pay*, 127. In 1894, Martin Terrell was listed as a delegate from Mt. Nebo Church to the tenth annual meeting of the Oolenoy River Baptist Association. Source: "Minutes of the Tenth Annual Session," 13. SC Baptist Historical Collection.

107. Andrews, *South since the War*, 112; Holt, *Making Freedom Pay*, 103; Megginson, *AAL*, quote about the Freedmen's Bureau on 221. See also Holt, *Making Freedom Pay*, 115–16.

108. Hendricks, "History and Present Status," 91. Cf. Megginson, *AAL*, 301 and 303. Supportive material about Ethel Hagood comes from *History: The Schools of Pickens County*, 277. Additional support for the quoted date about Ethel Hagood comes from "History Is Our Heritage," an undated and anonymous document in Johnson, Hightower, Ladd, Jameson, and Cruell, "Oolenoy River," n.p. (see note 54 to chapter 2). The specific quote about the school's description comes from Hendricks, "History and Present Status," 92, with additional information from 91–92.

109. Megginson, *AAL*, 300–310.

110. Pickens, *Bursting Bonds*, 5.

111. Ibid., 6. Megginson, *AAL*, 300–310, on rural schools; Tindall, *South Carolina Negroes*, 222–23; Holt, *Making Freedom Pay*, 122, on household income; Hahn, *Nation under Our Feet*, 276–80. For the assertiveness of black women, see Collins, *Black Feminist Thought*, 99 and 111.

112. Barnes, "Archaeology of Community Life," 696. See also Scott, *Art of Not Being Governed*, 105 for mutual interdependency.

113. Barnes, "Archaeology of Community Life," 696; Montell, *Saga of Coe Ridge*, 81.

114. Andrews, *South since the War*, 195.

115. Reece, *HPO*, 42; "mammies" are listed on 41. J. Reece, *Rambling from the Mountain*, 6.

116. Hunter, *Nickel and a Prayer*, 39 and 43 (second example).

117. De Forest, *Union Officer*, 72–73. See Gilmore, *Gender and Jim Crow*, 88, on the black male rapist myth.

118. Tindall, *South Carolina Negroes*, 296–98; added comment about mother's race from 296. Collins, *Black Feminist Thought*, 165. See also Hunter, *Nickel and a Prayer*, 31–32.

119. See also Gilmore, *Gender and Jim Crow*, 68.

120. Hunter, *Nickel and a Prayer*, 45; Scott, *Domination*, quotes on 208 and 210, respectively.

121. Hunter, *Nickel and a Prayer*, 38. See also Collins, *Black Feminist Thought*, 165.

122. Doyle, *Etiquette of Race Relations*, 142–59; the strain of violence quote is from Tindall, *South Carolina Negroes*, 233; for Reconstruction violence, see ibid., 234–36. For lynching, see ibid., 249–55; fear of violence quote from ibid., 259. Brundage, "Racial Violence," 308–13; quote from 308. See Taussig, "Culture of Terror," 469; and Dunaway, *African-American Family*, 244; her Pickens County observation is on 246. For more support, see also Megginson, *AAL*, 388–90.

123. Barnes, "Archaeology of Community Life," 679; Hunter, *Nickel and a Prayer*, 47.

124. See also Foner, *Reconstruction*, 432, and Sitton and Conrad, *Freedom Colonies*, 176–78, about black land loss in Texas.

125. Hunter, *Nickel and a Prayer*, all quotes from 58; Pickens, *Bursting Bonds*, 4.

126. Megginson, *AAL*, 404; Schweninger, *Black Property Owners*, 237.

127. Foner, *Reconstruction*, 78; see also Megginson, *AAL*, 404.

128. Foner, *Reconstruction*, 291; Tindall, *South Carolina Negroes*, 290. See also Holt, *Making Freedom Pay*, xxiii.

Chapter 4

1. For the general overview, see Fite, *Cotton Fields No More*, 30–34, quote on 30.

2. Hayes, *South Carolina and the New Deal*, land of cotton quote from xi; although see Baker, "'Recourse That Could Be Depended Upon,'" 36. For dependency, see Hemmingway, "Beneath the Yoke of Bondage," 187; and Hayes, *South Carolina and the New Deal*, 165.

3. On telephones, motor vehicles, and electricity, see Fite, *Cotton Fields No More*, 101.

4. Hahn, *Nation under Our Feet*, 465–67; Tolnay, *Bottom Rung*, 143–67; and Hemmingway, "Beneath the Yoke of Bondage," 254.

5. For menial jobs, see Gilmore, *Gender and Jim Crow*, 138–42; and Hemmingway, "Beneath the Yoke of Bondage," 181.

6. Foner, "Prologue," xxvii.

7. See Gilmore, *Gender and Jim Crow*, for the rise of the Klan. Edgar, *South Carolina*, 456–513, summarizes this period of South Carolina's history.

8. Schultz, *Rural Face of White Supremacy*, 10.

9. Hemmingway, "Beneath the Yoke of Bondage," 398–405; and Hayes, *South Carolina*, 160–61, quote from 160.

10. See Edgar, *South Carolina*, 456–513, for an overview. The quote is from Robertson, *Red Hills and Cotton*, 268–69. Fite, *Cotton Fields No More*, 94–100, for out-migration and 120–23, for the Depression.

11. Fite, *Cotton Fields No More*, 68–83, for agricultural changes and 139–49, for New Deal policies; and Hayes, *South Carolina*, 168–83, for black activism. See Fite, *Cotton Fields No More*, 156, and Hayes, *South Carolina*, 168–183 for the future.

12. Petty, "Jim Crow Section," 31. See also Fite, *Cotton Fields No More*, 20.

13. For information on McKinney's wife's family, see note 67 to chapter 3. Johnson, Hightower, Ladd, Jameson, and Cruell, "Oolenoy River," n.p. (see note 54 to chapter 2).

14. Edens, Elrod, and Gilcrease, *History of Oolenoy Baptist Church*, 161–62. Middy blouses were popular in the early twentieth century. See *The Vintage Traveler*, Antique and Vintage Photo Archive. Compiled by Sharon Elizabeth Adams Bramlett, http://fuzzylizzie.com/middy.html. Accessed June 27, 2017.

15. See Jimenez, "History of Grandmothers," 528, about the roles of black grandmothers at this time. The article's use of the term "fatty bread" for cornbread was an already outdated term, first appearing during the early colonial period when cooks began experimenting with Native American traditions by adding ingredients such as meat scraps, more closely approximating European traditions. See Burkette, "'Stamped Indian,'" 325.

16. I was unable to find any mention of the custom in Puckett (*Folk Beliefs of the Southern Negro*), but see the *Frank C. Brown Collection*, vol. 7 (*Popular Beliefs and Superstitions*), item no. 5131, 39.

17. Reece, *HPO*, 59; J. Reece, *Rambling from the Mountain*, 6, reprints the same photo.

18. Collins, *Black Feminist Theory*, 201–16.

19. Gilmore, *Gender and Jim Crow*, 147.

20. On black medical exclusion and midwives, see Chafe, Gavins, and Korstad, *Remembering Jim Crow*, 57.

21. Jimenez, "History of Grandmothers," 527, citing "Family Folklore," MS archive of folk custom, fols. 1–2, Folklife Reading Room, Library of Congress, Washington, DC.

22. Reece, *HPO*, 59; Lynch and Ellison, *Echoes*, 87. Very similar photos ("Emerson Kemp, 'boss slave,'" Easley E361 (see also "Emerson Kemp home," Easley, E382), may be viewed online in the Historical Photo Collection, Pickens County Library System, https://www.flickr.com/photos/pcls/255819988/in/photolist-oB9ns -oB9xT. Accessed November 7, 2016. See note 35 to this chapter.

23. Barnes, "Archaeology of Community Life," 694.

24. Bayne, personal recollection, in Johnson, Hightower, Ladd, Jameson, and Cruell, "Oolenoy River," n.p. (see note 54 to chapter 2).

25. Fulmer, "Analytical Study," 5; Reece's recollection is from *Rambling from the Mountain*, 13. According to the Agricultural census, by 1930 in Pickens County, cotton had replaced corn in total planted acreage (http://agcensus.mannlib.cornell .edu/AgCensus/censusParts.do?year=1930, USDA Census of Agriculture Historical Archive, Albert R. Mann Library, Cornell University). Accessed December 15, 2016. For a general overview of Piedmont life, see Coggeshall, *CPC* or Robertson, *Red Hills and Cotton*. For descriptions of "blackways" in the Upstate, see Lewis, *Blackways*; for a white perspective on life in an eastern Carolina community, see Taylor, *Carolina Crossroads*. For more general descriptions, see Tolnay, *Bottom Rung*, 25–72; Schultz, *Rural Face of White Supremacy*, 23–30; and Fite, *Cotton Fields No More*, 30–34.

26. Megginson, *AAL*, 330-1.

27. See also Fulmer, "Analytical Study," 24.

28. Ibid., 53.

29. See also Montell, *Saga of Coe Ridge*, 165–86, for moonshining.

30. Halperin, *Livelihood of Kin*, 3 (homeplace ties); 1–4, 146, for a general overview.

31. For the underground food economy, see Baker, "'Recourse That Could Be Depended Upon,'" 25.

32. Halperin, *Livelihood of Kin*, 67–68, and Baker, "'Recourse That Could Be Depended Upon,'" 35.

33. Fulmer, "Analytical Study," 23.

34. See Dunaway, *African-American Family*, 89; and Fite, *Cotton Fields No More*, 35–39 for similar housing descriptions.

35. Reece, *HPO*, 59; and McFall, *It Happened in Pickens County*, photo 6, after 96. Another photo ("Emerson Kemp, 'boss slave,'" Easley, E361), very similar to Reece's (note the small flowering tree [redbud?]), may be found online in the Historical Photo Collection, Pickens County Library System, https://www.flickr.com/photos/pcls/255819988/in/photolist-oB9ns-oB9xT. Accessed November 8, 2016. Kemp's home has a visible chimney. See also "Emerson Kemp home," Easley, E382, https://www.flickr.com/photos/pcls/255820593/in/album-72157594314212138/showing a younger couple by the same house. Might this be Emerson Kemp's son James and his wife?

36. See also Chafe, Gavins, and Korstad, *Remembering Jim Crow*, 57.

37. Coggeshall, *CPC*, 100–101.

38. See ibid., 103.

39. See also Schultz, *Rural Face of White Supremacy*, 116–18.

40. Burgess letter in "Black History/School/Soapstone," Vertical File, Faith Clayton Genealogy Room, Rickman Library, Southern Wesleyan University.

41. On automobile ownership, see Fulmer, "Analytical Study," 23.

42. The ownership transfer date comes from Victor Chastain, "Chastains of Pickens County, South Carolina 1790–1986" (n.p., 1986?), 33, a private manuscript viewed during the fifth annual "100 Year Reunion of Upstate Families," Southern Wesleyan University, April 26, 2014. Reece, *HPO*, 23. A photograph, "Pumpkintown General Store, Pumpkintown, 1930s," SA064, also exists online in the Historical Photo Collection, Pickens County Library System, https://www.flickr.com/photos/pcls/13625864024/in/set-72157643410503393. Accessed November 8, 2016.

43. "I Remember Oolenoy 1930," by Ruth Roper Hendricks, in Lynch and Ellison, *Echoes*, 129. Several photographs of the Edens Store exist: one, dating from the 1890s ("S. B. Edens' Store, Oolenoy, 1890s," SA047, Historical Photo Collection, Pickens County Library System, https://www.flickr.com/photos/pcls/13625816424/in/set-157643410503393), and a second one ("Sid Edens' Store, Oolenoy, 2000s," SA028, Historical Photo Collection, Pickens County Library System, https://www.flickr.com/photos/pcls/13625387765/in/set-72157643410503393), indicating the store had closed by 1952. Accessed November 8, 2016. As of this writing, the building is still standing, although abandoned.

44. See also Baker, "'Recourse That Could Be Depended Upon,'" 30.

45. L. Johnston, "Oolenoy River Baptist Association," 19, and in *Schools of Pickens County*, 277. The second photo also appears in McFall, *It Happened in Pickens County*, Photo 6, following 96. The 1899 date is from L. Johnson and the 1905 date is from the *Greenville News*, April 24, 1967.

46. See Barnes, "Archaeology of Community Life," 691; and Hemmingway, "Beneath the Yoke of Bondage," 300.

47. For the importance of black churches, see Schultz, *Rural Face of White Supremacy*, 102–3.

48. Gilmore, *Gender and Jim Crow*, 150–57.

49. Barnes, "Archaeology of Community Life," 694.

50. See also appendix 1. The "Nineteenth Annual Session," held in 1903, mentioned B. Terrell from Soapstone and J. S. Ferguson and E. T. Gowens from Mt. Nebo (3). In 1903, Mt. Nebo recorded a membership of sixty-nine people, with no listing at all from Soapstone. In 1907, A. B. Gowens attended the "Sunday School Convention" from Mt. Nebo, and Soapstone sent J. S. Ferguson and Miss Queen Anthony, at that time about fourteen years old (3). Soapstone had enrolled twenty-five members in Sunday school that year, while Mt. Nebo had thirty-four (3). The next year, Anderson [*sic*] Gowens, King Anthony, and his sister, now Mrs. Queen Ferguson (fifteen-year-old wife of Columbus Ferguson), attended from Soapstone (3); their church had twenty-eight members in Sunday school (11), but Mt. Nebo had thirty-one (12). The final church record came from the twenty-ninth annual session of the "Oolenoy River Baptist Association and Sunday School Convention," from 1913. Mt. Nebo sent M. Turle [Terrell] and several others, while Soapstone sent E. T. Gowens and S. M. Chasteen [Chastain] (3). According to the "Committee on Letters," Soapstone had forty-five church members, but Mt. Nebo was not listed (9). Source: SC Baptist Historical Collection.

51. "A History of Soapstone Baptist Church," private manuscript from Mable Owens Clarke, January 25, 2008. See also the 1913 Minutes (14), SC Baptist Historical Collection for alternate initials for Cureton's name (probably a typo in the original).

52. Fulmer, "Analytical Study," 34.

53. For the details of the school year and attendance figures, see Hendricks, "History and Present Status," 92.

54. The Chris Owens interview is from Edens, Elrod, and Gilcrease, *History of Oolenoy Baptist Church*, 251. For the information about Chris and Lula Owens's schooling, see the interview of Chris and Lula Owens by Elizabeth Ellison and Connie Rigdon, July 18, 1979, file 117, Elizabeth Ellison Notebook, 4, in the Mullinax-Ellison Collection, Faith Clayton Genealogy Room, Rickman Library, Southern Wesleyan University.

55. For the photo of the church as a schoolhouse, see *Schools of Pickens County*, 277. For the date of the "new" school, see Hendricks, "History and Present Status," 92.

56. Burgess letter in "Black History / School / Soapstone," Vertical File, Faith Clayton Genealogy Room, Rickman Library, Southern Wesleyan University.

57. Devlin, "South Carolina and Black Migration," 370. At this time Sears and Roebuck president Julius Rosenwald financially supported the construction of numerous black schools throughout the South. Although the extant Soapstone School looks like another "Rosenwald School," the building does not appear in the list

(http://shpo.sc.gov/res/Pages/Rosenwald.aspx, South Carolina Dept. of Archives and History, State Historic Preservation Office website). Accessed June 29, 2017.

58. Doyle, *Etiquette of Race Relations*, 151. See also Hemmingway, "Beneath the Yoke of Bondage," 158–71.

59. Fite, *Cotton Fields No More*, 137.

60. Chafe, Gavins, and Korstad, *Remembering Jim Crow*, 57.

61. Schultz, *Rural Face of White Supremacy*, 79.

62. Chafe, Gavins, and Korstad, *Remembering Jim Crow*, 155.

63. Wieder, "South Carolina School History," 31; Hemmingway, "Beneath the Yoke of Bondage," 150–51 (report) and 150–56 (self-esteem).

64. Schultz, *Rural Face of White Supremacy*, 66–67.

65. Reece, *HPO*, 43; McFall, *It Happened in Pickens County*, 87; Megginson, *AAL*, 330.

66. Schultz, *Rural Face of White Supremacy*, 5. See also Chafe, Gavins, and Korstad, *Remembering Jim Crow*, xxiii–xxiv, for the "Behind the Veil" project.

67. Schultz, *Rural Face of White Supremacy*, 6–7, quote on 7, humility comment from 52. Hayes, *South Carolina*, 161, quoting Hemmingway, "Beneath the Yoke of Bondage," 140–45 and 149–57.

68. Hemmingway, "Beneath the Yoke of Bondage," social customs discussed on 54–61, stores on 63, laws on 100.

69. Hayes, *South Carolina*, both comments from 159, citing Hemmingway, "Beneath the Yoke of Bondage," 53–64.

70. Schultz, *Rural Face of White Supremacy*, 10; Chafe, Gavins, and Korstad, *Remembering Jim Crow*, xxxiii.

71. Doyle, *Etiquette of Race Relations*, 155; Robertson, *Red Hills and Cotton*, 257–58. See also Schultz, *Rural Face of White Supremacy*, 84–88, for the etiquette of subordination. Additional comment about propinquity from 97.

72. Robertson, *Red Hills and Cotton*, 113.

73. Thurman, *Luminous Darkness*, 71. Also quoted in Chafe, Gavins, and Korstad, *Remembering Jim Crow*, 1.

74. Scott, *Domination*, 93.

75. Avery, *Dixie after the War*, 401–2.

76. Robertson, *Red Hills and Cotton*, 7, longer quote from 156.

77. Tindall, *South Carolina Negroes*, 295. In his book *Red Hills and Cotton*, Robertson does the same.

78. See also Schultz, *Rural Face of White Supremacy*, 91, for influential white patrons.

79. Duncan, Thompson, and Young, "Place Called Adamsville," 66. This statement illustrates the diversity of perspectives suggested by Schultz (*Rural Face of White Supremacy*), and perhaps also a public transcript of complacency suitable for white middle school interviewers.

80. J. Reece, *Rambling from the Mountain*, 6–7.

81. Fite, *Cotton Fields No More*, quote from 161. See also Schultz, *Rural Face of White Supremacy*, 122–27, for various forms of social interaction.

82. Brundage, "Racial Violence," 302–16. See also Schultz, *Rural Face of White Supremacy*, 76 and 128.

83. Chafe, Gavins, and Korstad, *Remembering Jim Crow*, 2.

84. Doyle, *Etiquette of Race Relations*, 142–59.

85. Schultz, *Rural Face of White Supremacy*, 131, black subservience discussion on 146; the "Behind the Veil" project in Chafe, Gavins, and Korstad, *Remembering Jim Crow*, senseless white power quote from xxx; Thurman, *Luminous Darkness*, 71; also cited in Chafe, Gavins, and Korstad, *Remembering Jim Crow*, 1.

86. For support of this behavior, see also Doyle, *Etiquette of Race Relations*, 149 and 153.

87. Schultz, *Rural Face of White Supremacy*, 163–74; quote from 170. See also Chafe, Gavins, and Korstad, *Remembering Jim Crow*, 1–2 and 268–70.

88. Dunaway, *Slavery*, 255. See also Collins, *Black Feminist Thought*, 274.

89. Witchcraft belief is well established in Euro-American folklore; for the African American beliefs in witches, see Puckett, *Folk Beliefs of the Southern Negro*, 79–166.

90. Chafe, Gavins, and Korstad, *Remembering Jim Crow*, 56–57; quote from 57.

91. Schultz, *Rural Face of White Supremacy*, 201.

92. See also ibid., 171–72, and Chafe, Gavins, and Korstad, *Remembering Jim Crow*, 3, for black women and retaliation.

93. Hayes, *South Carolina*, 122–27; Daniel, *Breaking the Land*, 92–109.

94. J. Reece, *Rambling from the Mountain*, 20. See also Hayes, *South Carolina*, 162–63; Hemmingway, "Beneath the Yoke of Bondage," 394–96.

95. Brundage, "Racial Violence," 309–10.

96. J. Reece, *Rambling from the Mountain*, 14. See also Sitton and Conrad, *Freedom Colonies*, 176. A descendant of this person still pressures Mable Clarke to sell him her family property, according to Mable.

97. Blakely, "McGowens Chronicle," n.p. (see note 48 to chapter 2). See also Hayes, *South Carolina*, 160, for a similar example.

98. Tindall, *South Carolina Negroes*, 296. See also Schultz, *Rural Face of White Supremacy*, 119–20.

99. Gilmore, *Gender and Jim Crow*, 67–72 for the black male rapist myth, white superiority, and racial impurity. See Schultz, *Rural Face of White Supremacy*, 147 for white female submissiveness and the Women's Rights movement.

100. For more information on this crime, see *H-Net: Humanities and Social Sciences Online*, http://h-net.msu.edu/cgi-bin/logbrowse.pl?trx=vx&list=h-gape&month=9904&week=c&msg=Ql3XYpVOlb788ZqIK3cgcQ&user=&pw=. I am indebted to historian Bruce Baker for locating the website.

101. Devlin, "South Carolina and Black Migration," 205; and Campbell, Johnson, and Stangler, "Return Migration," 514.

102. Specific quotes are from Devlin, "South Carolina and Black Migration," 206 and 247. Joint observations are from ibid., 257, and Edgar, *South Carolina*, 485; the Klan comments are from Devlin, "South Carolina and Black Migration," 277, and Edgar, *South Carolina*, 484. See also Hemmingway, "Beneath the Yoke of Bondage," 283–93.

103. For northern migration, see Foner, *Nothing but Freedom*, 73; Reece, *HPO*, 43; Edgar, *South Carolina*, 486–47. For boll weevil information, see Nickles, "Poisoning the Boll Weevil," 3 and 6–7.

104. Devlin, "South Carolina and Black Migration," 172 (quote) and 179; Brundage, "Roar on the Other Side of Silence"; Tindall, *South Carolina Negroes*, 306; see also Edgar, *South Carolina*, 484.

105. Scott, *Domination*, 208 and 210.

106. Edgar, *South Carolina*, 456–88; Fite, *Cotton Fields No More*, 20; Hemmingway, "Beneath the Yoke of Bondage," 292; and Devlin, "South Carolina and Black Migration," 347.

107. See Chafe, Gavins, and Korstad, *Remembering Jim Crow*, 205–8, for employment opportunities.

108. Reece, *HPO*, 43.

109. Beardsley, "Tuberculosis," 980–81. See also Hemmingway, "Beneath the Yoke of Bondage," 249. Caleb Klipowitz (personal communication) added that the stress of structural racism and violence would weaken immune systems and exacerbate the disease's spread, along with frequent visits by kin. Dr. Lynne Ogawa (personal communication) suggested that churches also might serve as vectors for spreading the disease since rural populations were otherwise more dispersed.

110. Devlin, "South Carolina and Black Migration," 361; for white acquisition of land, see also 367. See also Hayes, *South Carolina*, 166.

111. See also Hayes, *South Carolina*, 165–66.

112. Devlin, "South Carolina and Black Migration," 335–36; Fite, *Cotton Fields No More*, 161.

113. Sitton and Conrad, *Freedom Colonies*, 174.

114. Edgar, *South Carolina*, 513.

Chapter 5

1. Edgar, *South Carolina*, 527–29, on segregated schools.

2. Fite, *Cotton Fields No More*, 174.

3. Schultz, *Rural Face of White Supremacy*, 205–9; Fite, *Cotton Fields No More*, 163–64 and 175 (rayon); Daniel, *Lost Revolutions*, 41–42.

4. Daniel, *Breaking the Land*, 249; and Daniel, *Lost Revolutions*, 121–22.

5. Edgar, *South Carolina*, 518–19, on the right to vote.

6. For more information on Brynes's proposals, see Dobrasko, "Upholding 'Separate but Equal,'" 37; and Quint, *Profile in Black and White*. See also Daniel, *Lost*

Revolutions, inequalities between races discussion on 2, Lost Cause on 26, black male rapist myth on 37, and popular culture on 123.

7. End of segregation discussion from Edgar, *South Carolina,* 537–40; integration and quote from Daniel, *Lost Revolutions,* 305.

8. Edgar, *South Carolina,* 529. See Schultz, *Rural Face of White Supremacy,* sinking wreck quote on 223.

9. Coggeshall, "Mountains of Menace and Majesty."

10. Coggeshall, *CPC,* 204–5.

11. For kinship discussion, see ibid., 48–49.

12. Dunaway, *Slavery,* 255.

13. Coggeshall, *CPC,* 94–97.

14. Ibid., 121.

15. Ibid., 164.

16. Ibid., 165.

17. Ibid., 139–40.

18. Halperin, *Livelihood of Kin*; and Baker, "'Recourse That Could Be Depended Upon,'" underground food economy defined on 25.

19. Baker, "'Recourse That Could Be Depended Upon,'" discussion of strategies on 36.

20. Coggeshall, *CPC,* 103–4.

21. Although this belief sounds very traditional, I found nothing in the *Frank C. Brown Collection.* The closest idea in Puckett, *Folk Beliefs of the Southern Negro,* is a belief from the Sea Islands about a child being carried around on the ninth day after birth, mentioned on 335.

22. Coggeshall, *CPC,* 100–101.

23. On silver for charms, see ibid., 98; see also Puckett, *Folk Beliefs of the Southern Negro,* 288; photo 315.

24. See Glassie, *Folk Housing,* 144, for a structural analysis of this arrangement.

25. See Baker, "'Recourse That Could Be Depended Upon,'" 33, for the berries ripening idea. I am also appreciative of Baker (personal communication) for suggesting the link between walking and a closer tie to land.

26. Cornelison, Fant, Hembree, and Robertson, *Journey Home,* 19.

27. On job opportunities, see Coggeshall, *CPC,* 194–99; Lewis, *Blackways,* 121. See also Collins, *Black Feminist Thought,* 56–57.

28. Jaber, J. McCauley, M. McCauley, and Norman, "Dramatic Story of Caesar's Head," 24–25.

29. Cornelison, "James McJunkin," *Greenville News,* May 25, 1983, 4B.

30. See also Sitton and Conrad, *Freedom Colonies,* 174.

31. L. Johnson, "Oolenoy River Baptist Association"; and Johnson, Hightower, Ladd, Jameson, and Cruell, "Oolenoy River," n.p. (see note 54 to chapter 2); Tindall, *South Carolina Negroes,* 208 on church social importance.

32. L. Johnson, "Oolenoy River Baptist Association," 19.

33. Coggeshall, *CPC*, 154–57.

34. Hendricks, "History and Present Status," 92 and 94. For information on "Type B" lunches at this time, see Gordon Gunderson, "National School Lunch Act," website of the U.S. Dept. of Agriculture Food and Nutrition Service, http://www .fns.usda.gov/nslp/history_5. According to the National School Lunch Act of 1946, the Type B pattern was devised to provide a supplementary lunch in schools where adequate facilities for the preparation of a Type A lunch could not be provided. Accessed October 10, 2016. The Seneca Junior College provided additional educational opportunities for African Americans in the region; it was located in Seneca, Oconee County (see map 1). See Seneca Junior College—Seneca Institute, Wikipedia, https://en.wikipedia.org/wiki/Seneca_Institute_%E2%80%93_Seneca_Junior _College. Accessed May 4, 2017.

35. "The Doodlebug Song" may be found in Hand, *Popular Beliefs and Superstitions*, vol. 7 in the *Frank C. Brown Collection*, ed. White, items no. 7355–7368, 412–13.

36. For general information on the period, see Zwolandek, "'Right and Wise,'" 21–25. For the threat to close public schools, see Byrnes's address to the South Carolina Education Association, March 16, 1951 (box 12, folder 8, Mss 90), Byrnes Papers, 7.

37. James F. Byrnes letter to J. C. Long (Educational Finance Commission), July 6, 1954 (Governor Byrnes Papers, Governors' Papers, Columbia, SC), cited in Zwolandek, "'Right and Wise,'" 90.

38. Informal address by Governor James F. Byrnes to Boys State (box 14, folder 10, Mss 90), Byrnes Papers. The visualization quotes are from 5, and the trouble conclusion is on 7. On the general concern of Byrnes on miscegenation, see Zwolandek, "'Right and Wise,'" 120–21.

39. Johnson, Hightower, Ladd, Jameson, and Cruell, "Accomplishments/Legacy," in "Oolenoy River," n.p. (see note 54 to chapter 2). According to Ruth Adams (personal communication), both drivers became ministers as adults.

40. Daniel, *Lost Revolutions*, popular culture commentary on 9 and lewd and suggestive music discussed on 148.

41. Lewis, *Blackways*, 312; see also Doyle, *Etiquette of Race Relations*, for a detailed summary.

42. Lewis, *Blackways*, 24.

43. See also Schultz, *Rural Face of White Supremacy*.

44. See also ibid. for parallels in southern Georgia.

45. Lewis, *Blackways*, 197.

46. Scott, *Domination*, 112–13.

47. Lewis, *Blackways*, 113.

48. Ibid., 109.

49. See also Coggeshall, *CPC*, 182–88.

50. On tenant farming, see ibid., 186–87.

51. The episode is discussed in Quint, *Portrait in Black and White*, 40–41. Four of the eleven perpetrators received jail terms ranging from one to six years, with A. Marshall Rochester (head of the Greenville County Klan) receiving the maximum.

52. Historian Bruce Baker (personal communication) noted that in the late 1950s there was a resurgence of Klan activity in western North Carolina, but Mable is positive she was younger than she would have been in 1957 or 1958.

53. See Montell, *Saga of Coe Ridge*, 137–38 and 142–44, for other examples of white prostitutes in black communities. Glenda Gilmore (*Gender and Jim Crow*, 72) has argued that such living arrangements "blackened" the prostitutes, removing them from white female concern and reading them out of the white race, thus restoring the culturally acceptable white male–"black" female sexual relationship.

54. W. E. B. DuBois had proposed that the most effective way to stop white violence against blacks was for blacks to "keep and use arms in defense against lynchers and mobs." DuBois, "We Are a Nation of Murderers," 126. See also Montell, *Saga of Coe Ridge*, 102–5, for a similar story.

55. Schultz, *Rural Face of White Supremacy*, 223.

56. Coggeshall, "Mountains of Menace and Majesty."

Chapter 6

1. See the interview of Chris and Lula McJunkin Owens by Ellison and Rigdon in the Mullinax-Ellison Collection (see note 54 to chapter 4). This interview dates the fire to April 1968, but the newspaper accounts prove it was from the year before.

2. I submitted a Freedom of Information Act request to the SC State Law Enforcement Division (SLED) for a copy of the 1967 arson investigation on the Soapstone Baptist Church fire, but they have not located a report. SLED thought either the investigation was never completed or the report has been lost or misfiled. On May 6, 1967, the *Greenville News* reported (5) that three Marietta men had been arrested and charged with starting the Oolenoy area brush fires, but they were not charged with the Soapstone fire.

3. Dot Robertson, "Little Liberia's Heart of Gold," *Greenville News*, May 18, 1988, 1B. While it may seem difficult to believe that the church was rebuilt that quickly, Mable Clarke remembered that it was. There was no mention of the cornerstone laying in any local newspaper.

4. On othermothers, see Collins, *Black Feminist Thought*, 201–16; and Collins, "Shifting the Center," 49. For the "nameless" quote, see Collins, *Black Feminist Thought*, 192. See also Jimenez, "History of Grandmothers," 542–43, for the continuing social importance of black grandmothers to their families.

5. Collins, *Black Feminist Thought*, 194.

6. Ibid., 185.

Chapter 7

1. *Greenville News*, May 25, 2016, 6A.

2. Williams, *Homeplace*, 36.

3. Ibid., 125–26.

4. Ibid., inheritance of family land and division of land on 125.

5. Ibid., homeplace discussion on 130, and inheritance discussion on 126–28.

6. Cornelison, "Little Liberia," *Greenville News*, March 23, 1983, 1B.

7. Fite, *Cotton Fields No More*, quote from 231 and discussion of decline of family farms on 204.

8. Interview of Chris and Lula Owens by Ellison and Rigdon, Ellison Notebook, 2–3 (see note 54 to chapter 4).

9. Halperin, *Livelihood of Kin*, 4–7.

10. Ibid., 4.

11. Ibid., 7, for both economic and kinship activities.

12. Coggeshall, *CPC*, 51–52.

13. Sitton and Conrad, *Freedom Colonies*, 184.

14. For the dedication description, see the Mable Clarke press release, May 17, 2007. Loaned by Mable Clarke.

15. Cornelison, "Little Liberia," *Greenville News*, March 23, 1983, 1B.

16. On othermothers, see Collins, *Black Feminist Thought*, 201–16, quote from 288.

17. For example, see McFall, *It Happened in Pickens County*, 87; Reece, *HPO*, 43; and Megginson, *AAL*, 330.

18. Cornelison, "Little Liberia," 7B.

19. Fite, *Cotton Fields No More*, 225.

20. See also Daniel, *Lost Revolutions*.

21. See Stack, *Call to Home*, 7–18; and Campbell, Johnson, and Stangler, "Return Migration," 526.

22. Williams, *Homeplace*, 116–17.

23. Ibid., 131.

24. Ibid., 126–28.

25. Glassie, *Folk Housing*, 137.

Chapter 8

1. Richardson, "Introduction," 1; Casey, "How to Get from Space to Place," 14; Steele, *Sense of Place*, 11; Casey, *Getting Back into Place*, 314; Steele, *Sense of Place*, 131; see also Rowles, "Toward a Geography of Growing Old," 59–60.

2. Feld and Basso, "Introduction," in *Senses of Place*, 11; see also Buttimer, "Home, Reach, and the Sense of Place," 167, for the connection between identity and place.

3. Casey, "How to Get from Space to Place," 46; Basso, "Wisdom Sits in Places," 54. The shared experiences idea is discussed on 57, and the subsequent quote is from 87.

4. For the South in general, see Fulmer and Kell, "Sense of Place"; Allen, "Genealogical Landscape"; and Blu, " 'Where Do You Stay At?' " For South Carolina's Low Country, see Falk, *Rooted in Place*; and Dyer and Bailey, "Place to Call Home." For Appalachia, see Wagner, "Measuring Cultural Attachment."

5. Eller, "Place and the Recovery of Community," both quotes from 4. See also Blu, "'Where Do You Stay At?,'" 220; and Wagner, "Measuring Cultural Attachment," 245.

6. Williams, *Homeplace*, commentary on symbolic connection from 20, family reunion site discussion from 133, and narratives, including quote, from 135–36.

7. Beaver, "Appalachian Families," 150. See also Allen, "Genealogical Landscape," 156–61, quote from 163. Batteau, "Mosbys and Broomsedge."

8. Cox, "Topophilia and Technological Change," 249.

9. Wagner, "Measuring Cultural Attachment," 245; Cox, "Topophilia and Technological Change," 249. and Davis, "Epilogue," 215.

10. Geertz, "Thick Description," 6–10.

11. Cornelison, "Little Liberia," *Greenville News*, March 23, 1983, 7B.

12. This idea will be explored further in a later publication. See Coggeshall, "Mountains of Menace and Majesty," for a preliminary analysis.

Bibliography

Abbott, Martin. *The Freedmen's Bureau in South Carolina: 1865–1872*. Chapel Hill: University of North Carolina Press, 1967.

Allen, Barbara. "The Genealogical Landscape and the Southern Sense of Place." In *Sense of Place: American Regional Cultures*, edited by Barbara Allen and Thomas J. Schlereth, 152–63. Lexington: University Press of Kentucky, 1990.

Allen, Barbara, and William Lynwood Montell. *From Memory to History: Using Oral Sources in Local Historical Research*. Nashville: American Association for State and Local History, 1981.

Andrews, Sidney. *The South since the War, as Shown by Fourteen Weeks of Travel and Observation in Georgia and the Carolinas*, abridged by Heather Cox Richardson. Baton Rouge: Louisiana State University Press, 2004. Originally published Boston: Ticknor and Fields, 1866.

Anglin, Mary. "Lives on the Margin: Rediscovering the Women of Antebellum North Carolina." In *Appalachia in the Making: The Mountain South in the Nineteenth Century*, edited by Mary Beth Pudup, Dwight Billings, and Altina Waller, 185–209. Chapel Hill: University of North Carolina Press, 1995.

Avery, Myrta Lockett. *Dixie after the War: An Exposition of Social Conditions Existing in the South, during the Twelve Years Succeeding the Fall of Richmond*. New York: Doubleday, Page, 1906.

Baker, Bruce. "'A Recourse that Could Be Depended Upon': Picking Blackberries and Getting By after the Civil War." *Southern Cultures* 16 (2010): 21–40.

———. *What Reconstruction Meant: Historical Memory in the American South*. Charlottesville: University of Virginia Press, 2007.

Baker, Bruce, and Brian Kelly. "Introduction." In *After Slavery: Race, Labor, and Citizenship in the Reconstruction South*, edited by Bruce Baker and Brian Kelly, 1–15. Tallahassee: University Press of Florida, 2013.

Banks, Kristie, Wil Crapps, Brett Nix, Jonathon Richards, and Ryan Stinnett. "Cleveland, a Little Town in the Hills." *Echoes: Reflections of the Past* 7 (1991): 64–83.

Barnes, Jodi. "An Archaeology of Community Life: Appalachia, 1865–1920." *International Journal of Historical Archaeology* 15 (2011): 669–706.

Bass, Jack, and W. Scott Poole. *The Palmetto State: The Making of Modern South Carolina*. Columbia: University of South Carolina Press, 2009.

Basso, Keith. "Wisdom Sits in Places: Notes on a Western Apache Landscape." In *Senses of Place*, edited by Steven Feld and Keith Basso, 53–90. Santa Fe, NM: School of American Research Press, 1996.

Batteau, Allen. "Mosbys and Broomsedge: The Semantics of Class in an Appalachian Kinship System." *American Ethnologist* 9 (1982): 445–66.

Beardsley, Ed. "Tuberculosis." In *The South Carolina Encyclopedia*, edited by Walter Edgar, 980–81. Columbia: University of South Carolina Press, 2006.

Beaver, Patricia. "Appalachian Families, Landownership, and Public Policy." In *Holding On to the Land and the Lord: Kinship, Ritual, Land Tenure, and Social Policy in the Rural South*, edited by Robert Hall and Carol Stack, 146–54. Southern Anthropological Society Proceedings. Athens: University of Georgia Press, 1982.

Bethel, Elizabeth. *Promiseland: A Century of Life in a Negro Community*. Philadelphia: Temple University Press, 1981.

Blassingame, John. *The Slave Community: Plantation Life in the Antebellum South*. Rev. and enl. ed. New York: Oxford University Press, 1979. Originally published 1972.

Blaustein, Richard. Review of "Free Hill: A Sound Portrait of a Rural Afro-American Community," by Elizabeth Peterson and Tom Rankin (Tennessee Folklore Society). *Now and Then* 3, no. 1 (1986): 29–30.

Bleser, Carol. *The Promised Land: The History of the South Carolina Land Commission 1869–1890*. Columbia: University of South Carolina Press, 1969.

Blu, Karen. " 'Where Do You Stay At?' Home Place and Community among the Lumbee." In *Senses of Place*, edited by Steven Feld and Keith Basso, 197–227. Santa Fe, NM: School of American Research Press, 1996.

Bourdieu, Pierre. "Intellectual Field and Creative Project." *Social Science Information* 8 (1969): 89–119.

Brundage, W. Fitzhugh. "Racial Violence, Lynchings, and Modernization in the Mountain South." In *Appalachians and Race: The Mountain South from Slavery to Segregation*, edited by John Inscoe, 302–16. Lexington: University Press of Kentucky, 2001.

——. "The Roar on the Other Side of Silence: Black Resistance and White Violence in the American South, 1880–1940." In *Under Sentence of Death: Lynching in the South*, edited by W. Fitzhugh Brundage, 271–91. Chapel Hill: University of North Carolina Press, 1997.

Bryan, Ellen, and Julie Bryan. "The Kingdom of Happy Land." *Echoes: Reflections of the Past* 1 (1988): 15–25.

Burkette, Allison. " 'Stamped Indian': Finding History and Culture in Terms for American 'Cornbread.' " *American Speech* 86 (2011): 312–39.

Butcher, Jamie. "Religion, Race, Gender, and Education: The Allen School, Asheville, North Carolina, 1885 to 1974." *Appalachian Journal* 33 (2005): 78–109.

Buttimer, Anne. "Home, Reach, and the Sense of Place." In *The Human Experience of Space and Place*, edited by Anne Buttimer and David Seamon, 166–87. London: Croom Helm, 1980.

Byrnes, James F. Mss 90, James F. Byrnes Papers, Strom Thurmond Institute, Clemson University Libraries, Clemson, SC.

Campbell, Rex, Daniel Johnson, and Gary Stangler. "Return Migration of Black People to the South." *Rural Sociology* 39 (1974): 514–28.

Casey, Edward. *Getting Back into Place: Toward a Renewed Understanding of the Place-World*. Bloomington: Indiana University Press, 1993.

——. "How to Get from Space to Place in a Fairly Short Stretch of Time: Phenomenological Prolegomena." In *Senses of Place*, edited by Steven Feld and Keith Basso, 13–52. Santa Fe, NM: School of American Research Press, 1996.

Chafe, William, Raymond Gavins, and Robert Korstad, eds. *Remembering Jim Crow: African Americans Tell about Life in the Segregated South*. New York: New Press, 2001.

Clark, Rhonda, Letresa Foster, Keisha Lewis, and Marla Sorenson. "Memories of the Old Slave Days." *Echoes: Reflections of the Past* 7 (1991): 37–49.

Clifford, James. "Introduction: Partial Truths." In *Writing Culture: The Poetics and Politics of Ethnography*, edited by James Clifford and George Marcus, 1–26. Berkeley: University of California Press, 1986.

Coates, Ta-Nehisi. *Between the World and Me*. Melbourne, Australia: Text Publishing, 2015.

Coggeshall, John M. *Carolina Piedmont Country*. Jackson: University Press of Mississippi, 1996. Abbreviated *CPC*.

——. "Mountains of Menace and Majesty: Memories in the Jocassee Gorges Region of Upstate South Carolina." Paper presented at the Southern Anthropological Society annual meeting, Staunton, VA, 2008.

Collins, Patricia Hill. *Black Feminist Thought: Knowledge, Consciousness, and the Politics of Empowerment*. 2nd ed. New York: Routledge, 2000.

——. "Shifting the Center: Race, Class, and Feminist Theorizing about Motherhood." In *Mothering: Ideology, Experience, and Agency*, edited by Evelyn Nakano Glenn, Grace Chang, and Linda Rennie Forcey, 45–65. New York: Routledge, 1994.

Cornelison, Jimmy, Reese Fant, Mike Hembree, and Dot Robertson. *Journey Home*. Greenville, SC: Greenville News-Piedmont, 1988.

Cox, Gary. "Topophilia and Technological Change in Appalachia." In *Sense of Place in Appalachia*, edited by S. Mont Whitson, 248–56. Office of Regional Development Services, Morehead State University, Morehead, KY, 1988.

Craven, Della, ed. *The Neglected Thread: A Journal from the Calhoun Community 1836–1842*. Columbia: University of South Carolina Press, 1951.

Culpepper, Linda Parramore. "Black Charlestonians in the Mountains: African American Community Building in Post–Civil War Flat Rock, North Carolina." *Journal of Appalachian Studies* 8 (2002): 362–81.

Daniel, Pete. *Breaking the Land: The Transformation of Cotton, Tobacco, and Rice Cultures since 1880*. Urbana: University of Illinois Press, 1985.

———. *Lost Revolutions: The South in the 1950s*. Chapel Hill: University of North Carolina Press, 2000.

Davis, Donald. "Epilogue." In *Homeplace Geography: Essays for Appalachia*, 215–16. Macon, GA: Mercer University Press, 2006.

De Forest, John William. *A Union Officer in the Reconstruction*. Edited by James H. Croushore and David M. Potter. New Haven, CT: Yale University Press, 1948.

Dennis, Jeffrey. "American Revolutionaries and Native Americans: The South Carolina Experience." Ph.D. diss., University of Notre Dame, 2002.

Devlin, George Alfred. "South Carolina and Black Migration 1865–1940: In Search of the Promised Land." Ph.D. diss., University of South Carolina, 1984. Ann Arbor, MI: UMI.

Dobrasko, Rebekah. "Upholding 'Separate but Equal': South Carolina's School Equalization Program, 1951–1955." M.A. thesis, University of South Carolina, 2005.

Doyle, Bertram. *The Etiquette of Race Relations in the South: A Study in Social Control*. Port Washington, NY: Kennikat, 1937.

Drake, Richard. "Slavery and Antislavery in Appalachia." In *Appalachians and Race: The Mountain South from Slavery to Segregation*, edited by John Inscoe, 16–26. Lexington: University Press of Kentucky, 2001.

DuBois, W. E. B. "We Are a Nation of Murderers." Chapter 4 in *W. E. B. DuBois: The Crisis Writings*, edited by Daniel Walden, 118–27. Greenwich, CT: Fawcett Publications, 1972.

Dunaway, Wilma A. *The African-American Family in Slavery and Emancipation*. Cambridge: Cambridge University Press, 2003.

———. *The First American Frontier: Transition to Capitalism in Southern Appalachia, 1700–1860*. Chapel Hill: University of North Carolina Press, 1996.

———. "Put in Master's Pocket: Cotton Expansion and Interstate Slave Trading in the Mountain South." In *Appalachians and Race: The Mountain South from Slavery to Segregation*, edited by John Inscoe, 116–32. Lexington: University of Kentucky Press, 2001.

———. *Slavery in the American Mountain South*. Cambridge: Cambridge University Press, 2003.

———. "Speculators and Settler Capitalists: Unthinking the Mythology about Appalachian Landholding, 1790–1860." In *Appalachia in the Making: The Mountain South in the Nineteenth Century*, edited by Mary Beth Pudup, Dwight Billings, and Altina Waller, 50–75. Chapel Hill: University of North Carolina Press, 1995.

Duncan, Susan, Keesha Thompson, and April Young. "A Place Called Adamsville." *Echoes: Reflections of the Past* 4 (1988): 59–71.

Dyer, Janice, and Conner Bailey. "A Place to Call Home." *Rural Sociology* 73 (2008): 317–38.

Edens, Ethel, Evonne Edens Elrod, and Mildred S. Gilcrease, eds. *A History of Oolenoy Baptist Church and the Lives of the People Who Have Worked for It's* [sic] *Growth*. N.p., 1995. Captain Kimberly Hampton Memorial Library, Pickens County, South Carolina.

Edgar, Walter. *South Carolina: A History*. Columbia: University of South Carolina Press, 1998.

Eller, Ronald. "Place and the Recovery of Community in Appalachia." In *Sense of Place in Appalachia*, edited by S. Mont Whitson, 3–19. Office of Regional Development Services, Morehead State University, Morehead, Kentucky, 1988.

Falk, William. *Rooted in Place: Family and Belonging in a Southern Black Community*. New Brunswick, NJ: Rutgers University Press, 2004.

Feder, Ellen. "Power/Knowledge." In *Michel Foucault: Key Concepts*, edited by Dianna Taylor, 55–68. Durham, UK: Acumen Publishing, 2011.

Feld, Steven, and Keith Basso, eds. "Introduction." In *Senses of Place*, edited by Steven Feld and Keith Basso, 3–11. Santa Fe, NM: School of American Research Press, 1996.

Fite, Gilbert C. *Cotton Fields No More: Southern Agriculture, 1865–1980*. Lexington: University Press of Kentucky, 1984.

Fleming, Walter, ed. *Documents Relating to Reconstruction*. Morgantown: West Virginia University, 1904.

Foner, Eric. *Nothing but Freedom: Emancipation and Its Legacy*. Baton Rouge: Louisiana State University Press, 1983.

———. "Prologue." In *Forever Free: The Story of Emancipation and Reconstruction*, by Eric Foner with Joshua Brown, xix–xxx. New York: Alfred A. Knopf, 2005.

———. *Reconstruction: America's Unfinished Revolution 1863–1877*. New American Nation Series, edited by Henry S. Commager and Richard Morris. New York: Harper and Row, 1988.

Foner, Eric, with Joshua Brown. *Forever Free: The Story of Emancipation and Reconstruction*. New York: Alfred A. Knopf, 2005.

Foucault, Michel. *Introduction*. Vol. 1 of *The History of Sexuality*, translated by Robert Hurley. New York: Pantheon Books, 1978.

———. "Power and Strategies." In *Power/Knowledge: Selected Interviews and Other Writings 1972–1977*, edited by Colin Gordon; translated by Colin Gordon, Leo Marshall, John Mepham, and Kate Soper, 134–45. New York: Pantheon Books, 1980.

———. "Prison Talk." In *Power/Knowledge: Selected Interviews and Other Writings 1972–1977*, edited by Colin Gordon; translated by Colin Gordon, Leo Marshall, John Mepham, and Kate Soper, 37–54. New York: Pantheon Books, 1980.

Fulmer, Hal, and Carl Kell. "A Sense of Place, a Spirit of Adventure: Implications for the Study of Regional Rhetoric." *Rhetoric Society Quarterly* 20 (1990): 15–25.

Fulmer, Henry. "An Analytical Study of a Rural School Area." South Carolina Agricultural Experiment Station Bulletin 320 (June), 1939.

Geertz, Clifford. "Thick Description: Toward an Interpretive Theory of Culture." In *The Interpretation of Cultures*, 3–30. New York: Basic Books, 1973.

Gilmore, Glenda Elizabeth. *Gender and Jim Crow: Women and the Politics of White Supremacy in North Carolina, 1896–1920*. Chapel Hill: University of North Carolina Press, 1996.

Glassie, Henry H. *Folk Housing in Middle Virginia: A Structural Analysis of Historic Artifacts*. Knoxville: University of Tennessee Press, 1975.

Groover, Mark. "Evidence for Folkways and Cultural Exchange in the 18th-Century South Carolina Backcountry." *Historical Archaeology* 28 (1994): 41–64.

Hahn, Steven. *A Nation under Our Feet: Black Political Struggles in the Rural South from Slavery to the Great Migration*. Cambridge, MA: Belknap Press of Harvard University Press, 2003.

Halperin, Rhoda H. *The Livelihood of Kin: Making Ends Meet "the Kentucky Way."* Austin: University of Texas Press, 1990.

Harrison, Faye, and Ira Harrison. "Introduction: Anthropology, African Americans, and the Emancipation of a Subjugated Knowledge." In *African-American Pioneers in Anthropology*, edited by Ira E. Harrison and Faye V. Harrison, 1–36. Urbana: University of Illinois Press, 1999.

Hayden, Wilburn, Jr. "In Search of Justice: White Privilege in Appalachia." *Journal of Appalachian Studies* 8 (2002): 120–31.

Hayes, Jack Irby, Jr. *South Carolina and the New Deal*. Columbia: University of South Carolina Press, 2001.

Hemmingway, Theodore. "Beneath the Yoke of Bondage: A History of Black Folks in South Carolina, 1900–1940." Ph.D. diss., University of South Carolina, 1976.

Hendricks, Betty. "History and Present Status of the Negro Schools of Pickens County, South Carolina." M.A. thesis, Furman University, 1949.

A History: The Schools of Pickens County. N.p., n.d. 1995[?]. Historical Collection, Captain Kimberly Hampton Memorial Library, Pickens County, SC.

Hoffman, Marcelo. "Disciplinary Power." In *Michel Foucault: Key Concepts*, edited by Dianna Taylor, 27–39. Durham, UK: Acumen, 2011.

Holder, Frederick C. "Notes Relating to Pickens County, SC." Oconee County Historical Society, 1987. Captain Kimberly Hampton Memorial Library, Pickens County, South Carolina.

Holt, Sharon Ann. *Making Freedom Pay: North Carolina Freedpeople Working for Themselves, 1865–1900*. Athens: University of Georgia Press, 2000.

hooks, bell. *Feminist Theory: From Margin to Center*, 2nd ed. Cambridge, MA: South End Press, 2000.

———. *Talking Back: Thinking Feminist, Thinking Black*. Boston: South End Press, 1989.

———. *Yearning: Race, Gender, and Cultural Politics*. Boston: South End Press, 1990.

Hunter, Jane Edna. *A Nickel and a Prayer: The Autobiography of Jane Edna Hunter*, edited by Rhondda Robinson Thomas. Morgantown: West Virginia University Press, 2011.

Inscoe, John C. "Introduction." In *Appalachians and Race: The Mountain South from Slavery to Segregation*, edited by John Inscoe, 1–15. Lexington: University Press of Kentucky, 2001.

———. *Mountain Masters, Slavery, and the Sectional Crisis in Western North Carolina*. Knoxville: University of Tennessee Press, 1989.

———. "Race and Racism in Nineteenth-Century Southern Appalachia: Myths, Realities, and Ambiguities." In *Appalachia in the Making: The Mountain South in the Nineteenth Century*, edited by Mary Beth Pudup, Dwight Billings, and Altina Waller, 103–31. Chapel Hill: University of North Carolina Press, 1995.

———. *Race, War, and Remembrance in the Appalachian South*. Lexington: University Press of Kentucky, 2008.

Jaber, Nawal, Joanna McCauley, Mindy McCauley, and Melissa Norman. "The Dramatic Story of Caesar's Head." *Echoes: Reflections of the Past* 3 (1987): 15–29.

Jackson, Antoinette. "Shattering Slave Life Portrayals: Uncovering Subjugated Knowledge in U.S. Plantation Sites in South Carolina and Florida." *American Anthropologist* 113 (2011): 448–62.

Jimenez, Jillian. "The History of Grandmothers in the African-American Community." *Social Service Review* 76 (2002): 523–51.

Johnson, Luther, Jr. "Oolenoy River Education and Missionary Baptist Association of Pickens County, South Carolina." N.p.; revised 1982. Captain Kimberly Hampton Memorial Library, Pickens County, South Carolina.

Keefe, Susan E., and Jodie D. Manross. "Race, Religion, and Community: The Demolition of a Black Church." *Appalachian Journal* 26 (1999): 252–63.

Keith, John M. "To the Tenth Generation of the Descendants of Cornelius Keith in America." N.p., 1983. Manuscript, Pendleton Chapter of the South Carolina Genealogical Society, Pendleton District Historical and Recreational Commission, Pendleton, South Carolina.

King, Ronald. "Counting the Votes: South Carolina's Stolen Election of 1876." *Journal of Interdisciplinary History* 32 (2001): 169–91.

Klein, Rachel. *Unification of a Slave State: The Rise of the Planter Class in the South Carolina Backcountry, 1760–1808*. Chapel Hill: University of North Carolina Press, 1990.

Lewis, Hylan. *Blackways of Kent*. Chapel Hill: University of North Carolina Press, 1955.

Lynch, Alma, and Elizabeth Ellison. *Echoes: Oolenoy—Pumpkintown*. Easley, SC: Pace Printing, 1980.

Lynch, Richard. "Foucault's Theory of Power." In *Michel Foucault: Key Concepts*, edited by Dianna Taylor, 13–26. Durham, UK: Acumen, 2011.

Marcus, George, and Michael Fischer. *Anthropology as Cultural Critique: An Experimental Moment in the Human Sciences.* 2nd ed. Chicago: University of Chicago Press, 1999.

McFall, Pearl Smith. *It Happened in Pickens County.* Pickens, SC: Sentinel, 1959.

McGee, Charles M., Jr., and Ernest Lander Jr., eds. *A Rebel Came Home: The Diary and Letters of Floride Clemson, 1863–1866.* Rev. ed. Women's Diaries and Letters of the Nineteenth-Century South, edited by Carol Bleser and Elizabeth Fox-Genovese. Columbia: University of South Carolina Press, 1961.

Megginson, W. J. *African-American Life in South Carolina's Upper Piedmont, 1780–1900.* Columbia: University of South Carolina Press, 2006. Abbreviated *AAL.*

Montell, William Lynwood. *The Saga of Coe Ridge: A Study in Oral History.* Knoxville: University of Tennessee Press, 1970.

Montell, William Lynwood, and Michael L. Morse. *Kentucky Folk Architecture.* Lexington: University Press of Kentucky, 1976.

Murphy, Carolyn Hanna. *Carolina Rocks! The Geology of South Carolina.* Orangeburg, SC: Sandlapper, 1995.

Nash, Steven. *Reconstruction's Ragged Edge: The Politics of Post-War Life in the Southern Mountains.* Chapel Hill: University of North Carolina Press, 2016.

Neuffer, Claude. *Names in South Carolina.* Volumes 1–12, *1954–1965.* Vol. 11, *Winter 1964.* Columbia, SC: State Printing Co., 1967.

Nickles, C. B. "Poisoning the Boll Weevil in the Piedmont Section of South Carolina." Circular 33 (1925), South Carolina Agricultural Experiment Station, Clemson College, Clemson, SC.

Ostwalt, Conrad, and Phoebe Pollitt. "The Salem School and Orphanage: White Missionaries, Black School." *Appalachian Journal* 20 (1993): 264–75.

Overman, Flora Keith. "The Keith Family in South Carolina." Manuscripts Division, South Caroliniana Library, University of South Carolina, 1930.

———. "The Keiths." Reprinted in "Some Facts of History: Old Pickens." Walhalla, SC: Keowee Courier Print, 1930.

Perdue, Theda. *"Mixed Blood" Indians: Racial Construction in the Early South.* Athens: University of Georgia Press, 2003.

Petty, Adrienne. "The Jim Crow Section of Agricultural History." In *Beyond Forty Acres and a Mule: African American Landowning Families since Reconstruction,* edited by Debra Reid and Evan Bennett, 21–35. Tallahassee: University Press of Florida, 2012.

Pickens, William. *Bursting Bonds: The Autobiography of a "New Negro,"* edited by William Andrews. Bloomington: Indiana University Press, 1991.

Poole, W. Scott. *Never Surrender: Confederate Memory and Conservatism in the South Carolina Upcountry.* Athens: University of Georgia Press, 2004.

Puckett, Newbell Niles. *Folk Beliefs of the Southern Negro.* Chapel Hill: University of North Carolina Press, 1926.

Quint, Howard. *Profile in Black and White: A Frank Portrait of South Carolina*. Washington, DC: Public Affairs Press, 1958.

Reece, Bert Hendricks. *History of Pumpkintown—Oolenoy: Land of Grain and Water*. Greenville, SC: A Press, 2002. Originally published 1970. Abbreviated *HPO*.

Reece, Josef. *Rambling from the Mountain: My Life's Story*. N.p., 2007. Historical Collection, Captain Kimberly Hampton Memorial Library, Pickens County, SC.

Reid, Debra. "Introduction." In *Beyond Forty Acres and a Mule: African American Landowning Families since Reconstruction*, edited by Debra Reid and Evan Bennett, 1–18. Tallahassee: University Press of Florida, 2012.

——. "Researching African American Land and Farm Owners." In *Beyond Forty Acres and a Mule: African American Landowning Families since Reconstruction*, edited by Debra Reid and Evan Bennett, 297–315. Tallahassee: University Press of Florida, 2012.

Rhyne, Martha McJunkin. *McJunkin: A Family of Memories*. Greenville, SC: A Press, 1989. South Carolina Room, Hughes Public Library, Greenville County.

Rich, Peggy Burton, and Frederick Holder. "Oconee and Pickens Counties, South Carolina: 1868 Voter Registration." N.p., 1990. Pendleton Chapter of the South Carolina Genealogical Society, Pendleton District Historical and Recreational Commission.

Richards, T. Addison. "The Table Rock." *Orion* 2, no. 1 (November 1842): 1–4. Manuscript in the Clayton Collection, Miscellaneous File, Pickens County, Towns, Pumpkintown. Faith Clayton Genealogy Room, Rickman Library, Southern Wesleyan University.

Richardson, Miles. "Introduction." In *Place: Experience and Symbol*, edited by Miles Richardson, 1–2. Vol. 24 of *GeoScience and Man*. Baton Rouge: Louisiana State University, 1984.

Ringer, Fritz. "The Intellectual Field, Intellectual History, and the Sociology of Knowledge." *Theory and Society* 19 (1990): 269–94.

Robertson, Ben. *Red Hills and Cotton: An Upcountry Memory*. Columbia: University of South Carolina Press, 1942. Republished 1973.

Rowles, Graham. "Toward a Geography of Growing Old." In *The Human Experience of Space and Place*, edited by Anne Buttimer and David Seamon, 55–72. London: Croom Helm, 1980.

Saville, Julie. "A Measure of Freedom: From Slave to Wage Laborer in South Carolina, 1860–1868." Ph.D. diss., Yale University, 1986. Ann Arbor, MI: UMI.

Schultz, Mark. *The Rural Face of White Supremacy: Beyond Jim Crow*. Urbana: University of Illinois Press, 2005.

Schweninger, Loren. *Black Property Owners in the South, 1790–1915*. Urbana: University of Illinois Press, 1997.

Scott, James C. *The Art of Not Being Governed: An Anarchist History of Upland Southeast Asia*. New Haven, CT: Yale University Press, 2009.

———. *Domination and the Arts of Resistance: Hidden Transcripts.* New Haven, CT: Yale University Press, 1990.

Seaborn, Margaret Mills, ed. *Benjamin Hawkins's Journeys through Oconee County, South Carolina in 1796 and 1797.* Columbia, SC: R. L. Bryan, 1973.

Sitton, Thad, and James H. Conrad. *Freedom Colonies: Independent Black Texans in the Time of Jim Crow.* Austin: University of Texas Press, 2005.

Smith, Barbara Ellen. "De-gradations of Whiteness: Appalachia and the Complexities of Race." *Journal of Appalachian Studies* 10 (2004): 38–57.

Smith, Jennifer Lund. "Negotiating the Terms of Freedom: The Quest for Education in an African-American Community in Reconstruction North Georgia." In *Appalachians and Race: The Mountain South from Slavery to Segregation,* edited by John Inscoe, 220–34. Lexington: University Press of Kentucky, 2001.

Smith, Leroy. "Grandpa's Olden Days." Manuscripts Division, South Caroliniana Library, University of South Carolina, 1979.

South Carolina Baptist Historical Collection. African-American Baptist Annual Reports, SC, reel 76 (vol. 5), African-American Baptist Reference Materials, James B. Duke Library, Furman University.

Stack, Carol. *Call to Home: African Americans Reclaim the Rural South.* New York: BasicBooks, 1996.

Steele, Fritz. *The Sense of Place.* Boston: CBI, 1981.

Swanton, John. *The Indians of the Southeastern United States.* Washington, DC: Smithsonian Institution Press, 1987. Originally published 1946.

Taussig, Michael. "Culture of Terror—Space of Death: Roger Casement's Putumayo Report and the Explanation of Torture." *Comparative Studies in Society and History* 26 (1984): 467–97.

Taylor, Rosser Howard. *Carolina Crossroads: A Study of Rural Life at the End of the Horse and Buggy Era.* Murfreesboro, NC: Johnson, 1966.

Thurman, Howard. *The Luminous Darkness: A Personal Interpretation of the Anatomy of Segregation and the Ground of Hope.* New York: Harper and Row, 1965.

Tindall, George Brown. *South Carolina Negroes: 1877–1900.* Columbia: University of South Carolina Press, 1952.

Tolnay, Stewart. *The Bottom Rung: African American Family Life on Southern Farms.* Urbana: University of Illinois Press, 1999.

Tolnay, Stewart, and E. M. Beck. *A Festival of Violence: An Analysis of Southern Lynchings, 1882–1930.* Urbana: University of Illinois Press, 1995.

Turner, William H. "The Demography of Black Appalachia: Past and Present." In *Blacks in Appalachia,* edited by William H. Turner and Edward J. Cabbell, 237–61. Lexington: University Press of Kentucky, 1985.

Turner, William H., and Edward J. Cabbell. "Preface." In *Blacks in Appalachia,* edited by William H. Turner and Edward J. Cabbell, xiii–xv. Lexington: University Press of Kentucky, 1985.

Tyler, Stephen. "Post-Modern Ethnography." In *Writing Culture: The Poetics and Politics of Ethnography*, edited by James Clifford and George Marcus, 122–40. Berkeley: University of California Press, 1986.

Wagner, Melinda Bollar. "Measuring Cultural Attachment to Place in a Proposed Power Line Corridor." *Journal of Appalachian Studies* 5 (1999): 241–46.

Webster, Laura. *The Operation of the Freedmen's Bureau in South Carolina*, 2nd ed. New York: Russell and Russell, 1970.

White, Newman, gen. ed. *The Frank C. Brown Collection of North Carolina Folklore*. 7 vols. Durham, N.C.: Duke University Press, 1952–64.

Wideman, John Edgar. *Fatheralong: A Meditation of Fathers and Sons, Race and Society*. New York: Vintage Books, 1994.

Wieder, Alan. "South Carolina School History Textbooks' Portrayals of Race during Reconstruction: An Historical Analysis." *Journal of Thought* 30 (1995): 19–33.

Williams, David. "Georgia's Forgotten Miners: African-Americans and the Georgia Gold Rush of 1829." In *Appalachians and Race: The Mountain South from Slavery to Segregation*, edited by John Inscoe, 40–49. Lexington: University Press of Kentucky, 2001.

Williams, Leon. "The Vanishing Appalachian: How to 'Whiten' the Problem." In *Blacks in Appalachia*, edited by William H. Turner and Edward J. Cabbell, 201–6. Lexington: University Press of Kentucky, 1985.

Williams, Michael Ann. *Homeplace: The Social Use and Meaning of the Folk Dwelling in Southwestern North Carolina*. Athens: University of Georgia Press, 1991.

Williamson, Joel. *After Slavery: The Negro in South Carolina during Reconstruction, 1861–1877*. New York: W. W. Norton, 1975. Originally published 1965.

Woodward, C. Vann. *Origins of the New South: 1877–1913*. Vol. 9 of *A History of the South*, edited by Wendell H. Stephenson and E. Merton Coulter. Baton Rouge: Louisiana State University Press, 1951.

Wright, Louis. *South Carolina: A Bicentennial History*. New York: W. W. Norton, 1976.

Zerubavel, Yael. *Recovered Roots: Collective Memory and the Making of Israeli National Tradition*. Chicago: University of Chicago Press, 1995.

Zwolandek, Michael. "'Right and Wise': James F. Byrnes and South Carolina's Educational Revolution." M.A. thesis, Clemson University, 1997.

Index

French, Carl, 124, 193–94
Fulmer, Henry, 95, 96, 101
funeral homes, 145–46

gardens, family, 126, 180, 181
Glenn, Clarence, 83, 84, 118, 119, 123, 124, 129; death and burial of, 175, 211; white violence against, 161
Glenn, Ernest, 64, 83–84, 117
Glenn, Lonzo, 64, 83–84, 117
Glenn, William/Willis, 63, 64, 83
Gold Mine neighborhood, 139, 197
Gordon, Brooks, 115
Gowans, Thomas, 84, 231n64
Gowens, Andrew, 92, 214, 231–32n67
Gowens, Robert, 231n67
Gowens, Rosie Glenn. *See* Owens, Rosie Glenn
Great Depression, 82, 96, 112, 115
Greenville (city), SC, 82, 121, 181, 189
Greenville County, 26, 29, 37, 141, 151; black community in, 59, 60–61, 70–71, 75, 121, 200–201; Cleveland district of, 60–61, 63–64, 84, 85, 86, 123; Ku Klux Klan in, 159, 244n51
Greenville News, 168–69, 172, 173, 245n2
Groover, Mark, 25

Hagood, Ethel, 73, 235n108
Hampton, Wade, 48–49, 59
Hayes, Rutherford B., 48–49
Hendricks, Betty, 73–74
Hester, Abraham, 31
Hester, Alfred, 36, 226n50
Hester, James, 2, 31, 36, 37
hidden transcripts, 2, 111–12, 126; and countermemory, 23, 33–34, 42–43, 58, 103–5; counternarratives as, 8–9, 33–34; of interracial sexual relationships, 191–92; of Jim Crow, 80, 105, 110; Liberia as, 13, 24, 68, 83; of resistance, 110–13, 117; Scott concept

of, 9–10, 33, 34, 68; of slaves, 38, 43; of white benevolence, 113, 162. *See also* alternate histories; public transcripts
Hill, Allen, 127, 130, 131, 132, 137–38, 143
historical "truth": alternate versions of, 17, 23, 24, 43, 55, 75, 104; and black women, 16–17; as contested territory, 5–7; countering, 2, 9, 149; and local histories, 20, 21; power's manipulation of, 8, 103, 169
Holiday, Billie, 12
holidays, 128–30
homeplace, symbolic, 180–81, 197–98
home remedies, 134–35
houses, 97, 135–36; electrification of, 136, 167; and household clusters, 180; indoor plumbing in, 136; inheritance of, 180
Hunter, Jane Edna, 67, 76–77, 78, 79; on slavery, 34, 42
hunting, 130–32

Indians: Cherokee, 25–26, 27, 29, 94; as racial category, 18–19, 94–95
indoor plumbing, 136
intercommunity visits, 141–43
interracial sexual relations: in late nineteenth century, 76–77; legacy of, 191–93; under slavery, 40–41. *See also* miscegenation

Jackson, Alice, 108, 149
Jackson, Andrew, 27
Jameson, McElroy, 52, 229n32
Jim Crow, 11, 66, 110, 114, 167; hidden transcripts of, 80, 105; imposition of, 49–50; social hierarchy under, 80, 104–6. *See also* segregation
jobs and employment, 65–66, 96, 139–41, 181; differential pay for, 82; in textile mills, 117–18, 139–40

Johnson, Andrew, 47
Johnson, Lyndon, 168
Johnston, Luther, 145
Joseph (slave), 37, 38, 39. *See also* McJunkin, Joseph

Katie, Aunt, 36, 37, 62, 63, 66, 208–9; as mammy figure, 76. *See also* Owens, Katie
Keith, Cornelius, 27, 43, 62, 96, 112, 179
Keith, James, 31, 37
Keith, John M., 27
Keith, Samuel "Goob," 26, 36–37, 62–63, 83, 84, 85; obituary for, 93–94
Keith, William, 31–32
Kemp, Emerson "Empse," 14, 37, 62–63, 64, 80, 83, 84, 231n67; as boss-slave, 2, 31, 36, 37, 92; death and burial of, 91, 196; photo of, 91–92
Kemp, Hattie, 84, 85, 86, 119, 186
Kemp, James, 84–85, 93, 96, 118, 186, 214
"Kentucky way," 97, 133, 181
King, Martin Luther, Jr., 168–69
Ku Klux Klan: during Reconstruction, 48; resistance to, 158–59, 161–62; resurgence of, 82, 115, 117, 168, 245n52; and Soapstone Church fire, 1, 171

labor contracts, 51–53, 229n32
land: anthropomorphic appreciation of, 207–8; memory tied to, 141, 166–67, 203, 205–7; occupancy of, 167, 204; ties to ancestral, 2, 3–4, 123, 165–66, 196, 201–4, 208
land ownership, 83, 95, 176, 203–4, 208; black defense of, 112–13, 166, 189–90; former slaves' acquisition of, 53–54, 56–57, 59–60; white attempts to strip blacks of, 78–79, 112–13, 157–58, 165, 189–90
Laycock, George, 59

Liberia: census information on, 30, 60–61, 62–65, 83–86, 122–23; country life in, 95–99, 126–35; founding of, 37, 50–62; as hidden transcript, 13, 24, 68, 83; houses in, 97, 135–36, 180; intercommunity visits to, 141–43; kinship ties in, 119, 124, 125, 141, 196–97, 201, 206 land ownership in, 56–57, 59–60, 78–79, 83, 112–13, 157–58, 203–4, 208; location of, 54–58; naming of, 58–60; out-migration from, 84, 85, 115–19, 121, 163–65; population of, 60–61, 63, 64, 84, 85, 170, 181; returning to, 119, 165–67, 196–99; schools in, 73–74, 101–3, 147–52, 158; social life in, 135–39; as story of resistance, 9–10, 13, 15, 83, 110–13, 158–60; in twenty-first century, 179–83; white neighbors of, 152–62
Liberia (Africa) emigration movement, 59
Lost Cause rhetoric, 122
lynching, 12, 77, 78, 114–15, 116, 155

"mammy" stereotype, 32, 39, 74, 76
Marietta, SC, 66, 80, 125, 140, 175
Maxwell community, 14
McClain, William, 185
McCravy, John, 94
McGowens, Andrew, 174
McGowens, Sam, 140
McJunkin, Absalom "Joab," 64, 85, 111, 117
McJunkin, Daniel, 28–29, 37, 227n57
McJunkin, Emma, 64, 77, 84, 85, 86, 123, 124–25
McJunkin, James Monroe, 59, 98, 125, 136, 139, 140–41, 151, 165–66; defense of land by, 190; racist threats against, 159; slave grandfather's recollections told by, 20, 32–33, 35, 37–38, 42, 222n68; on white grandmother, 41

McJunkin, Joseph, 62, 63–64, 80, 156, 204, 209; as church official, 71–72, 173, 231n67; land owned by, 59–60, 176; and naming of Liberia, 58–59

McJunkin, Pamela, 165

McJunkin, Sarah, 37, 38, 39

McKinney, Ansel "Anse," 84, 85, 86, 92, 119, 123, 170–71; birth and death of, 63, 214

McKinney, George, 63

McKinney, Minnie, 124

medical care, 98, 133–35

memory, 85, 105–6, 115; and counter-memory, 2, 5–6, 7, 19, 23, 33–34, 43, 56, 58, 103–5, 210; dominant public, 5, 6, 39, 42–43, 57, 104; land and place tied to, 141, 166–67, 203, 205–7; selective, 20–21

midwives, 98, 133–34

Miles, John, 93

Miracle Hill Children's Home, 179, 190

miscegenation, 49, 77, 113–14, 150. See also interracial sexual relations

mixed-race individuals, 155–56

moonshining, 132

Moragne, Mary, 28

Mt. Nebo Baptist Church, 144–45, 155–56, 231–32n67; founding of, 71; membership of, 234n105, 239n50; and Soapstone Church, 72–73, 100

Mt. Nebo Cemetery, 89, 92

narratives, 21, 38, 103, 202; counternar-ratives as hidden transcripts to, 8–9, 33–34; public, 5; slave, 33–34, 38, 39, 40–41, 45, 90

New Deal, 82–84, 121

Nixon, Richard, 168

Obama, Barack, 188

obituaries, 19, 75–76, 87–90, 91–93

Oconee County, 26, 30

Oolenoy Baptist Church, 32, 43–44, 69–70, 71–72

Oolenoy River Baptist Missionary and Educational Association, 72, 143–44, 239n50

Oolenoy School, 101

Oolenoy Valley, 65, 69, 150–51; settlement of, 25–26, 27–29; social transformations in, 178–79; urban-ization in, 167

oral history, 1–2, 60, 75, 77, 90; and Behind the Veil project, 11, 20, 104, 111; on forms of resistance, 110–11; and personal memoirs, 67–69; postmodern view of, 17; as source, 20–22, 222–23n76

oral traditions, 37, 90, 114–15; of blacks under slavery, 33–34, 35, 41–42; and creation of black social world, 69, 111; efforts to preserve, 20, 35; on Liberia's founding, 54–55, 61; by oppressed peoples, 40, 111

othermother, 90, 175–76, 187–88, 194

out-migration, 84, 85, 115–19, 121, 163–65

Overman, Flora Keith, 28, 31, 51

Owens, Chris, 60, 85, 118, 134, 155–56, 157, 204; birth and death of, 64, 80, 212; and black resistance, 112, 159–60, 190; childhood of, 83, 84, 86, 87, 96, 101, 136, 138–39; defense of land by, 166, 190; racial discrimi-nation against, 109–10; respect for, 123–24, 193; return to Liberia by, 119, 166; and Soapstone Church, 71, 174; and white-black interactions, 108, 130–31, 152–53, 154, 173, 179–80, 185–86, 193–94, 195; on white land theft, 57, 158; and white threats, 114–15, 162

Owens, Don, 128, 131, 135, 138, 143, 157; on segregation, 151, 155; and Soapstone Church fire, 170, 173, 174

Williams, Pamela, 125, 138, 203, 204, 205, 206, 207
Williamson, Andrew, 25–26

Young, Angela McJunkin, 20, 41, 72, 100, 139, 140, 145; on land ownership, 59–60, 166, 203; and Liberia ancestral land, 197, 204; on Liberia naming, 58–59; on slave ancestors, 35, 38, 39; on white-black relations, 109, 156, 159
Young, Judith, 197
Young, Stephen, 139–40

Zimmerman, Colleen, 172, 175, 183

H. EUGENE AND LILLIAN YOUNGS LEHMAN SERIES

Lamar Cecil, *Wilhelm II: Prince and Emperor, 1859–1900* (1989).

Carolyn Merchant, *Ecological Revolutions: Nature, Gender, and Science in New England* (1989).

Gladys Engel Lang and Kurt Lang, *Etched in Memory: The Building and Survival of Artistic Reputation* (1990).

Howard Jones, *Union in Peril: The Crisis over British Intervention in the Civil War* (1992).

Robert L. Dorman, *Revolt of the Provinces: The Regionalist Movement in America* (1993).

Peter N. Stearns, *Meaning Over Memory: Recasting the Teaching of Culture and History* (1993).

Thomas Wolfe, *The Good Child's River*, edited with an introduction by Suzanne Stutman (1994).

Warren A. Nord, *Religion and American Education: Rethinking a National Dilemma* (1995).

David E. Whisnant, *Rascally Signs in Sacred Places: The Politics of Culture in Nicaragua* (1995).

Lamar Cecil, *Wilhelm II: Emperor and Exile, 1900–1941* (1996).

Jonathan Hartlyn, *The Struggle for Democratic Politics in the Dominican Republic* (1998).

Louis A. Pérez Jr., *On Becoming Cuban: Identity, Nationality, and Culture* (1999).

Yaakov Ariel, *Evangelizing the Chosen People: Missions to the Jews in America, 1880–2000* (2000).

Philip F. Gura, *C. F. Martin and His Guitars, 1796–1873* (2003).

Louis A. Pérez Jr., *To Die in Cuba: Suicide and Society* (2005).

Peter Filene, *The Joy of Teaching: A Practical Guide for New College Instructors* (2005).

John Charles Boger and Gary Orfield, eds., *School Resegregation: Must the South Turn Back?* (2005).

Jock Lauterer, *Community Journalism: Relentlessly Local* (2006).

Michael H. Hunt, *The American Ascendancy: How the United States Gained and Wielded Global Dominance* (2007).

Michael Lienesch, *In the Beginning: Fundamentalism, the Scopes Trial, and the Making of the Antievolution Movement* (2007).

Eric L. Muller, *American Inquisition: The Hunt for Japanese American Disloyalty in World War II* (2007).

John McGowan, *American Liberalism: An Interpretation for Our Time* (2007).

Nortin M. Hadler, M.D., *Worried Sick: A Prescription for Health in an Overtreated America* (2008).

William Ferris, *Give My Poor Heart Ease: Voices of the Mississippi Blues* (2009).

Colin A. Palmer, *Cheddi Jagan and the Politics of Power: British Guiana's Struggle for Independence* (2010).

W. Fitzhugh Brundage, *Beyond Blackface: African Americans and the Creation of American Mass Culture, 1890–1930* (2011).

Michael H. Hunt and Steven I. Levine, *Arc of Empire: America's Wars in Asia from the Philippines to Vietnam* (2012).

Nortin M. Hadler, M.D., *The Citizen Patient: Reforming Health Care for the Sake of the Patient, Not the System* (2013).

Louis A. Pérez Jr., *The Structure of Cuban History: Meanings and Purpose of the Past* (2013).

Jennifer Thigpen, *Island Queens and Mission Wives: How Gender and Empire Remade Hawai'i's Pacific World* (2014).

George W. Houston, *Inside Roman Libraries: Book Collections and Their Management in Antiquity* (2014).

Philip F. Gura, *The Life of William Apess, Pequot* (2015).

Daniel M. Cobb, ed., *Say We Are Nations: Documents of Politics and Protest in Indigenous America since 1887* (2015).

Daniel Maudlin and Bernard L. Herman, eds., *Building the British Atlantic World: Spaces, Places, and Material Culture, 1600–1850* (2016).

William Ferris, *The South in Color: A Visual Journal* (2016).

Lisa A. Lindsay, *Atlantic Bonds: A Nineteenth-Century Odyssey from America to Africa* (2017).

Mary Elizabeth Basile Chopas, *Searching for Subversives: The Story of Italian Internment in Wartime America* (2017).

John M. Coggeshall, *Liberia, South Carolina: An African American Appalachian Community* (2018).

CPSIA information can be obtained
at www.ICGtesting.com
Printed in the USA
LVHW01s2027011018
591856LV00004B/8/P

9 781469 640853